LEVEL BEST

3

DELIVERING
THE FRAMEWORK
FOR TEACHING
// ENGLISH //

Michael Ross // *Keith West*
Series Consultant: Mike Hamlin

Text © Michael Ross and Keith West 2002

Original illustrations © Nelson Thornes Ltd 2002

The right of Michael Ross and Keith West to be identified as authors of this work has been asserted by them in accordance with the Copyright, Designs and Patents Act 1988.

All rights reserved. No part of this publication may be reproduced or transmitted in any form or by any means, electronic or mechanical, including photocopy, recording or any information storage and retrieval system, without permission in writing from the publisher or under licence from the Copyright Licensing Agency Limited, 90 Tottenham Court Road, London W1T 4LP.

Any person who commits any unauthorised act in relation to this publication may be liable to criminal prosecution and civil claims for damages.

Published in 2002 by:
Nelson Thornes Ltd
Delta Place
27 Bath Road
CHELTENHAM
GL53 7TH
United Kingdom

01 02 03 04 05 / 10 9 8 7 6 5 4 3 2 1

A catalogue record for this book is available from the British Library

ISBN 0-7487-6261-2

Illustrations by Josephine Blake, Linda Jeffrey, Angela Lumley, Zhenya Matysiak, Linda Rogers and Harry Venning
Edited by Katherine James
Designed by Holbrook Design Oxford Limited

Printed and bound in Spain by Graficas Estella

Acknowledgements

The authors and publishers wish to thank the following for permission to reproduce copyright material and photographs in this book:

Malorie Blackman, Jamila Gavin and Jan Mark for short extracts written for this book;

John Brown Contract Publishing Ltd for material from *Hotline,* Virgin Trains complimentary magazine, Summer 2001, pp. 55, 71;

thecafe.org.uk for material from their website page;

Carcanet Press Ltd for Robert Herrick, 'To Daffodils' from *Selected Poems* by Robert Herrick, ed. David Jesson-Dibley (1980);

Faber and Faber Ltd for W H Auden, 'The Unknown Citizen' from *Collected Poems* by W H Auden (1976);

David Godwin Associates on behalf of the author for extracts from Ben Okri *Mental Fight: an anti-spell for the twenty-first century* by Ben Okri, Phoenix (1991) pp. 9, 55, 66;

HarperCollins Publishers Ltd for material from Frank McCourt, *Angela's Ashes*, Flamingo (1996) pp. 114–6;

David Higham Associates on behalf of the authors for material from Penelope Lively, *Oleander Jacaranda*, Penguin (1994); Penelope Lively, 'Next Term, We'll Mash You' in *Pack of Cards* by Penelope Lively, Heinemann (1986); and Jamila Gavin, *Coram Boy*, Mammoth (2000) pp. 8–9;

Hodder and Stoughton Ltd for material from David Almond, *Kit's Wilderness* (1999) pp. 9–10; Tanni Grey-Thompson, *Seize the Day* (2001) pp. xvii-xviv; and Jan Mark, *Heathrow Nights* (2000) pp. 1–3;

Independent Newspapers (UK) Ltd for Natasha Walter, 'We're all hooked by woolly thinking', *The Independent*, 1.8.01, p. 5;

Mike Jenkins for 'He Loved Light Freedom and Animals' included in *The Bright Field: An Anthology of Contemporary Poetry from Wales*, ed. Meic Stephens (1991);

Judith Nicholls for 'Ballad of the Sad Astronaut' from *Magic Mirror* by Judith Nicholls, Faber and Faber Ltd. Copyright © Judith Nicholls 1985;

Pan Macmillan for material from Karen E Bender, *Like Normal People*, Picador (2000) pp. 21–2;

Pathfinder for their Snowdonia activities leaflet;

Penguin Books Ltd for Benjamin Zephaniah, 'We Are the Cherokees' and 'The British' from *Wicked World* by Benjamin Zephaniah, Puffin (2000). Copyright © Benjamin Zephaniah, 2000; and material from Beverley Naidoo, *The Other Side of Truth*, Puffin (2000). Copyright © Beverley Naidoo, 2000;

Peters Fraser and Dunlop Group Ltd on behalf of the author for material from Michael Rosen, 'Clothes' in *Just Kids* by Michael Rosen, John Murray (1995) pp. 22–4. Copyright © 1995 Michael Rosen;

Philip Pullman for material from his adaption of *Frankenstein*, Oxford University Press (1990) pp. 42, 69;

Random House Group Ltd for Robert Frost, 'Nothing Gold Can Stay' from *The Poetry of Robert Frost*, ed. Edward Connery Latham, Jonathan Cape;

Scholastic Ltd for text and illustrations from Nick Arnold, *Horrible Science, Bulging Brains* (1999) pp. 8, 9, 10, 15, 32, 33. Text copyright © Nick Arnold 1999, illustrations copyright © Tony de Saulles 1999; and Terry Deary, 'The Ballad of Big Mac' from *Top Ten Shakespeare Stories* by Terry Deary, (1998). Text copyright © Terry Deary 1998, illustrations copyright © Michael Tickner 1998;

Scotrail for material from *Outlook*, complimentary magazine, 17, April–June 2001;

Seren for Sheenagh Pugh, 'Do You Think We'll Ever Get To See Earth, Sir?' from *Selected Poems*, Seren Books (1990);

The Society of Authors as the Literary Representative of the Estate of the author for W W Gibson, *The Monkey's Paw*;

Telegraph Group Ltd for Rupert Christiansen, 'We have to realise that it's wrong to drop litter', *Daily Telegraph*, 2.8.01, p. 22. Copyright © Telegraph Group Ltd 2001;

ticktock Media Ltd for material from *Modern Media: Music and Sound – 2000*, pp. 18–19;

Transworld Publishers, a division of Random House Group Ltd, for material from Oneta Malorie Blackman, *Noughts and Crosses*, Doubleday (2001) pp. 109–114; Bill Bryson, *Notes from a Big Country*, Black Swan (1998) pp. 72–5; and Bill Bryson, *Down Under*, Black Swan (2000);

The Watts Publishing Group Ltd for material from Jean Ure, *Get a Life*, Orchard Books (2001) p. 14.

Aerofilms, p. 6; Corel73(NT); Digital Vision 9 & 17 (NT), p. 96-97; Donald Cooper/Photostage, p. 184; Empics, p. 149; Eye Ubiquitous, p. 16, 117; Getty Images, p. 15; Ronald Grant Archive, p. 140; Simon Grossett p. 99; Peter Newark's Americana, p. 85; Yiorgos Nikiteas, p. 153 (all); Penguin/Penelope Lively, p. 31; People for the Ethical Treatment of Animals, p. 116; Rex Features, p. 68 middle left, middle right; Science Photo Library, p. 68 top left; Sony, p. 68 top right, 'Sony' is a registered trademark of Sony Corporation, Japan; The Western Mail/Cardiff, p. 148.

Every effort has been made to contact the copyright holders. The publishers apologise to anyone whose rights have been inadvertently overlooked, and will be happy to rectify any errors or omissions.

Contents

Introduction   4

1 Information and persuasion   5
On the move

2 Autobiography – fact and fiction   26
Lively Dickens

3 Portraying character   41
'And you are?'

4 Information, explanation and advice   62
Info A–Z

5 Poetry to persuade   83
Mental fight

6 Persuasive writing   104
Hooked

7 Creating drama   124
Frankenstein's monster

8 Report writing   147
Changing places

9 Creating and shaping stories   159
The Monkey's Paw

10 Exploring Shakespeare   177
Macbeth

Introduction

Welcome to *Level Best 3*! This book is the third in a series of three books designed to help you make real progress in English. It will help you to get the most out of the book if you know something about why it is written in the way it is. This introduction includes the principles outlined in the introductions to *Level Best 1* and *Level Best 2*, linking them where appropriate to the different skills being developed in *Level Best 3*. If you have used either *Level Best 1* or *Level Best 2*, or both, decide for yourself how far you made the best use of the opportunities outlined here.

- At the beginning of each unit there is a statement telling you what the purpose of the unit is. Here you also find out what skills you will be developing over the unit. It obviously helps you to achieve an aim if you know clearly what the aim is.

- In many of the activities you will first of all have a chance to discuss questions in small groups. This means you can try out ideas that you might not want to say straight away to everyone. Your small group can then decide which are the best ideas to share when you report back.

- Different people learn in different ways. Some learn best by looking, some by listening, and some by using a more active approach, such as through drama. There are opportunities in this book to learn in all these ways.

- When you are asked to write a character description, report, guide to a topic of your choice, or television script, you will be given plenty of support. For example, before writing a report yourself, you will be given advice on an appropriate style for a report. You will also be given help in planning the structure of your own report. These activities will help you to understand typical features of reports, so that you can be more confident in writing your own report in an effective way.

- At the end of each unit you are asked to think about what you have learned and what the next steps are for you. This will help you make the most of the work you have done through the course of the unit, and help make sure the benefits don't just fade away.

- There is also clear guidance at the end of each unit on how you can move on to higher levels in the future. This means that you can set yourself realistic and achievable targets to steadily increase your skills in speaking and listening, reading and writing.

- In many places in the book, words are given dictionary definitions, such as the ones below. These are intended to help you understand the word as it is used at that point in the book, but also to help you with the activity you are doing so that you can be confident and successful. It's worth having a good look at these, wherever they occur.

WORDS

- ▲ **best** • *adjective* (superlative of GOOD) most excellent, suitable or desirable.
- • *noun* **1** the most desirable quality or result. **2** the greatest effort; one's utmost.
- ▲ **do one's level best** to do one's very best; to make every effort.
- ▲ **level** *noun* a stage or degree of progress (e.g. *took exams at an advanced level*).
- ▲ **pun** *noun* the use of a word or phrase that can be understood in two different ways.

1 Information and persuasion
On the move

Your focus
The content of this unit is designed to:
- improve your skills in writing informatively and persuasively about places.

Your target
By the end of this unit you should be more able to:
- understand how authors select information and use persuasive language about places
- apply techniques authors use to write your own informative and persuasive text
- understand moving-image terminology and write a script for a television presentation.

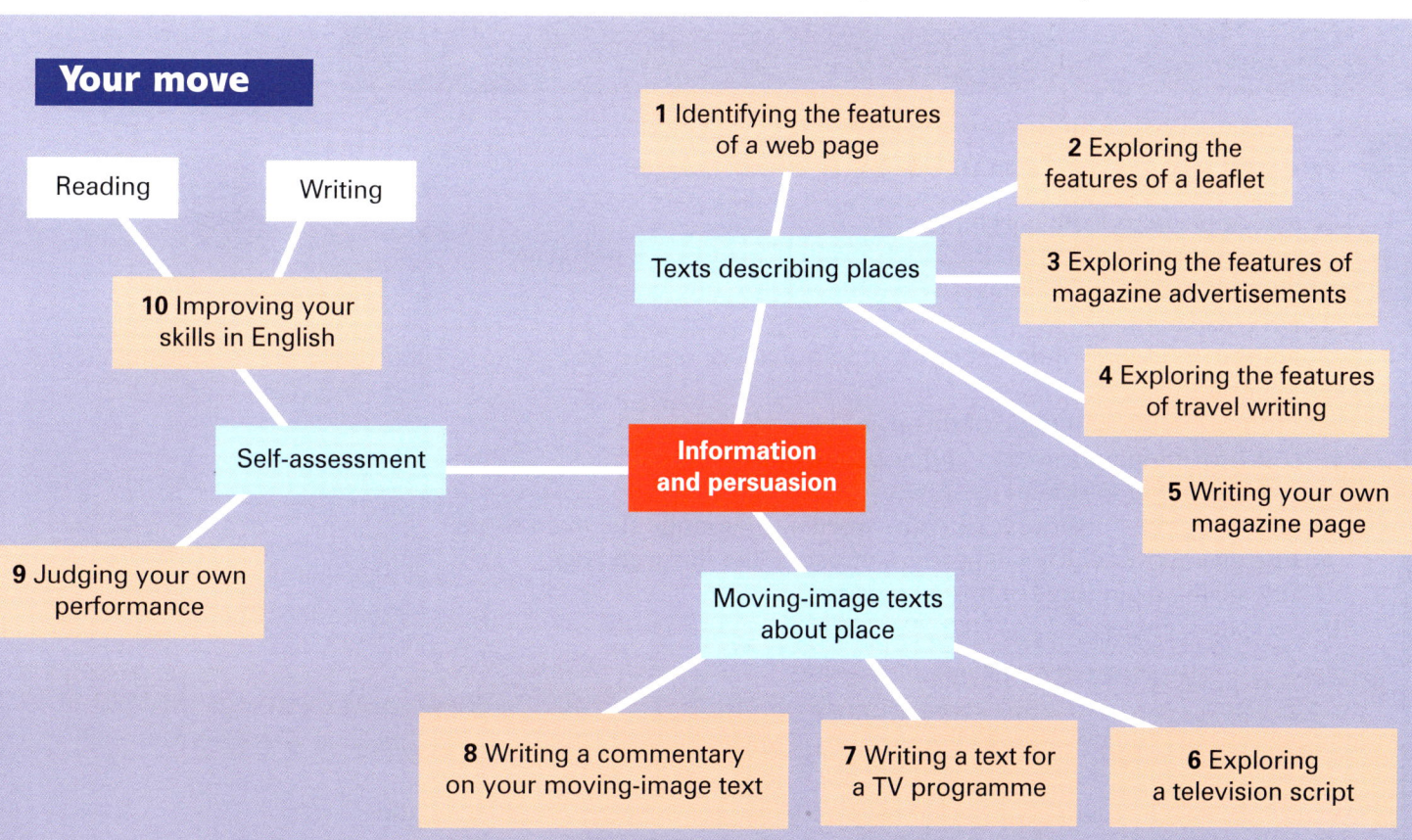

1 INFORMATION AND PERSUASION

Texts describing places

Writing to persuade is often connected with trying to change people's opinions about an issue, such as whether there should be curfews for young people (*Level Best 1*, Unit 6), or whether pig hearts should be used in humans (*Level Best 2*, Unit 6). However, persuasive writing is also used by authors trying to change the image of a place – perhaps persuading people to visit a certain place. *Travel writing* often explores both the positive and negative experiences associated with a particular place.

This unit is designed to help you explore how authors inform readers about places, and how authors try to change your image of places.

1 Identifying the features of a web page

▶ The text opposite is from a web page.
▶ Match up the letters A to J on the labels printed around the web page with the following descriptions. Use a table like the one below.
  1 advertisement
  2 graphic to identify different types of information
  3 hyperlink
  4 illustration of main topic of this page
  5 text providing information and also personal experience
  6 text providing information only
  7 text using only positive lexis (purr words) to describe the main topic
  8 title giving overall topic of a series of pages like this web page
  9 title giving main topic of this web page
  10 website address.

WORDS

▲ **breeze** *noun colloquial, especially North America* any job or situation that is effortless; a pleasantly simple task.
▲ **hyperlink** *noun computing* a link between pieces of information, so that one source of information may lead to another related source by a simple click or double-click on the mouse.

Letter	A	B	C	D	E	F	G	H	I	J
Number										

▶ Would you say the main purpose of this web page was to inform or to persuade? Be prepared to justify your point of view.
▶ How effective do you think it is in communicating to a reader?

6

On the move

Venues

Home
2002 Fixtures **New!**
Corporate Hospitality
Free E-mail News
Fixtures
OneOnOne Game
Virtual 6Nations
Results
Venues
Have Your Say
Teams
The Shopping Mall
Discussion Forum
Opinion Polls
Pub Guide
Rugby News
Rugby: The Game
Half Time
Links
Email Club

The use of the term 6 Nations on these pages is purely to describe the editorial nature of the content being covered in this site. No official or commercial association with the 6 Nations is implied or intended.

Millennium Stadium
Cardiff Arms Park
P.O. Box 22
Cardiff
CF1 1JI
Tel: +44(0)2920 781700
Fax: +44(0)2920 378472

Capacity: 72,500

Cardiff International Airport is located approximately 10 miles to the south-east of Cardiff City Centre. Trains into Cardiff Central station run every hour. The journey takes 25 minutes.

Cardiff Airport Telephone: +44(0)1446 711777

Cardiff has two rail stations, Cardiff Central (Tel: +44(0)1222 499 811) and Queen Street. Both are within walking distance of the stadium. Regular services from London Paddington.

From the east, take the M4 and leave at junction 29 and head into Cardiff on the A48(M). Then join the A4161 Newport Road and continue to the centre of Cardiff. Parking for the matches is a breeze. We drove straight to the centre of the town and parked in a multistorey car park 400 yards from the ground!

The central bus station is located within a short distance of the ground. For more detail call Cardiff Bus on +44(0)1222 396521.

Completed in time for the 1999 World Cup, the Millennium Stadium is one of the world's most spectacular sporting arenas, boasting a roof which can open or close depending on the weather conditions.

The shape of the seating bowl is the primary factor in the design of the stadium. Its form is optimised by computer analysis to bring spectators as close as possible to the in-field action and to provide a high standard of viewing and comfort for each seat.

It provides a wide range of accommodation on its three overlapping tiers while minimising the overall footprint and impact of the stadium on its city centre site.

The rear of the lower tier and its concourse link directly with the external podium, surrounding streets and river walk. This provides direct access for wheelchair users and other disabled people to their designated seating areas. Access to the middle and upper tier concourses is by escalators, lifts and stairs strategically placed around the building.

Upper and lower tier concourses offer hospitality suites, media facilities and the stadium control room all on its upper level with specialised refreshments and dining accommodation on its lower level concourse. Car parking, delivery access and back of house facilities are accommodated in the two levels below the podium.

http://www.6nations.co.uk/venues/millennium.asp

7

1 INFORMATION AND PERSUASION

SAFETY, EQUIPMENT & CLOTHING

We have all the specialist equipment you will need, and can provide waterproofs & rucsacs. On activities the instructors will carry group shelters, mobile phones and/or radios, first aid kits, and any other specialist equipment needed.

ALL INCLUSIVE ADVENTURE HOLIDAYS

We have a variety of accommodation, from secluded country cottages, fifty bed mountain centre, village B&B's, five star hotels, bunk houses, & camp sites, just tell us what you need and how long your break is, and leave the rest to us!

Mountain Activities remain our speciality, and we can put exciting and varied activities together for you wherever you choose to stay.

We provide for all, from the individual who prefers their own personal guide, up to larger groups needing several instructors, intensive training for company outings, interesting leisure for schools or clubs, to those with special needs.

WE OPERATE IN THE MOUNTAINS OF SNOWDONIA ALL YEAR ROUND

Bob Postings • The Coach House
Pencaenewydd • Pwllheli • Gwynedd • LL53 6RD

E-mail: bob@pathfindersnowdonia.co.uk
www.pathfindersnowdonia.co.uk

BOOKINGS & ENQUIRIES	07781 121820
HOME & EVENINGS ☎ & ✉	01766 810909
MOUNTAIN BOB	07702 233111

Pathfinder
SNOWDONIA MOUNTAIN, RIVER & LAKE ACTIVITIES

AALA Tel: 01222 755715
ADVENTURE ACTIVITIES LICENSING AUTHORITY

"In Safe Hands"

BOB POSTINGS MLC, SPSA

On the move

BOB POSTINGS MLC, SPSA

MOUNTAINEERING
HILL WALKING
ROCK CLIMBING
ABSEILING
GORGE SCRAMBLING
TYROLEAN TRAVERSES
KAYAKING
CANADIAN CANOEING

E-mail: bob@pathfindersnowdonia.co.uk
www.pathfindersnowdonia.co.uk

INTRODUCTION

Bob Postings and his hand picked team of Instructors all have a great love for the mountains of Snowdonia, and they take no greater delight than to help you enjoy the many exciting activities available among them. They are qualified, enthusiastic, experienced, and will help you achieve the impossible while soaking up the special atmosphere of the breathtakingly beautiful Snowdonia National Park.

MOUNTAINEERING WALKS

Snowdonia's mountains are very rugged, full of character, and can be a source of adventure. Learn something of their wild side by reaching high into their summits with an experienced guide. You will be rewarded with spectacular scenery if the weather is clear, and there is always a taste of that "special atmosphere".

SNOW & ICE ROUTES

Very specialised, one to one, or one to two instruction to get you started in arguably the most exciting aspect of mountaineering. Includes a study of equipment, clothing, conditions, and basic safe techniques.

ROCK CLIMBING AND ABSEILING

Instruction of basic climbing techniques on a suitable crag, this activity includes climbs of enjoyable height and difficulty while safely roped. After the climb abseiling down is always great fun! We also try to teach you something of the skills of ropework and the use of modern climbing equipment.

1 INFORMATION AND PERSUASION

LAKE & RIVER DAY

Canadian canoes, kayaks, raft building & racing, crossing the river by rope, make this a very varied & entertaining day! Any or all are just great for team building or just sheer amusement for all!

RADIO CONTROLLED MOUNTAIN EXERCISES

Often used in the mountains, radios can prove seriously useful, lots of fun, and sometimes life saving! Guide your "rescuers" to your exact mountain or forest location using no map or compass, *just* a radio and your observation and communication skills! - **Very entertaining!!**

RIVER GORGE CHALLENGE

Roped traverses along slippery rockwalls just inches above deep pools, tyrolean rope crossings, the "letter box", and the waterfall, are just some of the little challenges you get to try in this gorge, (which was used regularly by Royal Marines for adventurous training). You wear climbing harness and helmet for this exercise, and bring some spare dry clothing!

HUMAN RESOURCES - *STRESS MANAGEMENT*

Stress is a field of which no senior executive should be ignorant. The costs to industry are too high, and well documented. You will find that energetic and enjoyable mountain adventures work wonders to balance up the whole team's feeling of well being and calm. Activities are tailored to develop communication skills, self confidence, initiative, dynamic leadership, and foster good relationships. Your team will always benefit from these exercises, be they specifically targeted, or just an informal team adventure.
Improvements in attitude, performance and atmosphere in the workplace will be noticable!

MOUNTAIN ADVENTURE DAY

These are exciting and demanding courses. You will need to be strong, courageous and adventurous to succeed here, but the sense of achievement will be terrific!
Get to try tough classics such as Crib Goch, the North Ridge of Tryfan and Bristly Ridge. Very famous, very hairy, and very exciting, and yet quite within your grasp with our experienced instructors.

NAVIGATION TRAINING & ORIENTEERING

For the budding mountaineer or team leader this will prove invaluable. The absolute necessity of knowing where you are by day or night, cloud or whiteout, is a must! Learn to find your way around with serious mountain training, or make it educational fun with a leisurely orienteering course. Learn how to read a Map & use a Compass effectively, and we can even show you how to navigate by satellite.

SPECIAL NEEDS

It is Pathfinders policy and the goal of our instructors to do our utmost to help everyone to achieve success in the activities available in this beautiful area. *Whatever* your needs, or ability, we will definitely stretch your potential for sheer enjoyment of life! We shall try to fulfil this aim and see that you return home having enjoyed Snowdonia to the full.

On the move

2 Exploring the features of a leaflet

▶ On pages 8–10 there are six panels, designed to be folded into a leaflet:
  A WALES TOURIST BOARD
  B SAFETY, EQUIPMENT & CLOTHING
  C Pathfinder
  D INTRODUCTION
  E LAKE & RIVER DAY
  F MOUNTAIN ADVENTURE DAY
▶ Decide on the order in which you think it would be most logical to read the leaflet, assuming you read the whole leaflet at one time. Be prepared to justify your conclusions.
▶ Why is the word "rescuers" in quotation marks in the section 'RADIO CONTROLLED MOUNTAIN EXERCISES'?
▶ Why is the word 'just' in italics in the same section?
▶ Apart from giving details of the various types of activity available, how does the writer suggest there is something on offer for a wide range of people? Use the whole leaflet for this, and the following questions.
▶ How does the writer suggest the enjoyable side of the experiences on offer?
▶ How does the writer try to make some of the activities sound challenging, but also try to reassure the reader?
  In your answer you should consider:
  • the choice of words and details to reassure
  • the choice of words and details to suggest challenge
  • the use of pictures and illustrations.
▶ Would you say the main purpose of this leaflet was to inform or to persuade? Be prepared to justify your point of view.
▶ Overall, how effective do you think this leaflet is in communicating to the reader?

3 Exploring the features of magazine advertisements

The advertisements for Birmingham and Glasgow on pages 14 and 15 were published in the Virgin trains magazine, *HotLine*, available free to passengers on Virgin trains.
▶ In your group, identify as many of the techniques identified on pages 12 and 13 as you can.
▶ Write any examples you find into a table like those on pages 12 and 13.
▶ Look at the Advice panel. Which method will be most effective in terms of:
  • getting the answers filled in
  • understanding the techniques you will be using later
  • a sense of purpose and achievement for all?

WORDS

▲ MLC Mountain Leader Certificate SPSA Single Pitch Supervisors' Award
▲ **pitch** *noun mountaineering* the section of a route on a rock climb, sometimes equal to the full length of the rope, but often shorter.
▲ **seriously** *adverb colloquial* significantly.
▲ **tyrolean** *adjective* belonging or related to Tyrol, an east Alpine area that lies mainly in western Austria.
▲ **letter box** *noun* narrow gap between two rocks through which a person squeezes.
▲ **foster** *verb* encourage the development of (ideas, feelings, etc.).
▲ **hairy** *adjective colloquial*
1 dangerous, frightening or exciting.
2 difficult or tricky.
▲ **budding** *adjective* said of a person: developing; beginning to show talent in a specified area.
▲ **serious** *adjective* concerned with important matters; not inclined to flippancy or lightness of mood.

ADVICE

▲ Be aware of how your group is working. You could:
• all see what you can find individually, share ideas and then see what's missing
• work in pairs on one advertisement at a time
• all search at the same time, and say what you find when you find it
• have one pair working backwards and one pair working forwards through the questions
• match tasks to the different skills and interests in the group
• read the whole of each advertisement first *or* only scan for the detail you need.

1 INFORMATION AND PERSUASION

WORDS
▲ **alliteration** *noun* the repetition of the same sound at the beginning of words close to each other in a text.

ADVICE
▲ Each space represents one example.

▶ Playing with words

| Birmingham: | |

▶ Using the names of people who may be well known

| Birmingham: | |
| Glasgow: | |

▶ Using 'amazing' exhibits

| Birmingham: | |

▶ Using alliteration

| Birmingham: | |
| Glasgow: | |

▶ Using rhyme

| Birmingham: | |
| Glasgow: | |

▶ Using a question

| Birmingham: | |

▶ Using superlatives

| Birmingham: | |
| Glasgow: | |

▶ Using a comparison

| Glasgow: | |

▶ Making it sound unique/original

| Birmingham: | |
| Glasgow: | |

▶ Using words with positive connotations (purr words)

| Birmingham: | |
| Glasgow: | |

On the move

- Using colloquial/non-standard language

| Birmingham: | |
| Glasgow: | |

- Using non-standard spelling

| Glasgow: | |

- Using links to popular culture, e.g. designer labels, entertainment including football

| Birmingham: | |
| Glasgow: | |

- Using statistics to impress

| Birmingham: | |
| Glasgow: | |

- Using imperatives

| Birmingham: | |
| Glasgow: | |

- Using facts and figures: find one example of a price and one example of how to contact a business, etc

	Example of price given – write down what it refers to	Example of contact method given – write down who it refers to
Birmingham:		
Glasgow:		

- Using exceptions/qualifications: find any examples in the Fares box which tell you that the offer **may** not apply to you

| Birmingham: | |
| Glasgow: | |

- Would you say the main purpose of these advertisements was to inform or to persuade? Be prepared to justify your point of view.
- Overall, how effective do you think they are in communicating to the reader?

Self-assessment of the way you tackled Activity 3

- Decide in your group how effective you think your approach was.
- Would you do anything differently on another occasion, and why?

13

1 INFORMATION AND PERSUASION

DESTINATIONS
BIRMINGHAM

What to see and do

ART
- **The annual John Kobal Photographic Portrait Award** exhibition never fails to deliver innovative, quirky, atmospheric pictures of people, whether famous (such as David Beckham alone and waiting for a head-shave in a barber shop, below), infamous or unfamous. At the Cotton Gallery until 24 June. Free. Tel 0121 440 4221.
- **'Apocalypse Then: Graphic Art and the Great War'** offers a rare glimpse into the horrific events of that time through the eyes of some of the great artists of the early 20th century, such as Egon Schiele and Franz Marc. Ongoing at the Barber Institute of Fine Arts, Edgbaston. Tel 0121 414 7333.
- **'Egypt Revealed – Life & Death in Ancient Egypt'**. Pride of place at the exhibition goes to 'Gingerella', the dehydrated remains of a pre-dynastic woman who was buried in the hot desert sand. Children will also be lured by the mummified croc and cat. At the Gas Hall, from 23 June to 23 September. Tel 0121 303 2834.

ON STAGE
- **Blues in the Night** is a suitably sultry musical for a summer's evening, featuring some of the greatest jazz and blues songs ever written. At The Rep from 8 to 30 June. Tickets £4.99 to £16.50. Tel 0121 236 4455.
- **The annual Birmingham International Jazz Festival** offers yet more jazz, from trad to mad, 80 per cent of it free. From 6 to 15 July at venues across the city. Tel 0121 454 7020.
- **The Royal Shakespeare Company's** 2001 season offers familiar classics alongside eagerly awaited new work. The season runs in repertory until 13 October. Tickets £6 to £40. Tel 01789 403403.
- **The Crescent Theatre** hosts the two-week Birmingham Fringe Festival in August. Tickets £5.50 to £8.50. Tel 0121 643 5858.

WORTH A LOOK
- **Sherborne Wharf** runs daily hour-long Heritage Trips throughout summer, leaving the International Convention Centre at 11.30am, 1pm, 2.30pm and 4pm. £4/£3.50. Tel 0121 455 6163.
- **Jewellery Quarter**: the city's once-thriving bauble-making enclave is still home to hundreds of jewellers, many of whom sell direct to visitors. Start at the Discovery Centre in Vyse Street. £2/£1.50. Tel 0121 554 3598.

Take the plunge
Why do we do it? Why do we voluntarily subject ourselves to heart-stopping experiences such as plunging 180 feet earthwards at 50mph, strapped into a machine that is controlled only by a 'powerful magnetic field'? This is what Apocalypse, the world's first stand-up tower drop, does to its brave riders at Drayton Manor Park, Heart of England Tourist Board's Visitor Attraction of the Year 2000. The park also boasts Shockwave, Europe's only stand-up rollercoaster, and Stormforce 10, a wet thrill ride based on an RNLI rescue. Many less life-testing entertainments are available for the young, the elderly and the just-plain-sensible. Throughout the summer the X76 bus from Edgbaston Street (200 metres from New Street Station) deposits you at the main gate. Round trip £3.60/£2.40. Entrance to the park is £15 adults, £11 children, £47 for a family of four. Tel 01827 287979.

Where to eat, drink, dance, sleep

RESTAURANTS
Cheap eats: Verde, The Mailbox retail centre. Feel-good, super-fresh fast food has come to town with a stylish eat-in or take-out place which offers superb daytime panini, soups and salads. If this is the future of lunches on the hoof, count us in. Tel 0121 632 1444. **Karibunis**, Stratford Road, Hall Green. The restaurant in South Birmingham College's chef-training department has great bargains for hungry human guinea pigs. Friday two-for-one lunch gets you three courses apiece all for about £6. And it's good, too – everything from homemade samosas with tamarind dip to cajun blackened fish. Tel 0121 694 5000.
Mid-priced meals: Fish! Diner and Bar, Mailbox. The fish and chip shop comes of age. Grab a café-style table, choose your fish from the day's selection and pick a cooking method and sauce. Tel 020 7234 3333. **Ask**, 237 Hagley Road, Edgbaston, appeals to the Italian in all of us. Solid, competent dishes, just like mamma used to make (as they say) but served in rather more stylish surroundings. Tel 0121 454 2800.
Top nosh: Café Lazeez, Mailbox. The food here, based on 'evolved' north Indian fare, is as bang up to date as the *übermodern* interior. Hot stuff in cool surroundings. Tel 0121 643 7979.
Santa Fe, Mailbox. You don't know you want south-western American food until you eat here. Trip the spice fantastic with well-judged, robust dishes (chili pops up in a lot of it) in a great laidback restaurant in one of the Mailbox's best locations overlooking the canal. Yeehaw! Tel 0121 632 1250.

BARS AND CLUBS
Que Club, Central Hall, Corporation Street. You're told to dress to glow and promised three rooms of mayhem on Saturdays when Atomic Jam take over. Tel 0121 212 0550. **The Sanctuary in the Institute**, 78 Digbeth, is giving over its Fridays to host Slinky nights, the dance phenomenon which has already swept the south coast. Guaranteed admission available with £12 advance tickets. Tel 01202 646330.

HOTEL OFFER
The Plough and Harrow, 135 Hagley Road, Edgbaston. Tel 0121 454 4111. Since 1704, The Plough and Harrow has maintained its tradition for sumptuous comfort and plain courtesy. Conveniently situated less than a mile from the city centre – but still lucky enough to sit in its own spacious gardens. **The offer:** A special summer stop-over rate of £40 per room per night. (A saving of more than 60 per cent). Offer valid 1 June to 10 September 2001, subject to availability. Please quote *HotLine* Reader Offer when booking.

Information
- **New Street Station** is in the city centre. Take the escalator up to the shopping centre and follow the signs out to New Street.
- **Local transport** Call 0121 200 2700 for local bus and train information. Taxi rank at station.
- **Shopping** City Plaza, Cannon Street, for trendy clothes; The Pavilions, High Street, and New Street, for chain names. Corporation Street has Rackhams (House of Fraser), and the Virgin Megastore (0121 236 2523). The Jewellery Quarter is famous nationwide.
- **Banks** LloydsTSB and NatWest cash machines are at New Street station.
- **Entertainment** UGC cinema: Arcadian Centre, Hurst Street. Tel 0121 622 3323. Check out www.birminghamarts.org.uk for latest listings, or buy *What's On In Birmingham and Central England* (80p) from newsagents.
- **Tourist information** Birmingham Convention and Visitor Bureau, 2 City Arcade. Tel 0121 643 2514.

Fares
- **Virgin Value** off-peak returns to Birmingham New Street from Manchester start at £10; from London £15; from Edinburgh and Glasgow £29. Just book at least 14 days in advance. For all train and destination information go to www.virgin.com/trains or call 08457 222 333. Prices valid until 30 September 2001, subject to availability.

DEAN FREEMAN

On the move

DESTINATIONS
Glasgow

What to see and do

FUN ON THE WATER
- **GlasgowDucks** are the latest way to explore the city and its regenerated riverside – in a WWII amphibious vehicle. Be warned: these vehicles were not built for speed, even in the water. Adults £11.50, children £7.50. Tel 0870 0136140/0141 572 8381.
- **The Waverley**, aka 'the Pride of the Clyde', is the world's last remaining ocean-going paddle steamer. Day trips to Dunoon, Rothesay, Tarbert and Loch Fyne are conducted at a leisurely 1940s pace, although in modern splendour and elegance. Tours start from mid-June. Adults £10 to £27 round trip, children half price. Tel 0141 221 8152.
- **Seaforce**, as its name suggests, is just a tad speedier than The Waverley, being a powerboat. Exhilarating 30-minute trips start at the Tall Ship at Glasgow Harbour. Tall Ship admission, adults £4.50, one child free, others £2.50. Seaforce costs an additional £5/£2.50. Tel 0141 400 7737.

FESTIVALS
- **West End Festival**. The Midsummer Carnival Parade on Sunday 17 June is the focal point of this jolly jamboree. From 9 to 24 June. Tel 0141 341 0844.
- **Glenmorangie Glasgow Jazz Festival**. Names come big and even bigger at this very popular event: Chick Corea, George Melly, The Brecker Brothers and Jazz Jamaica are just a few of the performers appearing in 2001. From 30 June to 8 July. Tel 0141 552 3552.

ART
- **'Whistler in Venice'** includes etchings and pastels that the artist produced during his year in Venice. Particularly fine are those of the backwaters and bridges away from the crowds. At the Hunterian Art Gallery until 1 September. Tel 0141 330 5431.
- **'Ancient Egypt: Digging for Dreams'** is a major exhibition of Egyptology with many pieces being seen for the first time. Until 30 September. Timed tickets, adults £2, concessions £1, family £5. Tel 0141 287 2550.

WORTH A LOOK
- **The Museum of Scottish Football**, Hampden Park. Pride of place goes to the Scottish FA Cup, the oldest national trophy in the world. Adults £5, all concessions £2.50. Tel 0141 616 6100.

- **St Mungo Museum of Religious Life and Art**. Dali's *Christ of St John of the Cross* alone is worth a gander. Free. Tel 0141 553 2557.

The appliance of science
Glasgow's architecturally unique Science Centre finally fully opens this summer. The armadillo-like IMAX Theatre and the crescent-shaped Science Mall are the first buildings in the UK, and only the second in Europe, to be clad in titanium (the other being the much-acclaimed Guggenheim Museum in Bilbao). The Glasgow Tower, which takes the shape of an aircraft wing on its tip, is the only such structure in the world to revolve 360° from top to bottom. Since it opened last October, the giant cinema screen has already wowed 50,000 people; more than twice that many are expected to troop through the four floors of interactive science, technology and related exhibits in the Mall and downstairs in the Tower, which open this summer. The non-vertiginous should take a ride to the top of the Tower for spectacular views. Tel 0141 420 5000 or see www.gsc.org.uk

Where to eat, drink, dance, sleep

RESTAURANTS
Cheap eats: Italmania, 180-184 Argyle Street. Pizza, pasta and espresso to make your hair stand on end are on offer at this funky café-diner. Open until very late, it's ideal for a post-clubbing ciabatta. Tel 0141 248 1632.
Soba, 11 Mitchell Lane, surfs the trend for all things Oriental with a range of pan-Asian-inspired dishes including vast quantities of noodles. DJs and live bands add to the ambience as, of course, do the fashionable sake cocktails. Tel 0141 204 2404.
Mid-priced meals: Mussel Inn, 157 Hope Street. Building on the success of the Edinburgh original, this new branch serves much the same seafood menu but with a wider selection of specials. Tel 0141 572 1405. **The Other Side**, 53 Morrison Street. From eggs Florentine in the morning to carpaccio in the evening, The Other Side will keep the wolf from the door all day. Tel 0141 429 4042.
Top nosh: Gordon Yuill and Company, 257 West Campbell Street. After 17 years as Maitre d' at Rogano's, Mr Yuill has set up his own restaurant. Classic dishes with a twist mean that getting a table isn't easy. Tel 0141 572 4052.

BARS AND CLUBS
The Arches, 253 Argyle Street. Long-established and credible clubbing venue and arts centre which has just been fitted out with a stylish café-bar. Definitely a club for dancing rather than for being seen in, The Arches still manages to retain a degree of comfort. Tel 0141 565 1000.
Bloc +, 117 Bath Street. This new basement bar on a street that is rapidly coming to life looks to Eastern Europe for its vibe. The furniture is chunky and concrete solid, the beer Czech or German and the after-work crowd not in the least bit shy about letting their hair down. Old skool DJs keep the sounds fresh at the weekends. Tel 0141 579 6066.

HOTEL OFFER
Days Inn, 80 Ballater Street. Tel 0141 429 4233. Just a few minutes from the River Clyde and a short walk to the city centre, the cosy rooms offer all the usual amenities in great comfort.
The offer: £44.40 per room per night, including breakfast. (A saving of 20 per cent.) Offer valid for a minimum of two nights from 1 June to 10 September, subject to availability. Please quote *HotLine* Reader Offer when booking.

Information

- **Glasgow Central Station** is on Gordon Street; the nearest Underground is St Enoch. There is a taxi rank outside the station.
- **Local transport** Buses go from Buchanan Street bus station. For information on local trains, buses and Glasgow Underground, call Strathclyde Passenger Transport on 0141 332 7133.
- **Shopping** Princes Square Shopping Centre, Buchanan Street for Space NK and Vidal Sassoon. The Italian Centre in Merchant City for Armani, Versace, Joseph, DKNY, and Philippe Starck. Buchanan Galleries houses the biggest Habitat in Europe.
- **Banks** Royal Bank of Scotland and The Halifax at Glasgow Central; main banks on Bothwell Street and Sauchiehall Street.
- **Entertainment** UGC cinema: 1221 Gallowgate. Tel 0141 556 4282. Parks: Glasgow Green, Greendyke Street. Tel 0141 287 5511. See *The List* (£1.95), from newsagents.
- **Tourist information** 11 George Square. Tel 0141 204 4400.

Fares

- **Virgin Value** off-peak returns to Glasgow from Preston start at £20; from Birmingham New Street £29; and from London £29. Just book at least 14 days in advance. For all train and destination information go to www.virgin.com/trains or call 08457 222 333. Prices valid until 30 September 2001, subject to availability.

15

1 INFORMATION AND PERSUASION

4 Exploring the features of travel writing

Finding out about a place does not have to be through leaflets and advertisements, which will only select details providing a positive image of the place. In travel writing, authors will give a much fuller picture of what the place is like, from their particular point of view.

The following extract is taken from the opening chapter of Bill Bryson's *Down Under*. As you read it or hear it read, think about:

▶ how Bill Bryson tries to interest the reader
▶ how Bill Bryson may encourage the reader to read on after the first chapter
▶ whether he gives a positive or negative image of Australia.

Australia is the world's sixth largest country and its largest island. It is the only island that is also a continent, and the only continent that is also a country. It was the first continent conquered from the sea, and the last. It is also the only nation that began as a prison.

It is the home of the largest living thing on earth, the Great Barrier Reef, and of the most famous and striking monolith, Ayers Rock (or Uluru to use its now official, more respectful Aboriginal name). It has more things that will kill you than anywhere else. Of the world's ten most poisonous snakes, all are Australian. Five of its creatures – the funnel-web spider, box jellyfish, blue-ringed octopus, paralysis tick and stonefish – are the most lethal of their type in the world. This is a country where even the fluffiest of caterpillars can lay you out with a toxic nip, where seashells will not just sting you but actually sometimes *go* for you. Pick up an innocuous coneshell from a Queensland beach, as innocent tourists are all too wont to do, and you will discover that the little fellow inside is not just astoundingly swift and testy, but exceedingly venomous. If you are not stung or pronged to death in some unexpected manner, you may be fatally chomped by sharks or crocodiles, or carried helplessly out to sea by irresistible currents, or left to stagger to an unhappy death in the baking outback. It's a tough place.

And it is old. For 60 million years, since the formation of the Great Dividing Range, Australia has been all but silent geologically, which has allowed it to preserve many of the oldest things ever found on earth – the most ancient rocks and fossils, the earliest animal tracks and riverbeds, the first faint signs of life itself. At some undetermined point in the great immensity of its past – perhaps 45,000 years ago, perhaps 60,000, but certainly before there were modern humans in the Americas or Europe – it was quietly invaded by a deeply inscrutable people, the Aborigines, who have no clearly evident racial or linguistic kinship to their neighbours in the region, and whose presence in Australia can be explained only by positing that they invented and mastered ocean-going craft at least 30,000 years in advance of anyone else in order to undertake an exodus, then forgot or abandoned nearly all they had learned and scarcely ever bothered with the open sea again.

The world the first Englishmen found was famously inverted – its seasons back to front, its constellations upside down – and unlike anything any of them had seen before, even in the near latitudes of the Pacific. Its creatures seemed to have

5

10

15

20

25

30

evolved as if they had misread the manual. The most characteristic of them didn't run or lope or canter, but *bounced* across the landscape, like dropped balls. The continent teemed with unlikely life. It contained a fish that could climb trees; a fox that flew (it was actually a very large bat); crustaceans so big that a grown man could climb inside their shells.

In short, there was no place in the world like it. There still isn't. Eighty per cent of all that lives in Australia, plant and animal, exists nowhere else. More than this, it exists in an abundance that seems incompatible with the harshness of the environment. Australia is the driest, flattest, hottest, most desiccated, infertile and climatically aggressive of all the inhabited continents. (Only Antarctica is more hostile to life.) And yet it teems with life in numbers uncounted.

This is a country that is at once staggeringly empty and yet packed with stuff. Interesting stuff, ancient stuff, stuff not readily explained. Stuff yet to be found.

Trust me, this is an interesting place.

▶ Would you say the main purpose of this writing was to inform or to persuade? Be prepared to justify your point of view.
▶ Overall, how effective do you think this writing is?
▶ Study the cards printed on pages 18 and 19, and match up a red card to a green card to a blue card.
▶ Use a table like the one on the next page, writing down the matching numbers and letters.

ADVICE

▲ The numbers on the red cards refer to line numbers in the printed passage.
▲ You may find it easier to match the red and green, then match the blue.
▲ Keep a careful record of the cards you have used already.

WORDS

▲ **monolith** *noun* **1** a single, tall block of stone, especially one shaped like or into a column or pillar. **2** anything resembling one of these in its uniformity, immovability or massiveness.
▲ **toxic** *adjective* poisonous.
▲ **innocuous** *adjective* harmless, inoffensive.
▲ **wont** *adjective chiefly formal, literary or old use* accustomed, habitually inclined.
▲ **testy** *adjective* irritable, bad-tempered, touchy.
▲ **irresistible** *adjective* too strong to be resisted; overpowering.
▲ **inscrutable** *adjective* hard to understand or explain; mysterious; enigmatic.
▲ **kinship** *noun* **1** family relationship. **2** a state of having common properties or characteristics.
▲ **posit** *verb* put forward as a possible explanation.
▲ **exodus** *noun* a mass departure of people.
▲ **invert** *verb* (**inverted, inverting**) to turn upside down or inside out.
▲ **constellation** *noun* a group of stars.
▲ **canter** *verb* to move or cause to move at a pace between trotting and galloping.
▲ **teem** *verb* (usually **teem with people** or **...things**) to be full of them or abound in them.
▲ **crustacean** *noun* animal without a backbone such as crab, lobster, shrimp, barnacle, woodlouse, etc.
▲ **incompatible** *adjective* inconsistent; not in agreement.
▲ **desiccated** *adjective* dried up.

WORDS

▲ **juxtaposition** *noun* positioning close together or side by side.

1 INFORMATION AND PERSUASION

Quotation and line reference	Techniques 1–3	Effects of techniques A–M
largest island 1 largest living thing 5 most famous 6 most poisonous/lethal 8/10		
not just sting you but actually sometimes *go* for you 12		
If you are not… you may be… or… or… 15–18		
fatally chomped 16		
It's a tough place. 18		
60 million years… 19		
most ancient rocks and fossils 21–22 earliest animal tracks and riverbeds 22		
can be explained only by positing… 27–28		
misread the manual 35		
bounced across the landscape, like dropped balls 36		
a fish that could climb trees; a fox that flew 37/38		
staggeringly empty and yet packed with stuff. 46		
Trust me, this is an interesting place. 48		

On the move

11 Use of superlatives.

I Makes it seem that if Australia does not kill *you* you, the reader in one way, it will find another way to do it.

7 Use of italics
Use of second person pronoun

6 Use of italics
Use of an image – a simile

4 Use of contradiction

12 Use of superlatives

J Makes the Aborigines seem skilled and fascinating, with unsolved mysteries about their past.

G Makes Australia today sound special and interesting because it has extremes.

L One word is fairly informal and light-hearted, the other word suggests death. Putting them together helps to make the text shockingly entertaining.

D Intrigues readers, making them want to read on and find out more about this extraordinary place.

9 Use of a short sentence at the end of a paragraph

10 Use of statistics

K Makes the reader wonder how both these statements can be true at the same time. Intrigues the reader.

A Direct appeal to the reader to have confidence in the writer – and therefore to read the rest of the book.

8 Use of second person pronoun
Use of 'listing'

5 Use of imperative
Use of first person pronoun

M Sums up the paragraph. Adds to the impact by summing it up briefly and directly.

H Makes it seem as if the seashells deliberately set out to attack *you* – makes it sound threatening.

C Indicates the kangaroo in a fun way without naming it. Makes the way it moves sound extraordinary and amazing.

F Makes Australia's history seem special and unique.

13 Use of surprising juxtaposition

E Makes Australia seem impressive and different.

2 Use of alliteration
Use of an image – a metaphor

B Helps to amuse the reader by imagining animals reading. The alliteration adds to the absurdity of the idea and the sense of fun in presenting it this way.

1 Describing an event in history as if it is almost impossible to believe

3 Use of amazing facts that sound impossible

1 INFORMATION AND PERSUASION

 ## Writing your own magazine

Now that you have studied some examples of the way places are described, you are in a good position to try to use some of the techniques on your own. You will be writing an advertisement similar to the ones published by Virgin Trains for Birmingham and Glasgow. Since it is an advertisement, you will obviously only refer to the *good* points about the place you choose.

▶ Write your own one-page advertisement for attractions near your home or school to encourage people to come and visit.

ADVICE

▲ The overall feel and look should match the Birmingham and Glasgow pages fairly closely. Treat it as real – as if this page might really be used by a train or coach company.
▲ However, you may wish to create an 'over-the-top' version of the material, but if so make it clear to your teacher that that is what you intend! Check with your teacher first.
▲ You must include:
- A section headed 'What to see and do'.
- A photograph/instruction to the designer of where and how the photograph should be taken.
- An Information section including how to get there.
- A Fares section including sample realistic prices by rail/rail + bus.
- A 'Where to eat, drink, dance, sleep' section.
- Attractions to suit different ages and interests.
- Words with positive connotations to attract people.
▲ You could include:
- use of alliteration
- use of different-coloured fonts
- use of rhyme
- use of playing with words
- use of superlatives
- names of famous people
- statistics.
▲ You will need to be able to explain your reasoning for using any of these. It would not be appropriate to use them just because they are listed here.

WORDS

▲ **XCU Extra close-up**: from just above the eyebrows to just below the mouth.
▲ **CU Close-up**: head and shoulders only.
▲ **MS Mid-shot**: shows the figure from approximately the waist to the head.
▲ **LS Long shot**: shows the figure from head to toe.

Moving-image texts about place

 ## Exploring a television script

Another way of creating or changing an image of a place is through television.
▶ Look in detail at the way the script on pages 21–22 is written.
▶ What image of the Millennium Stadium is being created?
▶ How would the pictures and sound-effects affect the television audience's reaction?

On the move

Sound	Vision
Studio Presenter: *Now for our regular Friday feature looking at places of interest which viewers might like to visit. Over to our reporter (name) ....* Theme music for Six Nations Championship.	CU Studio Presenter. Background screen showing map of UK with Cardiff indicated.
Fade out gradually, including over first part of commentary.	Bird's-eye shot: Slow pan across open roof of Millennium Stadium looking down at the pitch. Caption moving across bottom of screen: *Millennium Stadium, Cardiff* *Reporter: ....*
Voice-over: *You don't have to be a rugby or football supporter to have seen the inside of this magnificent stadium. It's been used for Robbie Williams concerts, religious gatherings and a whole range of other events.*	Cut to 3-second LS of Robbie Williams concert. Cut to 3-second LS of religious gathering. LS Pan around stadium when full.
If and when you do get to be here, you're part of an audience of up to 72,500 people.	
Sound of stadium crowd with capacity audience cheering/clapping/reacting to events.	Clips of stadium crowd to match sound.
The stadium can be used in so many different ways and in any weather because of its amazing sliding roof. Twenty minutes is all it takes from fully open to fully closed.	LS Slow pan from below across open stadium roof. Cut to same angle, LS stadium roof closed. CU Foundation stone plaque – 5-second clip.
The national status of the stadium was recognised from the beginning when the foundation stone was laid by the Prime Minister.	
Sound-track of Tony Blair laying the foundation stone.	Clip to match sound-track. LS Pan showing walkway built out over River Taff.
To cope with the huge crowds attending events at the Millennium Stadium, this riverside walkway has been built alongside the River Taff.	
If you look down at your feet as you walk along you can see the flags of many of the rugby teams which played in the 1999 Rugby World Cup. Look even closer, and you can see the names of some of the players engraved below the flags.	CU 2-second clips of emblems of England, France, Ireland, Italy, Scotland, Wales. XCU Names of English team including Delaglio.
For a small fee, you can have your own name engraved on the walkway – and perhaps even have the lettering finished in gold.	MS Man painting gold lettering.

1 INFORMATION AND PERSUASION

Sound	Vision
Even if you don't go inside the stadium, it's well worth a visit to see the impressive architecture, including the unique roof held up by four towers and dominating the city centre.	LS One of the supporting towers, panning across to Cardiff Castle and the City Centre. Statistics run across bottom of screen: 13,500 Foundation Piles... Masts each 90 metres high... 56,000 tonnes of concrete and steel... Bowl volume – 1,500,000 cubic metres... Roof 38,000 metres square... Seating 72,500 spectators...
Theme music for Six Nations Championship fades in and out over next 15 seconds.	
So don't wait for your team to be playing at the Millennium Stadium. Arrive at the train or coach station in Cardiff, and within two minutes you can be at the Millennium Stadium.	LS Pan from Central Station façade to bus station to Millennium Stadium.
Next week, we'll be having a look at the oldest surviving theatre in the region. But for now, back to the studio.	CU Presenter standing in front of main entrance. Tilt-up during commentary to give sense of scale and height of the building. CU Studio Presenter.

On the move

 Writing a text for a TV programme

One day each week, your local television company includes in its news broadcast a description of one building or place of interest in the local area. The buildings could be chosen because of an interesting history, their present use, their design, or a variety of factors. The places could be chosen because of an interesting history, because they are beauty spots, or because tourists might be encouraged to visit.

You have been asked to write the script about one building or place that interests you. You should follow the type of layout explored in Activity 6. Possibilities include:
- a beauty spot such as a waterfall, a viewpoint, an Area of Outstanding Natural Beauty
- a building that has a preservation order on it which means it cannot be demolished
- a cathedral/church/mosque etc.
- a concert venue
- a football/sports stadium
- a house with the latest energy-saving devices
- a leisure centre
- a town hall

– but you may have other ideas, which you could discuss with your teacher.
- You need to include the script for the presenter, but you should also include any interviews which are part of the programme, so that a reader understands how all the parts of your programme fit together. You should definitely include:
  - camera directions and a short description of what the audience will see on screen
  - details of any on-screen captions
  - presenter's script and any sound-effects which the audience will hear.

  Content – suggestions for what to include:
  - a brief link from the studio presenter at the beginning and end
  - a brief introduction, explaining why this place has been included
  - details of the materials used/the design/interesting features of this particular building/place
  - brief interviews with people who work there or visit the building/place
  - a brief account of why this building/place is special to you/especially interesting to you.

  Layout
  - Use a play-form layout, but instead of stage directions briefly write down what the camera would be showing/how it would be moving, e.g. close-up, pan, track.

  Style
  - When writing your presenter's text, make sure it will sound like spoken English when read aloud from an autocue.
  - When writing the text for the presenter (who may be on camera or simply heard as a voice-over), make references to what the television audience can see, e.g. Here... This...
  - You should include standard punctuation. Any pauses etc. must be deliberately planned for your presenter.
  - You may wish to show how unscripted speech is different from scripted speech in your 'transcript' of any interviews you include.

WORDS

▲ **bird's-eye shot:** the camera looks vertically down on the subject
▲ **high-angle shot:** the camera points downwards
▲ **low-angle shot:** the camera points upwards, usually making the subject seem more impressive.
▲ **pan** *verb* pivoting the camera horizontally left or right
▲ **tilt** *verb* pivot the camera vertically up or down
▲ **track** *verb* move the camera towards or away from the subject, or following a moving subject
▲ **zoom** *verb* keep the camera in one place, but vary the lens to give the impression of movement towards/away from subject.
▲ **autocue** *noun, trademark* TV screen hidden from the camera which slowly displays a script line by line; the speaker can read the script but appears to speak without a prompt.
▲ **transcript** *noun* written/typed/printed copy of spoken text.
▲ **voice-over** *noun* the voice of an unseen narrator in a film, TV ad or programme.

ADVICE

▲ Aim to write 2–3 sides of A4 paper.
▲ Try reading the spoken part of your script aloud to see if it sounds like natural speech.

1 INFORMATION AND PERSUASION

 Writing a commentary on your moving-image text
- Write a commentary of no more than half a page of A4 paper.
- Explain some of the choices you made in writing your script:
  - the effect you intended from some of your choices of camera angles
  - an explanation for some shot types you chose to use (LS, CU, etc.)
  - an explanation of how a sample of the spoken text was written to sound like speech rather than written English
  - the feelings you hoped to create in your viewers with your choice of music/sound-effects
  - how you have tried to link the commentary with what the viewer will see
  - any methods you used to try to make the programme sound and look like a real television programme about a place.

Self-assessment

 Judging your own performance
- From the list below:
  a select three points on which you feel you have made the most progress
  b select one point on which you most need to improve.
  I can identify the different features and purposes of parts of a web page.
  I can judge how far a text is informative or persuasive.
  I understand the layout and purpose of a leaflet.
  I can work as part of a team in oral work, planning, carrying out the plan and reflecting on strengths and weaknesses.
  I can identify techniques used by writers to inform and persuade, and comment on their effect.
  I can write an informative and persuasive text about a place I know, using techniques I have identified in texts I have read.
  I understand the meaning of key terms used when referring to moving images.
  I can write a text for a moving-image presentation which would be effective on television.
  I can write a commentary on my text, explaining and justifying the choices I have made.

 Improving your skills in English

Select one or two skills you need to concentrate on to improve your skills in reading and writing.
(The descriptions of levels are a guide only.)

	Reading skill	From	To
1	Show understanding of significant ideas and themes	Level 3	Level 4
2	Refer to the text when explaining views, locating and using ideas and information	Level 3	Level 4
3	Show understanding of a range of texts, selecting essential points and using inference and deduction where appropriate	Level 4	Level 5
4	Identify key features and select sentences, phrases and relevant information to support views	Level 4	Level 5
5	Identify different layers of meaning and comment on their significance and effect	Level 5	Level 6
6	Summarise a range of information from different sources	Level 5	Level 6

		From	To
7	Show understanding of the ways in which meaning and information are conveyed in a range of texts	Level 6	Level 7
8	Select and synthesise a range of information from a variety of sources	Level 6	Level 7
9	Show appreciation of, and comment on, a range of texts, evaluating how authors achieve their effects through the use of linguistic, structural and presentational devices	Level 7	Level 8
10	Select and analyse information and ideas, and comment on how these are conveyed in different texts	Level 7	Level 8
11	Confidently sustain responses to a demanding range of texts, developing ideas and referring in detail to aspects of language, structure and presentation	Level 8	E.P.
12	Make apt and careful comparison between texts, including consideration of audience, purpose and form	Level 8	E.P.

	Writing skill	From	To
1	Ideas are organised appropriately for an advertisement or television presentation	Level 3	Level 4
2	Writing is thoughtful, and ideas are sustained and developed in interesting ways	Level 3	Level 4
3	Writing is varied and interesting, conveying meaning clearly in an appropriate form for an advertisement or television presentation	Level 4	Level 5
4	Vocabulary choices are imaginative and words are used precisely	Level 4	Level 5
5	Writing engages and sustains the reader's interest, showing some use of style appropriate to an advertisement or television presentation	Level 5	Level 6
6	Pupils use a range of sentence structures and varied vocabulary to create effects	Level 5	Level 6
7	Writing is confident, and shows an appropriate choice of style for an advertisement or television presentation	Level 6	Level 7
8	Ideas are organised and coherent, with grammatical features and vocabulary accurately and effectively used	Level 6	Level 7
9	Writing is coherent, showing selection of specific features or expressions to convey particular effects and to interest the reader	Level 7	Level 8
10	The use of vocabulary and grammar enables fine distinctions to be made or emphasis achieved	Level 7	Level 8
11	Writing has shape and impact, and control of the style appropriate for an advertisement or television presentation	Level 8	E.P.
12	The writing is coherent, reasoned and persuasive, using a variety of grammatical constructions	Level 8	E.P.

2 Autobiography – fact and fiction
Lively Dickens

Your focus
The content of this unit is designed to:
- help you understand how authors build on their own experience
- help you use your own experiences effectively in your own writing.

Your target
By the end of this unit you should be more able to:
- recognise how writers transform their own experience into fiction
- vary the choice of tense and point of view appropriately to different stories
- write a story, effectively building on your own experience.

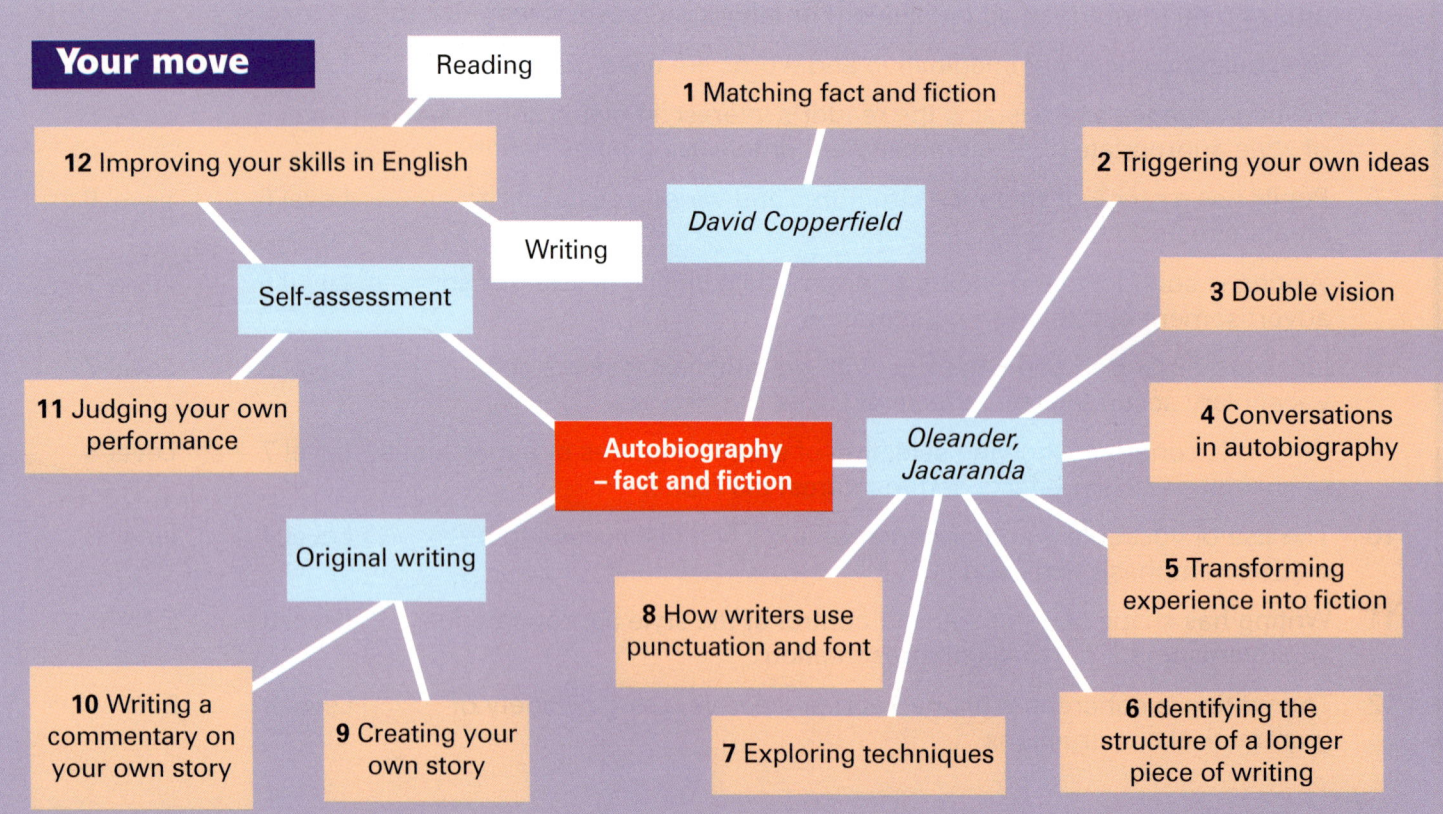

David Copperfield

At some stage in writing stories, some pupils feel that they are being asked to lie. There is probably no other subject in the curriculum that sometimes involves 'making it up as you go along'.

Strange as it may seem, the majority of what is seen on television or at the cinema, and the majority of books in most bookshops, are made up of 'lies', or fiction. This includes soap operas, plays, films, novels, short stories and so on.

Even if a film is made of a famous person, such as Gandhi, no-one seeing the film seriously thinks that events happened in exactly the way shown, with exactly those words spoken. After all, actors play the roles, not the real people involved in the real experiences. And even the real people, if they were still alive, could not recreate exactly what happened at an earlier time. Documentaries which show 'real lives' are usually edited down selectively; in any case the people in the documentaries usually know they are on camera, which will affect their behaviour.

So the boundary between fact and fiction is trickier than it may at first seem.

Most fiction writers make use of facts, including their own experiences, in their writing of fiction. In this unit you will be exploring some of the ways in which writers do this, and some possible reasons why. This will lead on to your own writing of fiction based on autobiographical elements.

Matching fact and fiction

When the author Charles Dickens was ten years old, he was sent to work by his parents, who were short of money. He wrote about his experiences in what he intended to be his autobiography. He changed his mind later, but used some of these early memories in his novel *David Copperfield*. The part of the novel from which you will be reading extracts comes at a time after David Copperfield's mother has died. His father died before he was born.

▶ What similarities and differences can you find between the two accounts?
▶ Can you suggest any possible reasons for significant similarities and differences?

Extracts from Charles Dickens's planned autobiography	***David Copperfield* Chapter XI** **First person narrative: 'I' = David Copperfield**
...in an evil hour for me, as I often bitterly thought. The chief manager (of the blacking business), James Lamert, the relative who had stayed with us in Bayham Street, seeing how I was employed from day to day, and knowing what our domestic circumstances then were, proposed that I should go into the blacking warehouse, to be as useful as I could, at a salary, I think, of six shillings a week. I am not clear whether it was six or seven. I am inclined to believe, from my uncertainty on this head, that it was six at first and seven afterwards. At any rate, the offer was accepted very willingly by my father and mother, and on a Monday morning I went down to the blacking warehouse to begin my business life. *see over*	I BEGIN LIFE ON MY OWN ACCOUNT, AND DON'T LIKE IT I know enough of the world now, to have almost lost the capacity of being much surprised by anything; but it is matter of some surprise to me, even now, that I can have been so easily thrown away at such an age. A child of excellent abilities, and with strong powers of observation, quick, eager, delicate, and soon hurt bodily or mentally, it seems wonderful to me that nobody should have made any sign on my behalf. But none was made; and I became, at ten years old, a little labouring hind in the service of Murdstone and Grinby. Murdstone and Grinby's warehouse was at the *see over*

It is wonderful to me how I could have been so easily cast away at such an age. It is wonderful to me that, even after my descent into the poor little drudge I had become since we came to London, no one had compassion enough on me – a child of singular abilities: quick, eager, delicate, and soon hurt, bodily or mentally – to suggest that something might have been spared, as certainly it might have been, to place me at any common school. Our friends, I take it, were tired out. No one made any sign. My father and mother were quite satisfied. They could hardly have been more so, if I had been twenty years of age, distinguished at a grammar-school, and going to Cambridge.

The blacking warehouse was the last house on the left-hand side of the way, at old Hungerford Stairs. It was a crazy, tumble-down old house, abutting of course on the river, and literally overrun with rats. Its wainscoted rooms and its rotten floors and staircase, and the old grey rats swarming down in the cellars, and the sound of their squeaking and scuffling coming up the stairs at all times, and the dirt and the decay of the place, rise up visibly before me, as if I were there again. The counting-house was on the first floor, looking over the coal-barges and the river. There was a recess in it, in which I was to sit and work. My work was to cover the pots of paste-blacking: first with a piece of oil-paper, and then with a piece of blue paper; to tie them round with a string; and then to clip the paper close and neat all round, until it looked as smart as a pot of ointment from an apothecary's shop. When a certain number of grosses of pots had attained this pitch of perfection, I was to paste on each a printed label; and then go on again with more pots. Two or three other boys were kept at similar duty downstairs on similar wages. One of them came up, in a ragged apron and a paper cap, on the first Monday morning, to show me the trick of using the string and tying the knot. His name was Bob Fagin; and I took the liberty of using his name, long afterwards, in *Oliver Twist*.

Our relative had kindly arranged to teach me something in the dinner-hour; from twelve to one, I think it was; every day. But an arrangement so incompatible with counting-house business soon died away, from no fault of his or mine.

water side. It was down in Blackfriars. Modern improvements have altered the place; but it was the last house at the bottom of a narrow street, curving down hill to the river, with some stairs at the end, where people took boat. It was a crazy old house with a wharf of its own, abutting on the water when the tide was in, and on the mud when the tide was out, and literally overrun with rats. Its panelled rooms, discoloured with the dirt and smoke of a hundred years, I dare say; its decaying floors and staircase; the squeaking of the old grey rats down in the cellars; and the dirt and rottenness of the place; are things, not of many years ago, in my mind, but of the present instant. They are all before me, just as they were in the evil hour when I went among them for the first time, with my trembling hand in Mr Quinion's.

Murdstone and Grinby's trade was among a good many kinds of people, but an important branch of it was the supply of wines and spirits to certain packet ships. I forget now where they chiefly went, but I think there were some among them that made voyages both to the East and West Indies. I know that a great many empty bottles were one of the consequences of this traffic, and that certain men and boys were employed to examine them against the light, and reject those that were flawed, and to rinse and wash them. When the empty bottles ran short, there were labels to be pasted on full ones, or corks to be fitted to them, or seals to be put upon the corks, or finished bottles to be packed in casks. All this work was my work, and of the boys employed upon it I was one.

There were three or four of us, counting me. My working place was established in a corner of the warehouse, where Mr Quinion could see me, when he chose to stand up on the bottom rail of his stool in the counting-house, and look at me through a window above the desk. Hither, on the first morning of my so auspiciously beginning life on my own account, the oldest of the regular boys was summoned to show me my business. His name was Mick Walker, and he wore a ragged apron and a paper cap.

The deep remembrance of the sense I had, of being utterly without hope now; of the shame I felt in my position; of the misery it was to my young heart to believe that day by day what I had learned, and thought, and delighted in, and raised my fancy and my emulation up by, would pass away from me, little by little, never to be brought back any more; cannot be written.

Lively Dickens

Reading other writers can both set off ideas in your own mind about what you might write about and suggest how you can write about experiences.

ADVICE

▲ As you explore the ideas in this unit, note down any memories of your own that are suggested by what you read and discuss. For example, you could note down any memories you have of:
- feeling you have been badly treated
- earning money for the first time.

WORDS

▲ **wonderful** *adjective* **1** arousing amazement or bafflement, extraordinary. **2** excellent, splendid.
▲ **abut** *verb* (**abutted**, **abutting**) said of buildings etc.: to join, touch or lean against another.
▲ **recess** *noun* space, such as a niche or alcove, set in a wall.
▲ **apothecary** *noun, old use* a chemist licensed to dispense drugs
▲ **incompatible** *adjective* not able to work together.
▲ **hind** *noun, old use* **1** a farm worker. **2** a peasant.
▲ **literally** *adverb* in keeping with the straightforward meaning of a word or expression; not to be taken metaphorically.
▲ **counting-house** *noun* formerly a building, room, or office used for keeping account books and transacting business.
▲ **auspiciously** *adverb* favourably, in a way promising future success (used ironically in the extract).
▲ **emulation** *noun* close imitation of something or someone, especially in order to equal them.

Tracking whose point of view: from what point in time; in what tense

If the narrator is looking back on events that happened to them some time ago, it is possible to write in two different ways:
- writing from the viewpoint of the younger person, without the understanding of the older person – not using hindsight
- writing from the viewpoint of the younger person, with the understanding of the older person – using hindsight.

For example, in *David Copperfield*, Charles Dickens writes: 'it is matter of some surprise to me, even now, that I can have been so easily thrown away at such an age'. He is commenting on the earlier events from the viewpoint of the adult.

A different way of writing about the past is shown in Jean Ure's novel, *Get a Life!*, written as if by a fourteen-year-old boy.

WORDS

▲ **hindsight** *noun* wisdom or knowledge after an event.
▲ **cryptic** *adjective* puzzling, mysterious, obscure or enigmatic.

> ...there is nothing now that can change what happened. All I can do is write about it. And the only way I can do that is to try and get inside the person that I was then, a year ago. Try to be thirteen years old again, without any knowledge of what is to come.
>
> I have a feeling it will not be easy, as it is impossible to totally blot things out of your mind. But it will not work if I am for ever thinking ahead and making cryptic comments. By cryptic comments I mean remarks such as 'What I didn't realise at the time' or, 'As I was to discover later,' etc. and so on. This, I think, would be cheating. I am going to have to watch and not do it.

Authors use both methods, and you can decide which will work best for you in your own writing. One method is not better than the other – but be aware of the choice and which choice suits a particular story.

It may require some imagination to think yourself back even a year or so, to imagine what you thought and felt at the time of any events you narrate.

29

2 AUTOBIOGRAPHY – FACT AND FICTION

	Time events happen in real or fictional time: past tense	Adult looking back at these events: present tense
Autobiography Charles Dickens = 'I'	on a Monday morning I went down to the blacking warehouse to begin my business life.	It is wonderful to me how I could have been so easily cast away at such an age.
David Copperfield David Copperfield = 'I'	I became, at ten years old, a little labouring hind in the service of Murdstone and Grinby.	it is matter of some surprise to me, even now, that I can have been so easily thrown away at such an age.

Oleander, Jacaranda

2 Triggering your own ideas

In the next activities you will be reading extracts from a book by Penelope Lively called *Oleander, Jacaranda*, which is about her own childhood. She is writing about events that happened some five decades earlier. You will be exploring the way she writes about the past and how far she comments on it from her adult viewpoint. Reading about other people's experiences can remind us of events in our own past, so make a note of any memories of your own that Penelope Lively's memories bring back.

In this extract, Penelope Lively describes an incident when she was a young girl visiting a zoo in Egypt.

> The hippos float in a small lake. Summoned by their keeper, they approach the shallows, molten mud streaming from their backs, and they open pink maws edged with craggy brown teeth. For a few more piastres you can buy a scoop of potatoes from the keeper which you then hurl into the gaping mouths. This is a great sport – a test of aim but also a matter of trying to target the small hippos – females and infants – who get shouldered aside by the dominant males. When sated, the hippos shut up shop – you hear a great scrunch as their jaws close – and slide away down into the water until there is nothing visible but nostrils and an oval glistening snout.

▶ From the above extract, select what you consider to be the five most effective single words.
▶ In your selection, include **at least one noun, one verb and one adjective**.
▶ Be prepared to justify your choice to the other groups.

WORDS

▲ **maw** *noun* the jaw, throat or stomach of an animal that eats food in large quantities.
▲ **piastre** *noun* a unit of money in Egypt worth one-hundredth of an Egyptian pound.
▲ **sate** *verb* to satisfy an appetite to the full or to excess.

ADVICE

▲ Note down any vivid memories you have of feeding animals, or visits to places where animals are on view.

Lively Dickens

Tracking whose point of view: from what point in time; in what tense

	Time events happen in real time	Adult looking back at these events
Autobiography	The hippos float in a small lake.	(No evidence in extract of adult viewpoint.)
Tense used	The adult Penelope Lively describes the events **as if** they are happening now, using the present tense.	

3 Double vision

In this instance, Penelope Lively is reminded of her experiences as a child by looking at a photograph. She tries to recall the incident from her memory, and then reflects on the different view of events she has now as an adult looking back.

The Mercury basin is empty of water. It is cracked, making the surface uneven, and there is a scum of leaves in the bottom. I ride my bicycle round and round it, as around a Wall of Death at a fun-fair. This is thrilling and hazardous – there is always the risk of falling off.

Looking at the photograph of the Mercury basin, it seems to me that the diameter is only some five or six feet. A small bicycle, it must have been. A small child. My perspective of that space is dizzily distorted. I see it with double vision – the reality of the photograph in front of me, and that inward eye which insists upon a sweeping expanse, a great curve around which I hurtle. Both, though, are accurate. It is I who am the inconstant feature.

▶ Choose a memory of your own from your childhood. This might be triggered by a photograph which includes you in the picture.
▶ Write one paragraph on this incident as you remember it:
  a Describe the place.
  b Try to relive your thoughts and feelings as clearly and honestly as you can.
  c Comment on how you (as a child) think your family/friends reacted.
▶ In the second paragraph, comment with your present perspective:
  a Does the place look different from how you remember it?
  b What do you now think of what you did then?
  c How do you actually think others were reacting?
  d Reflect back on the whole incident with the benefit of hindsight.

WORDS

▲ **hindsight** *noun* wisdom or knowledge after an event.

2 AUTOBIOGRAPHY – FACT AND FICTION

Tracking whose point of view: from what point in time; in what tense

	Time events happen in real time	Adult looking back at these events
Autobiography Penelope Lively = 'I'	I ride my bicycle round and round it, as around a Wall of Death at a funfair	Looking at the photograph of the Mercury basin, it seems to me that the diameter is only some five or six feet.
Tense chosen	The adult Penelope Lively describes the events **as if** they are happening now, using the present tense.	The adult Penelope Lively comments on how she now sees this event in her past, using the present tense.

4 Conversations in autobiography

The following is another extract from the same book. Lucy was a Londoner who was employed by Penelope Lively's parents to look after Penelope. She acted, in effect, as a surrogate (substitute) mother.

> I have met up with Ahmed in the place behind the bamboo clump, both of us in flight from authority – I from Lucy, he from Mansour.
>
> 'I dare you to eat earth,' says Ahmed. 'Look…'
>
> He scoops up a handful of earth, grinning. He crams it into his mouth.
>
> I watch, stonily, waiting for him to expire. He does not. 'Now you,' challenges Ahmed, grinning hugely.   5
>
> I am in a fix. If I do it, I will surely die. If I do not, I shall lose face, irrevocably.
>
> There is really no choice. I gather a handful of earth, shove it into my mouth. My teeth grind on the gritty bits. I swallow.   10

As well as retelling incidents from her childhood in *Oleander, Jacaranda*, Penelope Lively also comments on the way she writes about these incidents. The following is part of her commentary on the earth-eating episode:

> Ahmed would have been about twelve, I think. He was Mansour's minion, employed to fetch and carry and to do those tasks beneath the dignity of Mansour. The earth-eating episode is of course embellished with a touch of hindsight. The conversation cannot have run quite like that – there was a language barrier. Suffice it to say that we understood each other perfectly.

WORDS

▲ **expire** *verb*
1 to come to an end or cease to be valid. 2 to breathe out. 3 to die.
▲ **irrevocable** *adjective* unable to be changed, stopped or undone. **irrevocably** *adverb* in a way that cannot be changed, stopped or undone.

▲ **minion** *noun* a slavishly obedient attendant.
▲ **embellish** *verb* to make (a story etc.) more interesting by adding details which may not be true.
▲ **suffice it to say** it is enough to say.

Lively Dickens

- Choose five verbs from lines 1–10 of the passage on page 32 that you think are particularly powerful. Try to think of alternative verbs that could fit in one or two of these places.
- Now select one or two pairs – the author's choice and your alternative – and prepare to explain your findings to the other groups. Which is more powerful, and why?
- Why do you think Penelope Lively has chosen to use the present tense when retelling this incident?
- In your group, decide why you think conversation in autobiography may not be accurate. Think up as many reasons as you can.

Now prepare to report back on the following questions:
- Does it matter if you don't give the exact words spoken when writing about events in your own autobiography?
- Are there any 'rules' you should follow, do you think?

5 Transforming experience into fiction

Passage A

In this extract from *Oleander, Jacaranda*, Penelope Lively describes a car journey she made with her parents when she was a young girl living in Egypt.

> We are going by car from Bulaq Dakhrur to Heliopolis. I am in the back. The leather of the seat sticks to my bare legs. We travel along a road lined at either side with oleander and jacaranda trees, alternate splashes of white and blue. I chant, quietly: 'Jacaranda, oleander… Jacaranda, oleander…' And as I do so there comes to me the revelation that in a few hours' time we shall return by the same route and that I shall pass the same trees, in reverse order – oleander, jacaranda, oleander, jacaranda – and that, by the same token, I can look back upon myself now, thinking this – but it will be then, not now.
>
> And in due course I did so, and perceived with excitement the chasm between past and future, the perpetual slide of the present.

Penelope Lively used some of her memories of this incident when writing her short story *Next Term We'll Mash You* (*Level Best 1*, Unit 9).

Passage B

- As you read these extracts from the short story, decide what details you can trace back to her actual memories, as described in passage A. For each link you make, note down how Penelope Lively has changed the details while keeping something the same. Use a table like the one at the top of the next page.

> Inside the car it was quiet, the noise of the engine even and subdued, the air just the right temperature, the windows tight-fitting. The boy sat on the back seat, a box of chocolates, unopened, beside him, and a comic, folded.
>
> His mother half-turned to speak to him. 'Nearly there now, darling.'
>
> The father glanced down at his wife's wrist. 'Are we all right for time?'
>
> 'Just right. Nearly twelve.'
>
> The car turned right, between white gates and high, dark, tight-clipped hedges. The whisper of the road under the tyres changed to the crunch of gravel. The child, staring sideways, read black lettering on a white board: 'St. Edward's Preparatory School. Please Drive Slowly.' The child shifted on the seat, and the leather sucked at the bare skin under his knees, stinging.

☆ ☆ ☆ ☆ ☆

> He is with his parents again, and they are getting into the car, and the high hedges skim past the car windows once more, in the other direction, and the gravel under the tyres changes to black tarmac.
>
> He looks straight ahead of him, at the road coiling beneath the bonnet of the car. His face is haggard with anticipation.

33

2 AUTOBIOGRAPHY – FACT AND FICTION

Links between passage A and passage B	How Penelope Lively has changed a detail, if at all

Tracking whose point of view: from what point in time; in what tense

	Time events happen in real or fictional time	Adult looking back at these events
Autobiography: Penelope Lively = 'I', writing in the present tense as if describing events as they happen. Past tense for commenting on her reaction.	We are going by car from Bulaq Dakhrur to Heliopolis. I am in the back.	And in due course I did so.
Short story: boy = 'he'; past tense for most of story, present tense used for effect when the boy feels particularly under pressure.	The boy sat on the back seat, a box of chocolates, unopened, beside him, and a comic, folded. He is with his parents again, and they are getting into the car…	No adult point of view from the boy in the story.

6 Identifying the structure of a longer piece of writing

Read the following extract from the same book, and match up each paragraph to these paragraph summaries:

Paragraph summaries

- A fuller description of the context, reflecting on the child's feelings at the time
- Looking back on Lucy's experience and the child's experience
- Lucy's role
- The plan
- Expecting trouble
- The setting
- Success – by ignoring Lucy

The water is just below waist level, which is precisely right. Any higher, and I would not be able to push off with my feet at the crucial moment. I have to be able to lean forward and launch myself with a kick at the exact moment that the wave is breaking.

I stand facing the shore with my head turned, assessing each approaching wave, clutching the surfboard. If they have already broken they are no good to me. Those that are still swelling must be allowed to go, lifting me temporarily off my feet as they do so. What I am after is the one that is ripening to a peak which frills with white as it begins to turn in on itself. Then I can fling myself forward with it and if the timing is right I will swoop down the slope of water and hurtle in with the wave – a glorious involuntary rush which will leave me washed up on the beach.

Out of the corner of my eye I can see Lucy. She is waving. Not in greeting but in summons. I am to come out. I pretend I have not seen her. I go on waiting my moment. Great white broken waves charge through me. I bob up and down with the swells. And then the right one comes, and I have timed it right, the wave has me in its grip, and I am racing for the beach.

The wave dies, and deposits me on the sand. Lucy is looking thunder, and I brace myself for an earful.

This was not, I hasten to say, surfing on a Hawaiian scale. There were adults who were doing ostentatious things with proper surfboards, way out in the deep water. My surfboard was a child's version of the kind most surfing camp-followers used – an oblong board with a rounded end over which you placed your hands, shaped to the waist at the other. Mine was made to measure, and had my initials on it in green paint – P.M.L. It was my most treasured possession. I was a good swimmer, and fancied myself as a surfer. I was passionate about it. I saw waves in my dreams, flaunting those alluring glassy flanks. When we went to the surfing beach I was in a state of tension, awaiting the colour of the flag. No flag meant no danger, and therefore possibly no waves either. Red meant hazardous, and therefore good waves, but an argument with Lucy about the degree of hazard. Black meant swimming forbidden.

Lucy never bathed. She would set up an encampment on the sand – sun umbrella, rug and stool, Thermos flask, knitting – and from there she would supervise my activities, making forays to check up on me. Lucy must have been condemned to many an afternoon's edgy patrolling of the shore while I plunged off into the Mediterranean. Occasionally, when my flouting of her shouts and waves became entirely blatant, she would despatch some total stranger to admonish me. And once, the *gaffir* – the beach watchman – who came racing out with a life-belt and hauled me back: an appalling humiliation.

I have every sympathy with Lucy, now. I'd do the same myself. A few people drowned off that beach every summer. In fact, I knew about the treachery of the inviting water, but I never let on to anyone. Once I had been caught in a current in a trough of deep water fifty yards from the shore, and found myself pulled terrifyingly out to sea. And on several occasions I had misjudged the size of a wave or positioned myself wrongly and turned head over heels, banging against the surfboard, caught up helplessly, hideously, in a roaring cauldron of water. I kept an expedient silence about such things. Surfing was essential; surfing was the whole point of existence. I have never surfed since, but I have always felt a sneaking empathy with those obsessives who traipse the globe in search of waves. I knew how they feel, once.

2 AUTOBIOGRAPHY – FACT AND FICTION

7 Exploring techniques

▶ Match these quotations and techniques to the 'effect of technique' statements below:

Line	Quotation	Technique	Effect of technique
4	I stand facing the shore	Use of present tense	
4–5	facing … assessing … clutching	Use of –ing form of verbs	
7	one that is ripening to a peak	Use of imagery – a metaphor	
8–9	fling … swoop … hurtle	Use of dynamic verbs	
11	She is waving.	Use of short sentence	
13	Great white broken waves charge through me.	Use of tripling of adjectives. Use of powerful verb 'charge'	
14–15	And then the right one comes … racing for the beach.	Use of longer sentence	
18 23–24	This was not … fancied myself …	Switch to past tense …	
41	found myself pulled **terrifyingly**	Use of adverb	
44	roaring cauldron of water	Use of imagery – a metaphor	

Effect of technique

A Compares a wave to fruit on a tree etc. at the point where it becomes perfect to eat/the wave becomes perfect to surf.	B Creates an impression of large quantities of fast moving water that could trap you underwater.	C Gives a feeling of immediacy, as if the events are happening now.	D Makes the waves seem powerful and unstable and as if they will stop for nothing.	E Makes this sentence seem important. Lucy waving is a threat to PML's enjoyment.
F Modifies 'pulled' and makes the event seem significant and dangerous.	G Suggests movement and action and energy.	H Switch to older person reflecting on the earlier events.	I The longer sentence mirrors the length of time she is surfing the waves. Starting with 'And' helps to create the feeling that the right moment has finally arrived.	J These verbs suggest waiting for something to happen rather than acting, the waiting perhaps lasting some time.

WORDS

▲ **cauldron** *noun* 1 a large open metal pot used for cooking over an open fire. 2 something that resembles a boiling cauldron.
▲ **empathy** *noun* the ability to share, understand and feel another person's feelings.
▲ **expedient** *adjective* practical and advantageous, rather than morally correct.
▲ **involuntary** *adjective* not subject to conscious control; reflex.

Lively Dickens

8 How writers use punctuation and font

▶ Look closely at the use of:
- dashes
- the colon
- italics

in the following passage, and explain why you think they are being used.

> She would set up an encampment on the sand – sun umbrella, rug and stool, Thermos flask, knitting – and from there she would supervise my activities.
>
> And once, the *gaffir* – the beach watchman – who came racing out with a life-belt and hauled me back: an appalling humiliation.

Tracking whose point of view: from what point in time; in what tense

	Time events happen in real time	Adult looking back at these events
Autobiography Penelope Lively = 'I'	I stand facing the shore with my head turned, assessing each approaching wave, clutching the surfboard.	I was a good swimmer, and fancied myself as a surfer. I have every sympathy with Lucy, now.
Tense chosen	The adult Penelope Lively describes the events **as if** they are happening now, using the present tense.	The adult Penelope Lively uses the past tense to describe herself as a child. She uses the present tense to describe her present feelings about those past events.

37

2 AUTOBIOGRAPHY – FACT AND FICTION

Original writing

9 Creating your own story

'The exciting thing about the writing of younger children is the way in which so many manage to incorporate influences while retaining a freshness and idiosyncrasy. That individual vision survives, for a while.'

Penelope Lively

Now that you have explored some of the different ways authors use different points of view from different points in time, you may find you have opened up more choices for your own writing.

Choices

Whose point of view: You can write about events as if they are happening to you (I). You can write about some events that happened to you as if they happened to someone else (David Copperfield; the boy in *Next Term We'll Mash You*). You can write about these events as if they happened to the 'I' of the story (David Copperfield = 'I'), or as if they happened to the 'he/she' of the story (the boy = 'he'). You can write about events you have been involved in from a different perspective. For example, Penelope Lively could write a story about her surfing from the viewpoint of Lucy. Or you could write Lucy's story, using Penelope Lively's descriptions but also your imagination.

You can choose any person's point of view to tell your story, but you need to make that person's point of view convincing and interesting.

From what point in time: You can write about events as if you only know what you knew at the time of the events. Or you can write about events and comment on them, using the benefit of hindsight. Or, most commonly, you can use a combination of the two.

There are all sorts of possibilities for point of view in time – later that day, that week, a year later, 'now'… And in each case you may be commenting on things happening at this new time, or reflecting back on what happened earlier:

Describing events as they happen	Describing events happening at this new position in time	Reflecting back from this new position in time
That day was the most significant in my life so far …	Later that day I found …	Later that day I realised I had made a terrible mistake …. how lucky I had been
	A week later my parents got to hear that I was involved …	A week later I was glad I had made that decision …
	After a year the real truth came out …	A year later I regretted saying those things even more …
	We are now speaking again, but only just …	I now think that the choice I made then has …

WORDS

▲ **idiosyncrasy** *noun* any personal way of behaving, reacting or thinking.

▲ **incorporate** *verb* to include something as part of the whole.

ADVICE

▲ Your aim should be to learn from other writers, but not let your own style be drowned. Don't copy others, just learn from them!

In what tense: You can use the present tense or the past tense or a combination. Usually it is probably wise to stick to the past tense, but you may like to experiment in at least one story, either by seeing if it works to write the whole story in the present tense, or if you can achieve the effect you want by just using a short part in the present tense. You could try using Penelope Lively's technique of describing an event as it happened (as you remember it) in the present tense and then commenting on it in the past tense.

> **ADVICE**
> ▲ For this unit, do not worry about events being real or imaginary, autobiographical or invented. You are developing your craft as a writer, exploring how you can write about any events convincingly and powerfully.
> ▲ But remember that a basis in fact can often provide your writing with some of its power.

10 Writing a commentary on your own story

▶ Having completed your story, write a commentary in which you explain your decisions on:
- choice of point of view – whose point of view your story is told from
- choice of point in time – what point in time your story is told from
- choice of tense – past or present (or a deliberate and planned mixture)

and how far you think your writing has improved by thinking about these choices.

Self-assessment

11 Judging your own performance

▶ From the list below:
  a select three points on which you feel you have made the most progress
  b select one point on which you most need to improve.
I can explain how an author has changed fact into fiction.
I can explain why an author might choose to write from a particular point of view.
I can explain why an author might choose to write from a particular point in time.
I can write a story making use of my own experiences.
I can choose the most effective point of view for a particular story.
I can use present and past tense appropriately.
I can write a story which engages the interest of the reader.
I can comment on my own writing, explaining my choices.

12 Improving your skills in English

▶ Select one or two skills you need to concentrate on to improve your skills in reading. Then do the same for your writing skills. (The descriptions of levels are a guide only.)

	Reading skill	From	To
1	Show understanding of significant ideas, themes, events and characters, beginning to use inference and deduction	Level 3	Level 4
2	Refer to the text when explaining their views	Level 3	Level 4

2 AUTOBIOGRAPHY – FACT AND FICTION

3	Select essential points and use inference and deduction where appropriate	Level 4	Level 5
4	Identify key features, themes and characters and select relevant sentences and phrases to support their views	Level 4	Level 5
5	Identify different layers of meaning and comment on their significance and effect	Level 5	Level 6
6	Give a personal response, referring to aspects of language, structure and themes in justifying their views	Level 5	Level 6
7	Show understanding of the ways in which meaning and information are conveyed in a range of texts	Level 6	Level 7
8	Articulate personal and critical responses, showing awareness of thematic, structural and linguistic features	Level 6	Level 7
9	Evaluate how authors achieve their effects through the use of linguistic, structural and presentational devices	Level 7	Level 8
10	Select and analyse information and ideas, and comment on how these are conveyed in different texts	Level 7	Level 8
11	Refer in detail to aspects of language, structure and presentation	Level 8	E.P.
12	Make apt and careful comparison between texts, including consideration of audience, purpose and form	Level 8	E.P.

	Writing skill	From	To
1	Vocabulary choices are adventurous and words are used for effect	Level 3	Level 4
2	Writing is lively and thoughtful, and is sustained and developed in an interesting way	Level 3	Level 4
3	Vocabulary choices are imaginative and words are used precisely	Level 4	Level 5
4	Writing is varied and interesting, conveying meaning clearly	Level 4	Level 5
5	Use a range of sentence structures and varied vocabulary to create effects	Level 5	Level 6
6	Writing engages and sustains the reader's interest	Level 5	Level 6
7	Grammatical features and vocabulary are accurately and effectively used	Level 6	Level 7
8	Characters and settings are developed	Level 6	Level 7
9	The use of vocabulary and grammar enables fine distinctions to be made or emphasis achieved	Level 7	Level 8
10	Control of characters, events and settings, and shows variety in structure	Level 7	Level 8
11	A variety of grammatical constructions and punctuation is used accurately and appropriately and with sensitivity	Level 8	E.P.
12	Use structure as well as vocabulary for a range of imaginative effects	Level 8	E.P.

3 Portraying character
'And you are?'

Your focus
The content of this unit is designed to:
- help you understand the choices authors make in writing about character
- give you the skills to use the same techniques yourself.

Your target
By the end of this unit you should be more able to:
- recognise and appreciate some of the techniques authors use to create characters
- use some of these techniques in your own writing
- choose an appropriate structure for your writing.

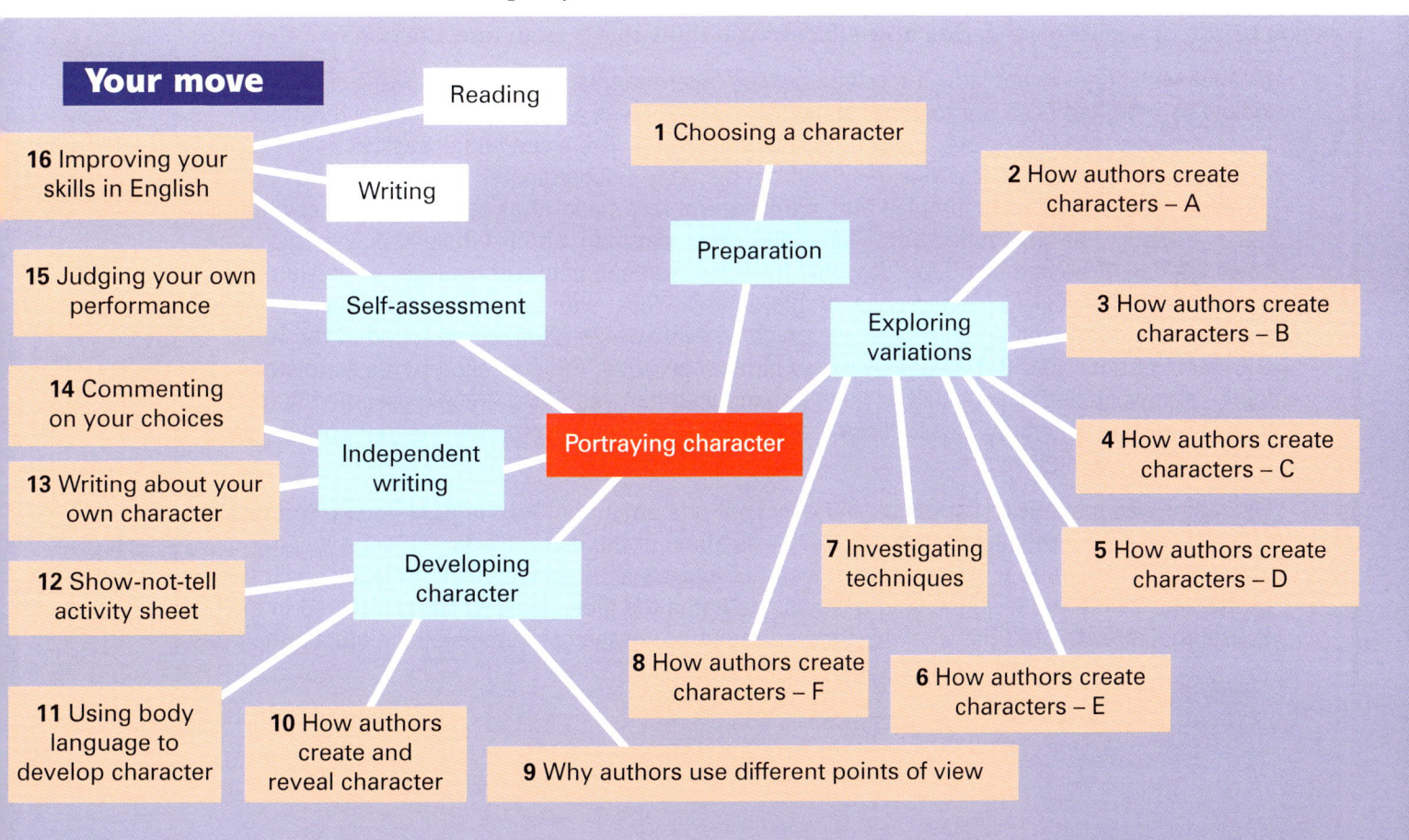

Your move

- Reading
- Writing
- Self-assessment
- Independent writing
- Developing character
- Preparation
- Exploring variations
- Portraying character
- Investigating techniques

1. Choosing a character
2. How authors create characters – A
3. How authors create characters – B
4. How authors create characters – C
5. How authors create characters – D
6. How authors create characters – E
7. Investigating techniques
8. How authors create characters – F
9. Why authors use different points of view
10. How authors create and reveal character
11. Using body language to develop character
12. Show-not-tell activity sheet
13. Writing about your own character
14. Commenting on your choices
15. Judging your own performance
16. Improving your skills in English

3 PORTRAYING CHARACTER

Preparation

1 Choosing a character

Over the course of this unit you will be writing parts of what will become a longer text focusing on description of character. It will be helpful if you decide early on who you will be writing about. Descriptions usually sound most convincing if they are based on real people, but of course you can combine elements of different people in creating a new character of your own.
You could base your initial description on:
- a brother or sister
- a friend
- someone who gets you involved with activities you wouldn't get involved with on your own
- someone you don't like/don't get on with
- an adult who has influenced you in some way
- a character in a story you are writing which you could develop further.

Exploring variations

2 How authors create characters – A

This is an extract from a novel first published in 2000, but set in England in the 18th century. As you read it or hear it read, decide how effective you think this is as an introduction to a character.

> Meshak was an awkward lad. At fourteen he was taller than his father and growing. But he looked as if he had been put together all wrong; his body was all over the place, his head too large, his ears too sticking out, his lips never quite closing. There seemed always to be a sleeve at his runny nose. His arms and legs dangled from his body, uncoordinated and clumsy; he dropped things, tripped over things, fumbled and stumbled. All this meant that people – especially his father – shouted at him, cuffed him, jeered and sneered at him, so his whole look was that of a cowering dog. If he had had a tail, it would have always been between his legs, as he slunk by waiting for the next kick. He had a vulnerable, infantile look, with his pale-freckled face beneath a stack of wild red hair, and his large, watery, blue eyes, which often stared round at the world with incomprehension. But no one ever saw him cry or laugh. People called him a simpleton – a loon – and wondered why his father hadn't abandoned him years ago. People assumed that he was nothing but an empty vessel, lacking all substance, feeling or emotion; neither able to love nor in need of being loved.
>
> His father was mean with the lamps and only kept one up in front for the road ahead, so Meshak hated being out on the highway at night. He was afraid of the dark. It was not just the spirit world which frightened him, but the real world of robbers and highwaymen, especially near the forest. And then there were the wild animals. He hated the green eyes which glimmered in the dense undergrowth, and the scufflings and gruntings of unseen creatures stalking among the trees.

From Coram Boy *by Jamila Gavin*

▶ Find one piece of evidence for each of the following:

Information about Meshak	Example in the text	Line reference
age		
height		
physical description		
typical behaviour		
treatment by others		
comparison		
how other people see him		
what Meshak's feelings are		

▶ What are your thoughts and feelings about Meshak?
▶ How has the author created these thoughts and feelings?

Tracking point of view

▶ Is this extract written in the first person (I) or the third person (he or she)?
▶ How far does the author let you know the feelings of any of the characters?

Drafting elements of your own writing

▶ Write a description in about five lines of your chosen character. This should concentrate on a physical description.

ADVICE

▲ Notice how the author uses rhyming to add impact to the description:
- *fumbled and stumbled*
- *jeered and sneered*.

▲ You could try using this technique selectively in your own writing.

ADVICE

▲ You could use some of the headings in the table above, or briefly match key descriptions of *your* character against key descriptions of Meshak.

3 How authors create characters – B

The passage about Meshak is in the third person, and is largely an external view of how others see him, rather than telling us how Meshak reacts to other people. The next extract is **similar** in being in the third person also.

▶ How is it **different**?

Shelley had stopped. And this became worst of all when she was left behind by her friends and they became her former friends. They moved on to their new selves in junior high school, and she was left watching them as though through a pane of glass.

Her former friends were a gang of girls with whom she had hung out in elementary school. They were named Denise, Wendy, Tracy, Lisa, and Tami. She could count on them to get together every Sunday afternoon to ride their bikes or play elephant tag. But once they moved to junior high, everything suddenly changed. 5

On the first day of junior high, Shelley spent half an hour looking for her friends. The school was large, fed from elementary schools all over Los Angeles; it was like being in a brand-new city. Finally, she found them sitting around a cafeteria table, but she did not recognize them at first. Each girl had drawn a line of blue on her eyelids, and each was wearing a camisole top and a thin cotton skirt. No one had told her that they had planned these outfits. 10

43

3 PORTRAYING CHARACTER

She sat beside them, but it was clear that she was not part of them anymore. They spoke in darting, urgent whispers, erupting into laughter that sounded like shrieks of pain. Their old selves had been discarded, forgotten. Some new and magical truth seemed sealed within them, remote and inaccessible to her.

It became a true loss when she called them and they had become busy. If she called on a Friday afternoon at four o'clock, they'd already made plans, and these plans excluded her. They seemed to know of a crucial calling time, and she had missed it and would never learn what it was. 'Sorry,' they'd say, their voices airy. 'We have our plans.' She tried calling at different times – three o'clock on Thursday, eight on Wednesday, but it was always the same.

She began to hate Sundays, the long hot stretch of time when she sat alone in the dull glare of her front yard. Sometimes she'd walk quickly around the block as though she, too, had exciting plans and was off somewhere; she'd try not to stare at her friends' houses to see what was going on inside. But she had no plans.

From Like Normal People *by Karen E. Bender*

▶ What part of this passage do you find most helpful in understanding Shelley's feelings? Be prepared to justify your choice.
▶ What are your thoughts and feelings about Shelley?
▶ How has the author created these thoughts and feelings?

Tracking point of view

▶ Is this extract written in the first person (I) or the third person (he or she)?
▶ How far does the author let you know the feelings of any of the characters?

Drafting elements of your own writing

▶ Make a note of one or two incidents which reveal your chosen character in particular ways. This may be something they do, or how they react to something someone else does.
▶ Write five lines showing how they react to one particular incident which clearly reveals something about your chosen character.

> **ADVICE**
> ▲ Many parts of the passage could be chosen. The important point is to be able to explain *why* you find a particular part of the passage effective.

> **ADVICE**
> ▲ It can be most interesting to explore what happens when your character is put in a challenging position. This may not mean a dangerous position – Shelley is put in a challenging position when she feels isolated from her previous friends.

4 How authors create characters – C

Unlike the first two extracts, the next one is in the first person, from the point of view of Kit Watson. The character being introduced, however, is not Kit Watson but Askew.
▶ As you read this passage or hear it read, decide whether you think Askew is being presented in a positive or negative way – does each detail make you like and respect him more, or less?

I'd been in Stoneygate a week when Askew found me. I was alone at the edge of the wilderness, standing against the broken fence. I stared out across this new place, the wide space of beaten grass where dozens of children played.

'Kit Watson?'

I turned and found him there. He climbed over and stood beside me. He was broad-faced, broad-shouldered. His hair hung heavy on his brow. A thin moustache was visible on his lip. He held a sketch pad under his arm, had a pencil behind his ear. I'd already seen him in school, lounging bitterly outside a closed classroom door.

'Kit Watson?' he repeated.

I nodded. I caught the scent of dog on him. I shifted away from him. I felt the skin crawling on my neck.

'What is it?' I said. My throat felt dry, my tongue felt too big for my mouth.

He smiled, and pointed to our house, across the potholed lane behind us, behind its own fence and its narrow garden.

'Just moved in, eh?'

'My Dad came from here. And my grandfather.'

I tried to say it proudly, to let him know I had the right to be here in Stoneygate.

'I know that, Kit.' He held out a packet of sweets. 'Go on. Take one.'

I chewed the sweet.

'You're from the old families. That's good, Kit. You're one of us.' He contemplated me. 'Been watching you, Kit, ever since you come.'

He waved his arm, indicating the kids at their games: football, fighting, little kids skipping or playing shops and houses. 'There's something to you,' he said. 'Something different to this rabble.' He stared, like he was waiting for me to reply.

'What d'you mean?'

'What do I mean? That you're like me, Kit.'

I looked at him, the thick body, the darkness in his eyes. '*No*,' I thought. '*No. I'm not like you*.'

He pointed out again. 'What do you see out there?'

'Eh?'

'Eh? Eh? Out there. What d'you see?'

I looked across the wilderness. 'Kids. Grass. River. Same as you see.'

He grinned. 'Aye. That's right. That's all, eh?'

I looked again. 'Yes.'

He laughed and shook his head. He slid a piece of paper from his sketch pad. 'Made this for you,' he said. 'Go on.'

It was me, a charcoal drawing. Me sitting against the chain link fence at school, as I had two days ago, staring down into the grass.

'Good, eh?' he said. 'Just like you, eh?'

I nodded.

'Best artist in the school. Not that it counts for nothing in that blasted place.'

I held it towards him. He laughed. 'Go on,' he said. 'It's yours. Take it home and pin it on your wall. An Askew original. Collector's item.'

From Kit's Wilderness *by David Almond*

3 PORTRAYING CHARACTER

▶ For each of the following quotations, decide if they give a positive or negative impression of Askew, and explain why. Rate a quotation at +2 for a very positive impression of him, −2 for a very negative impression of him, and 0 if you don't think it affects your opinion of him at all.
▶ Be prepared to justify your conclusions to the other groups.
▶ Look back at the quotation in context before you decide.
▶ Use a table like the one below.

Line	Quotation	Rating +2, +1, 0, −1, −2	Explanation of why you have given this rating to this quotation
6	broad-faced, broad-shouldered		
8–9	lounging bitterly outside a closed classroom door		
12	felt the skin crawling on my neck		
13–14	throat felt dry, my tongue felt too big for my mouth		
19	I tried to say it proudly (What effect is Askew having on him?)		
27	'Something different to this rabble.'		
31	the thick body, the darkness in his eyes		
31–32	'No. No, I'm not like you.'		
45	'Not that it counts for nothing in that blasted place.'		
47	'An Askew original. Collector's item.'		

▶ Characters can be introduced in a number of ways. Match up each of the techniques below with a relevant quotation from those included at the top of the next page (or select your own from the passage). More than one example is given for some techniques.

Technique to introduce character	Example from passage
Describe what they look like.	
Describe how they react to treatment by others.	
Describe how they are treated by others.	
Describe the sensations of someone meeting them.	
Use their speech to indicate their character.	
Describe how other people speak to them.	
Describe what they do.	
Give the thoughts of another character about them.	

'And you are?'

| A ... outside a closed classroom door | B 'No. No, I'm not like you.' |

| C 'Something different to this rabble.' | D 'Not that it counts for nothing in this blasted place.' |

| E 'An Askew original. Collector's item.' | F broad-faced, broad-shouldered |

| G felt the skin crawling on my neck | H throat felt dry, my tongue felt too big for my mouth |

| I He slid a sheet of paper from his sketch pad. (He is an artist; he is generous?) |

| J I tried to say it proudly | K lounging bitterly ... |

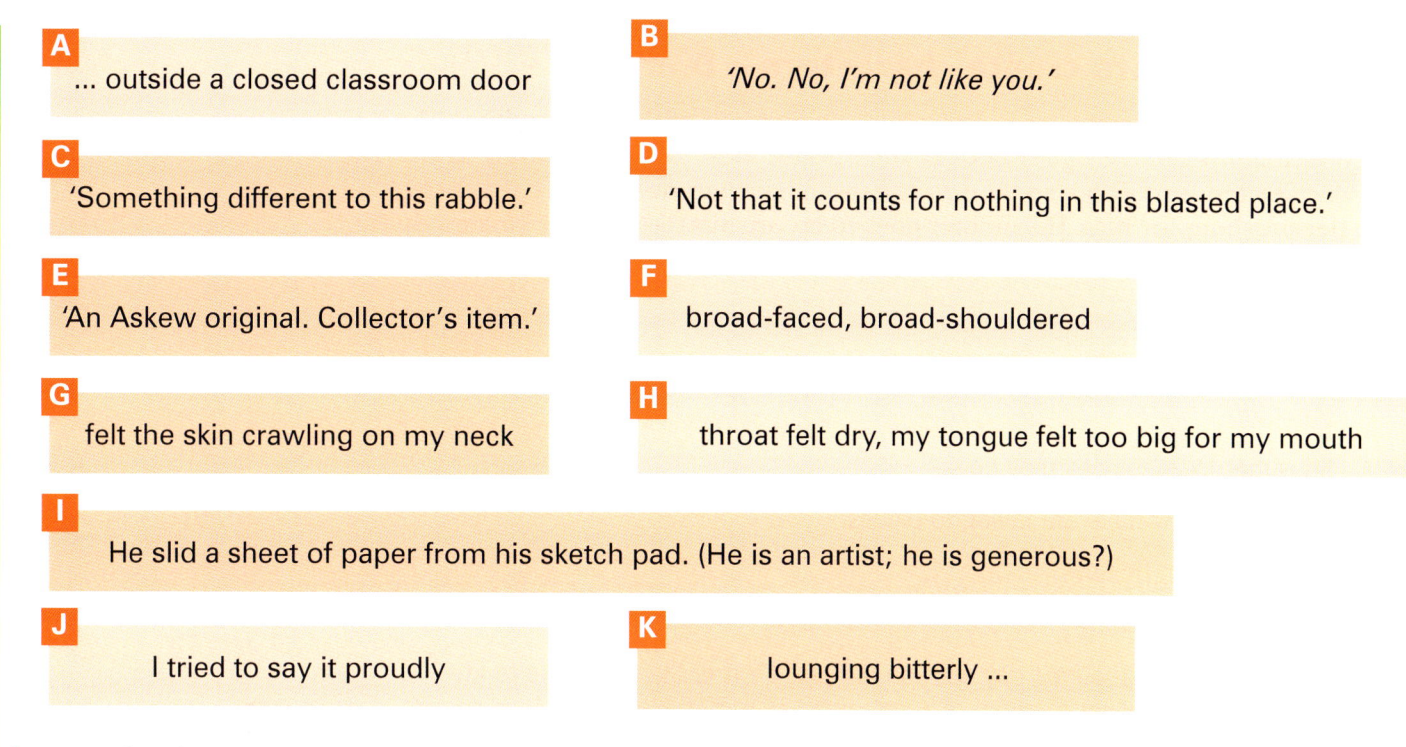

▶ Now decide in your group which of these were most helpful in forming a clear impression of this character. Be prepared to justify your choices.

Most effective techniques	Reason why you chose this technique
1	
2	
3	

Having explored these techniques, now come to a decision as a group:
▶ Do you think Askew is presented as someone who is more likely to be a 'hero' or a 'villain' in the rest of the novel? Explain your reasoning.

Tracking point of view

▶ Is this extract written in the first person (I) or the third person (he or she)?
▶ How far does the author let you know the feelings of any of the characters?

Drafting elements of your own writing

▶ Write about five lines on your own chosen character, indicating in some way if you are approving or disapproving of this character. This could be based on a particular incident.

ADVICE

▲ Showing approval or disapproval could be quite subtle, as in the case of the way Askew is presented, or quite blunt, saying exactly what you think of them.

47

3 PORTRAYING CHARACTER

5 How authors create characters – D

Frank McCourt is growing up in Ireland in the first half of the 20th century. The McCourt family call the upper floor of their house 'Italy' as it is relatively warm. The downstairs tends to flood, so they do not use it. His parents do not have enough money for decent shoes for him. His mother goes to an organisation, the St Vincent de Paul Society, to ask for charity, but his father objects to this.

Don't you have any pride, begging for boots like that?

And what would you do, Mr Grand Manner? Would you let them go barefoot?

I'd rather fix the shoes they have.

The shoes they have are falling to pieces. 5

I can fix them, he says.

You can't fix anything. You're useless, she says.

He comes home the next day with an old bicycle tire. He sends me to Mr Hannon next door for the loan of a last and a hammer. He takes Mam's sharp knife and he hacks at the tire till he has pieces to fit on the soles and heels of 10 our shoes. Mam tells him he's going to destroy the shoes altogether but he pounds away with the hammer, driving the nails through the rubber pieces and into the shoes. Mam says, God above, if you left the shoes alone they'd last till Easter, at least, and we might get the boots from the St. Vincent de Paul. But he won't stop till the soles and heels are covered with squares of rubber 15 tire which stick out on each side of the shoe and flop before and behind. He makes us put on the shoes and tells us our feet will be good and warm but we don't want to wear them anymore because the tire pieces are so lumpy we stumble when we walk around Italy. He sends me back to Mr Hannon with the last and hammer and Mrs Hannon says, God above, what's up with your 20 shoes? She laughs and Mr Hannon shakes his head and I feel ashamed. I don't want to go to school next day and I pretend to be sick but Dad gets us up and gives us our fried bread and tea and tells us we should be grateful we have any shoes at all, that there are boys in Leamy's National School who go to school barefoot on bitter days. On our way to school Leamy's boys laugh at 25 us because the tire pieces are so thick they add a few inches to our height and the boys say, How's the air up there? There are six or seven barefoot boys in my class and they don't say anything and I wonder if it's better to have shoes with rubber tires that make you trip and stumble or to go barefoot. If you have no shoes at all you'll have all the barefoot boys on your side. If you 30 have rubber tires on your shoes you're all alone with your brother and you have to fight your own battles. I sit on a bench in the schoolyard shed and take off my shoes and stockings but when I go into the class the master wants to know where my shoes are. He knows I'm not one of the barefoot boys and he makes me go back to the yard, bring in the shoes and put them on. Then he 35 says to the class, There is sneering here. There is jeering at the misfortune of others. Is there anyone in this class that thinks he's perfect? Raise your hands.

There are no hands.

Is there anyone in this class that comes from a rich family with money galore to spend on shoes? Raise your hands.

There are no hands.

He says, There are boys here who have to mend their shoes whatever way they can. There are boys in this class with no shoes at all. It's not their fault and it's no shame. Our Lord had no shoes. He died shoeless. Do you see Him hanging on the cross sporting shoes? Do you, boys?

No, sir.

What is it you don't see Our Lord doing?

Hanging on the cross and sporting shoes, sir.

Now if I hear of one boy in this class jeering and sneering at McCourt or his brother over their shoes the stick will come out. What will come out, boys?

The stick, sir.

The stick will sting, boys. The ash plant will whistle through the air, it will land on the backside of the boy that jeers, the boy that sneers. Where will it land, boys?

On the boy that jeers, sir.

And?

The boy that sneers, sir.

The boys bother us no more and we wear our shoes with the rubber tires the few weeks to Easter when the St Vincent de Paul Society gives us the gift of boots.

From Angela's Ashes *by Frank McCourt*

- What are your thoughts and feelings about Frank here?
- How has the author created these thoughts and feelings?
- What are your thoughts and feelings about the teacher here?
- How has the author created these thoughts and feelings?
- Do you find the lack of punctuation for speech an advantage or disadvantage? Be prepared to justify your views.

Tracking point of view

- Is this extract written in the first person (I) or the third person (he or she)?
- How far does the author let you know the feelings of any of the characters?

Drafting elements of your own writing

- Write about five lines describing how your character reacts to an embarrassing situation, or how your character puts someone else in an embarrassing situation.

WORDS

▲ **last** *noun* the wooden or metal form on which a shoe or boot is fashioned or repaired.

ADVICE

▲ Set the scene briefly, but spend most of your energy on trying to describe what they do, what they say, how they react. This will probably include body language.

3 PORTRAYING CHARACTER

6 How authors create characters – E

The following extract is taken from *Noughts & Crosses* by Malorie Blackman. Callum is a 'nought', and Sephy is a 'Cross'. Crosses have all the top positions in this society, noughts all the lowest positions, and they can be easily identified by their skin colour. This part of the story is told by Callum, who is 15.

▶ As you read it or hear it read, decide whose side you are taking and how the author leads you to take this side.

The train journey from hell, that's what it was. A journey which ruined the rest of the day as far as I was concerned. We were on our way to Celebration Park. There were only three more stops to go – when they got on. Police officers on a routine inspection. Two of them, boredom plastered over their faces.

'ID passes please. ID passes please.'

Sephy looked surprised. I wasn't. We both dug out our ID cards as they made their way up the first-class train carriage. I watched the cursory glances they gave the ID passes of all the Crosses in the carriage. I was the only nought. Would they stop and ask me lots of questions? Huh! Is pig poo smelly?

An officer of trim build and sporting a pencil-thin moustache stood right in front of me. He looked at me then took my ID pass without a word.

'Name?' he snapped out.

What's the matter? Can't you read?

'Callum McGregor.'

'Age?'

'Fifteen.'

Can't read numbers either, huh? That's too bad.

'Where are you going?'

None of your business.

'Celebration Park.'

'Why?'

To cut my toenails.

'Picnic.'

'Where d'you live?'

On the moon.

'Meadowview.' Meadowview by euphemistic name only. Rubbishshackview would've been more appropriate. The officer looked from my ID card to my face and back again. My thumbprint was on the card. Was he going to break out a magnifying glass and ask me to hold out my right hand so he could compare the imprint on the card to my print? It wouldn't've surprised me.

'You're a long way from home, boy.'

50

I bit down on the inside of my bottom lip, not trusting myself to speak. Both officious officers stood in front of me now. There was barely enough room to get a paperclip between their legs and my knees. I sighed.

Ladies and gentlemen, for your delectation and delight, another performance of 'You're a nought and don't you ever forget it, blanker boy.'

'Let me see your ticket.'

I handed it over.

'Where did you get the money to buy this kind of ticket?'

I looked up at them, but didn't speak. What was there to say? They had the scent of blood in their nostrils and I didn't stand a chance, no matter what I said or did. So why bother?

'I asked you a question,' Moustaches reminded me.

As if I'd forgotten.

'Did you buy this ticket?' Moustache's accomplice asked.

The truth or prevarication? What was Sephy thinking? I couldn't see her. The no-brain brothers were in the way. If only I could see her face.

'I asked you a question, boy. Did you buy this ticket?'

'No, I didn't,' I replied.

'Come with us, please.'

Time to get my posterior pummelled. Time to get my derrière dealt with. Time to get my bum bounced right off the train.

How dare a nought sit in first class? It's outrageous. It's a scandal. It's disgusting. Disinfect that seat at once.

'Officer, he's with me. I bought the tickets.' Sephy was on her feet. 'Is there a problem?'

'And you are?'

'Persephone Hadley. My dad's the Home Office Minister, Kamal Hadley. Callum is my friend,' Sephy said firmly.

'He is?'

'Yes, he is.' Sephy's voice had a steely tone to it that I'd never heard before. Not from her anyway.

'I see,' said Moustaches.

'I can give you my father's private phone number. I'm sure he'll sort all this out in a moment. Or you'll be able to talk to Juno Oyeleye, his personal secretary.'

Careful, Sephy. I'm tripping over all those names you're dropping.

'So is there a problem, Officer?' repeated Sephy.

Sniff! Sniff! Was I imagining things or was there the definite hint of a threat in the air? And I wasn't the only one to smell it. Moustaches handed back my ID pass.

'Would you like to see my ID pass as well?' Sephy held out her pass.

3 PORTRAYING CHARACTER

'That won't be necessary, Miss Hadley.' Moustaches almost bowed.

'I really don't mind.' Sephy thrust it under Moustaches' nose. 70

'That won't be necessary,' Moustaches repeated, looking straight at Sephy. He didn't even glance at her ID card.

Sephy sat back down again. 'Well, if you're sure.'

She turned to look out of the window. Moustaches was effectively dismissed. Sephy's mother would've been proud. Moustaches glared at me like it was my fault. He'd been humiliated, and by a child, no less, and he wanted to take it out on someone. Sephy was off-limits, and now, so was I. He was burning to re-establish his authority but he couldn't. Not with us anyway. Moustaches and his colleague moved off down the carriage. 75

From Noughts & Crosses *by Malorie Blackman*

- ▶ Try reading lines 2–3 out loud in your group.
- ▶ Decide as a group what effect the dash is intended to have.
- ▶ What are your thoughts and feelings about Callum in the passage?
- ▶ How has the author created these thoughts and feelings?
- ▶ What are your thoughts and feelings about Sephy in the passage?
- ▶ How has the author created these thoughts and feelings?
- ▶ What are your thoughts and feelings about the police officers in the passage?
- ▶ How has the author created these thoughts and feelings?

Tracking point of view

- ▶ Is this extract written in the first person (I) or the third person (he or she)?
- ▶ How far does the author let you know the feelings of any of the characters?

Drafting elements of your own writing

- ▶ Write about five lines exploring how your chosen character reacts to authority or acts when in a position of authority.

ADVICE

▲ Think of an incident that really happened as a basis for your account. But this incident need not have happened in *this* way to *your* character. However, you should try to match the reaction to how your individual character would react.

WORDS

▲ **cursory** *adjective* hasty, quick, usually superficial.

▲ **euphemism** *noun* a mild word which is used as a substitute for a word that might be considered harsh or offensive, especially connected with religion, sex, death, or excreta.

▲ **officious** *adjective* unnecessarily precise and abrupt in carrying out their duties.

▲ **accomplice** *noun* a person who helps another in committing a crime.

▲ **prevaricate** *verb* to speak or act falsely or evasively with the intention of deceiving.

▲ **posterior** *noun* the buttocks.

▲ **pummel** *verb* strike repeatedly with the fists, or as if with the fists.

▲ **derrière** *noun* a euphemistic word for the buttocks.

▲ **name-dropping** *noun, informal* the practice of referring frequently to famous or fashionable people, especially as though they were intimate friends, in order to impress others.

▲ **humiliate** *verb* to hurt the pride of/lower the dignity of.

▲ **plosive** *noun* a consonant or sound made by the sudden release of breath after stoppage, such as /p/, /t/, /k/, etc.; a shortening of **explosive**.

'And you are?'

7 Investigating techniques

▶ You have been given the quotation and the technique. Try to explain what the effect of each technique is. It will usually help if you look back at the passage to see how the quotation fits in to that part of the story.

Line	Quotation	Technique	Effect of technique
1	The train journey from **hell**	Choice of noun	
1–2	A journey which ruined the rest of the day as far as **I** was concerned.	Use of first person narrative	
8–9	Would they stop and ask me lots of questions? Huh! Is pig poo smelly?	Use of questions and exclamation	
13	*What's the matter? Can't you read?*	Use of italics	
25	*On the moon.*	Use of sarcasm in character's thoughts	
31	'You're a long way from home, **boy**.'	Choice of noun	
32	I bit down on the inside of my bottom lip	Use of body language	
40–41	They had the scent of blood in their nostrils	Use of metaphor	
44	accomplice	Choice of noun	
50–51	**p**osterior **p**ummelled/**d**errière **d**ealt with/ **b**um **b**ounced right off the train	Use of alliteration Use of plosives	
69	'That won't be necessary, Miss Hadley.'	Use of character's name	
75–76	He'd been humiliated, and by a child, no less	Use of contrast	

8 How authors create characters – F

This extract comes from a novel set in about 1996. Sade and Femi have arrived in London from Nigeria after the death of their mother. Their father, a journalist who has carried out a campaign against a brutal military dictatorship, is being detained near Oxford for trying to enter the country on a false passport. Sade is taking her younger brother Femi to the centre of London, hoping to get to a television studio and publicise what has happened to their father.

Once off the bus, the children steered their way through figures wrapped securely in coats and scarves. Shops and offices were closing and people were going home. A plump Father Christmas and an airy Snowman twinkled down at them above the street lights. Giant stars and Christmas trees flickered above the traffic. However, around the corner, the road was not lit so brightly. Cars and taxis still roared past, but there were less shops and people. More shadows. 5

'Listen child. London streets are full of strangers – and some are very sick, you know. Your daddy is trusting me and Uncle Roy to take good care of you.'

Aunt Gracie's words echoed in Sade's head. She remembered Darth Vader of the Alley lunging out at them on their first night in the new city.

3 PORTRAYING CHARACTER

'How far is it?' Femi mewled. Sade was peering through the gloom at each new entrance, searching for signs and brass number plates. She had no idea what kind of building they were looking for.

'It can't be far.'

'You lie! How do you know? You haven't been here before!' It was the whine that always got on her nerves.

'Then why ask me such a stupid question?!' Sade bit her lip. The moment the words were out she knew that they were a mistake. Femi stamped to a halt.

'If I'm so stupid, why do you need me? I'm going home! Give me my bus money!'

'Don't be so – 'Sade swung around. Femi's jaw jutted out fiercely. He was serious. He might even try to walk all the way if she refused to give him his busfare. Her whole plan was going to be ruined.

'Oh don't let's argue!' Sade pleaded. 'I'm sorry. It's me that's stupid. We won't help Papa if we fight.'

Slowly Femi's jaw and shoulders relaxed. Like a bristling cat letting its hair down. They set off again in silence. Ahead of them most of the buildings were shrouded in darkness. Was this really the right street? Sade would have liked to check her map under one of the pools of light but she dare not let Femi see any doubt. Her face prickled with the cold and her fingers stiffened despite her gloves.

A glow of light and two taxis pulling up alongside a row of great white pillars were the first signs. When they drew nearer, they could see the building was quite different from the rest. Behind the pillars, the pavement sloped up towards two large revolving glass doors. The entire wall was made of glass. Inside a brilliantly lit hall, glossy-green trees grew in huge tubs and televisions hung from the walls like decorations. For a little while they stared without speaking at this world inside a world. They could see everything but hear nothing. People walked briskly from the revolving doors to a man behind a desk. The buttons on his uniform glinted as he nodded and pointed.

'Will that man let us in?' Femi asked.

From The Other Side of Truth *by Beverley Naidoo*

▶ What are your thoughts and feelings about Femi here?
▶ How has the author created these thoughts and feelings?
▶ What are your thoughts and feelings about Sade here?
▶ How has the author created these thoughts and feelings?

Tracking point of view

▶ Is this extract written in the first person (I) or the third person (he or she)?
▶ How far does the author let you know the feelings of any of the characters?

Drafting elements of your own writing

▶ Write about five lines describing how your chosen character reacts when in conflict with another character. This could be someone in authority, a brother or sister (as with Femi and Sade), yourself/the 'I' of your text, a parent …

ADVICE

▲ Describe the situation briefly, but spend most of your energy describing **how** this person reacts to a situation of conflict with another person. This could include:
- what they say
- how they say it
- if they tend to react by 'fight' (arguing back), 'flight' (avoiding the situation), or something in between.

Developing character

9 Why authors use different points of view

▶ Brainstorm ideas for why authors use:
- first person narrative
- third person narrative as an external view
- third person narrative following one character.

> **ADVICE**
> ▲ It will probably help you to look back at examples of each type in this unit, and decide the advantages and disadvantages of each choice.
> ▲ As you read other books and extracts from books, be aware of the point of view and think about why the author may have chosen this point of view for this book.

10 How authors create and reveal character

It would be possible to draw up a list of adjectives you could use to describe your character, such as *brave, generous, kind, passive, selfish* ... Theophrastus divided characters into groups such as:

the boor – someone who regularly lowers the tone of the conversation ...
the grouch – someone who regularly moans ...
the liar
the sponge – someone who regularly relies on someone else to pay.

However, it may be advisable to avoid using these words on many occasions. This is because if a writer simply tells you someone is 'selfish', this is just an assertion, an unsupported statement of belief. However, if a writer tells a story in which readers can decide for themselves that a particular character has acted selfishly, this can be far more powerful and effective.

For example, Femi could be described as stubborn. Having read the extract, you may agree that Femi has acted stubbornly, but the story is much richer than that, and you may well have sympathy for this character which might be lacking if you had simply been told 'Femi was a stubborn boy'.

One effective way of describing character is therefore through 'showing' rather than 'telling', and this can be achieved in a number of ways, including descriptions of body language.

▶ Match up techniques authors use to reveal character (below) with the extracts from the passages at the top of the next page.

Letting the reader know the inner thoughts of a character	
Suggesting tone of voice	
Stating tone of voice	
Using body language to show what a character is thinking or feeling or to reveal their attitude	
Using speech to show how a character reacts	
Putting the character in a tense situation and showing how they react	
Using first person narrative to show what one character thinks/feels about another character	
Using first person narrative to let you know what the central character is thinking/feeling	
Using third person narrative to let you know how one character is feeling	
Using third person narrative to show what one character thinks/feels about another character	

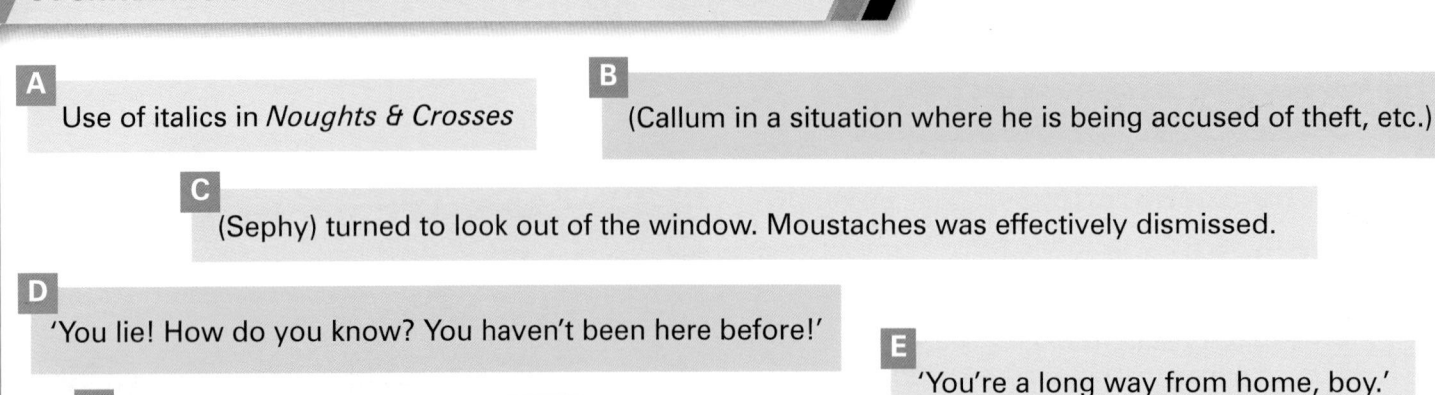

3 PORTRAYING CHARACTER

A Use of italics in *Noughts & Crosses*

B (Callum in a situation where he is being accused of theft, etc.)

C (Sephy) turned to look out of the window. Moustaches was effectively dismissed.

D 'You lie! How do you know? You haven't been here before!'

E 'You're a long way from home, boy.'

F Careful, Sephy. I'm tripping over all those names you're dropping.

G Femi's jaw jutted out fiercely. He was serious. He might even try to walk all the way if she refused to give him his busfare.

H Sephy's voice had a steely tone to it.

I They had the scent of blood in their nostrils and I didn't stand a chance, no matter what I said or did. So why bother?

J The moment the words were out she knew that they were a mistake.

▶ Add any examples of your own from the passages printed in this unit.

11 Using body language to develop character

Many of the authors you have been reading extracts from in this unit use body language to help the reader understand a character more fully.

▶ Match up each of the descriptions below, taken from the extracts in this unit, with the clearest equivalent you can find on the next page.

Page/line reference	Quotation	Feeling/emotion/idea conveyed
42: 4/5	he dropped things, tripped over things, fumbled and stumbled.	K
42: 6/7	his whole look was that of a cowering dog	J
44: 23	Sometimes she'd walk quickly around the block	
45: 11/12	I felt the skin crawling on my neck.	F
45: 13/14	My throat felt dry, my tongue felt too big for my mouth.	
51: 32	I bit down on the inside of my bottom lip, not trusting myself to speak.	I
52: 69	Moustaches almost bowed	E
52: 70	Sephy thrust it under Moustaches' nose.	D
52: 74	She turned to look out of the window.	
54: 17	Femi stamped to a halt.	
54: 19	Femi's jaw jutted out fiercely.	H
54: 24	Slowly Femi's jaw and shoulders relaxed. Like a bristling cat letting its hair down.	

'And you are?'

A Doing something not because the person wants to do it but because they want to be seen to have something to do.

B Feeling of embarrassment, lack of relaxation, tension.

C Indicating that the person knows they should show respect even if they do not want to.

D Indicating some lack of respect for the person and suggesting they should look even if they don't want to.

E Indicating that the other person is not needed now and can leave.

F Sense of something disturbing, perhaps even unnatural/supernatural.

G This indicates stubbornness and a determination not to do anything this person doesn't want to do.

H This indicates that the person means business and will not give way.

I This indicates that the person's anger and tension is gradually disappearing.

J This indicates that the person involved expects to be beaten or hurt in some way.

K This suggests the person involved is un-coordinated at times and can be clumsy.

L Trying to stop expressing the real anger felt inside.

▶ Make a note of any habits or mannerisms or ways of reacting that are special to or typical of your chosen character.

ADVICE

▲ It may help to think how they reveal particular emotions, such as anger, embarrassment, fear, happiness, pride, stress, stubbornness, feeling upset…

57

3 PORTRAYING CHARACTER

12 Show-not-tell activity sheet

▶ Work out how you can express the feelings referred to in the left-hand column without actually using the word for that feeling. Be original, but give a strong impression of the feeling involved. Try to include description of body language. Use a table like the one below.

ADVICE

▲ You could copy good examples from authors you read (including those represented in this unit), and also invent your own ways of expressing emotions.
▲ You could try to describe the body language that would indicate each feeling.

I was tired.	
I was angry.	
I was feeling proud.	
I was feeling sad.	
I was feeling disappointed.	
I was nervous.	
I was happy.	
I was determined.	
I was ashamed.	
I was irritable.	

'And you are?'

Independent writing

13 Writing about your own character

▶ Write about two sides of A4 paper on your chosen character, using the understanding you have gained from tackling this unit, and the advice on this page.

'So what's literature?'

'Literature is where you read a book and feel you could put a little mark under every line because it's true.'

'Because it's true? I don't get it.'

'When every sentence is simply right. When it reveals something about the world. And life. When every phrase gives you the feeling that you would have behaved or thought exactly the same way the character in the book does. That's when it's literature.'

'Where did you get that from?'

'I just think so, that's all.'

From Crazy *by Benjamin Lebert, translated from the German by Carol Brown Janeway*

Making your writing 'true' is not so much about not lying as about writing in a way that convinces other people. When other people read your work, do they have the sense that it 'rings true', that even if events did not happen in exactly the way you describe, the writing 'gives you the feeling that you would have behaved or thought exactly the same way the character in the book does'?
In writing about your chosen character, check against this statement, rather than against whether it is literally (actually) true.

ADVICE

▲ Characters often reveal themselves most clearly when put in a difficult situation, as with Callum and Sephy or with Femi and Sade.
▲ You could consider placing your character in a challenging but realistic situation.
▲ Think back to the descriptions of character you have read in this unit. Which one did you find most effective? Can you use some of the techniques of that author in your own writing?
▲ You may wish to use some of the drafts you have written during the course of this unit, but some re-drafting will almost certainly be necessary to link parts into a coherent whole.

Point of view

In this unit you have seen authors using a variety of points of view to present characters:
- Third person, not privileging or 'taking sides' with one character. (Meshak)
- Third person, privileging or 'taking sides' with one character. (Shelley, Sade)
- First person, revealing another character. (Kit Watson revealing Askew)
- First person, revealing first person (and more). (Callum, Frank)

▶ You could deliberately decide to use one of these four approaches that you have not used in your writing before.

3 PORTRAYING CHARACTER

14 Commenting on your choices

▶ Write no more than half a side of A4 paper, reflecting on your decisions and explaining your choices. Be honest and open about how far you think you have been successful.

You could comment on:
- your choice of point of view
- any techniques you have used that you have noticed other authors using
- any use you have made of descriptions of body language
- how you think a reader will judge your character – and why you think a reader may have this reaction
- how you have structured your writing in paragraphs.

Self-assessment

15 Judging your own performance

▶ From the list below:
  a select three points on which you feel you have made the most progress
  b select one point on which you most need to improve.

I can identify ways writers create characters and influence our views on characters.
I can use some of these techniques in my own writing.
I understand why writers may choose first or third person narrative.
I have used first and third person narrative in my own writing.
I can comment on the advantages and disadvantages of first and third person narrative.
I can identify examples of authors describing body language to reveal feelings.
I make use of descriptions of body language in my own writing to reveal feelings.
I can write about character in a powerful and logically structured way.
I can comment effectively on my choices in writing about character.

16 Improving your skills in English

▶ Select one or two skills you need to concentrate on to improve your skills in reading. Then do the same for your writing skills. (The descriptions of levels are a guide only.)

	Reading skill	From	To
1	Show understanding of characters, beginning to use inference and deduction	Level 3	Level 4
2	Refer to the text when explaining views, locating and using ideas and information	Level 3	Level 4
3	Select essential points, using inference and deduction where appropriate	Level 4	Level 5
4	Select sentences, phrases and relevant information to support views	Level 4	Level 5
5	Identify different layers of meaning and comment on their significance and effect	Level 5	Level 6
6	Give a personal response to texts, referring to aspects of language and structure in justifying views	Level 5	Level 6
7	Articulate personal and critical responses to texts	Level 6	Level 7

		From	To
8	Show awareness of structural and linguistic features	Level 6	Level 7
9	Appreciate and comment on a range of texts	Level 7	Level 8
10	Evaluate how authors achieve their effects through the use of linguistic, structural and presentational devices	Level 7	Level 8
11	Sustain responses to a demanding range of texts, developing ideas and referring in detail to aspects of language, structure and presentation	Level 8	E.P.
12	Make apt and careful comparison between texts	Level 8	E.P.

Writing skill		From	To
1	Vocabulary choices are often adventurous, and words are used for effect	Level 3	Level 4
2	Writing is lively and thoughtful, and ideas are sustained and developed in interesting ways	Level 3	Level 4
3	Writing is varied and interesting, conveying meaning clearly in a form appropriate for writing about character	Level 4	Level 5
4	Vocabulary choices are imaginative and words are used precisely	Level 4	Level 5
5	Writing engages and sustains the reader's interest, showing some use of style appropriate to writing about character	Level 5	Level 6
6	Pupils use a range of sentence structures and varied vocabulary to create effects	Level 5	Level 6
7	Writing is confident, and shows an appropriate choice of style for writing about character	Level 6	Level 7
8	Characters are developed, grammatical features and vocabulary are accurately and effectively used	Level 6	Level 7
9	Selection of specific features or expressions to convey particular effects and to interest the reader	Level 7	Level 8
10	Control of characters, variety and structure	Level 7	Level 8
11	Writing has shape and impact, and control of the style appropriate for writing about character	Level 8	E.P.
12	Maintains the interest of the reader throughout, with structure as well as vocabulary used for a range of imaginative effects	Level 8	E.P.

4 Information, explanation and advice
Info A–Z

Your focus
The content of this unit is designed to:
- improve your skills in writing information, explanation and advice.

Your target
By the end of this unit you should be more able to:
- judge why a text is effective or not in informing, explaining or advising
- choose the most appropriate style and structure for your own text
- write an effective text which informs, explains and advises.

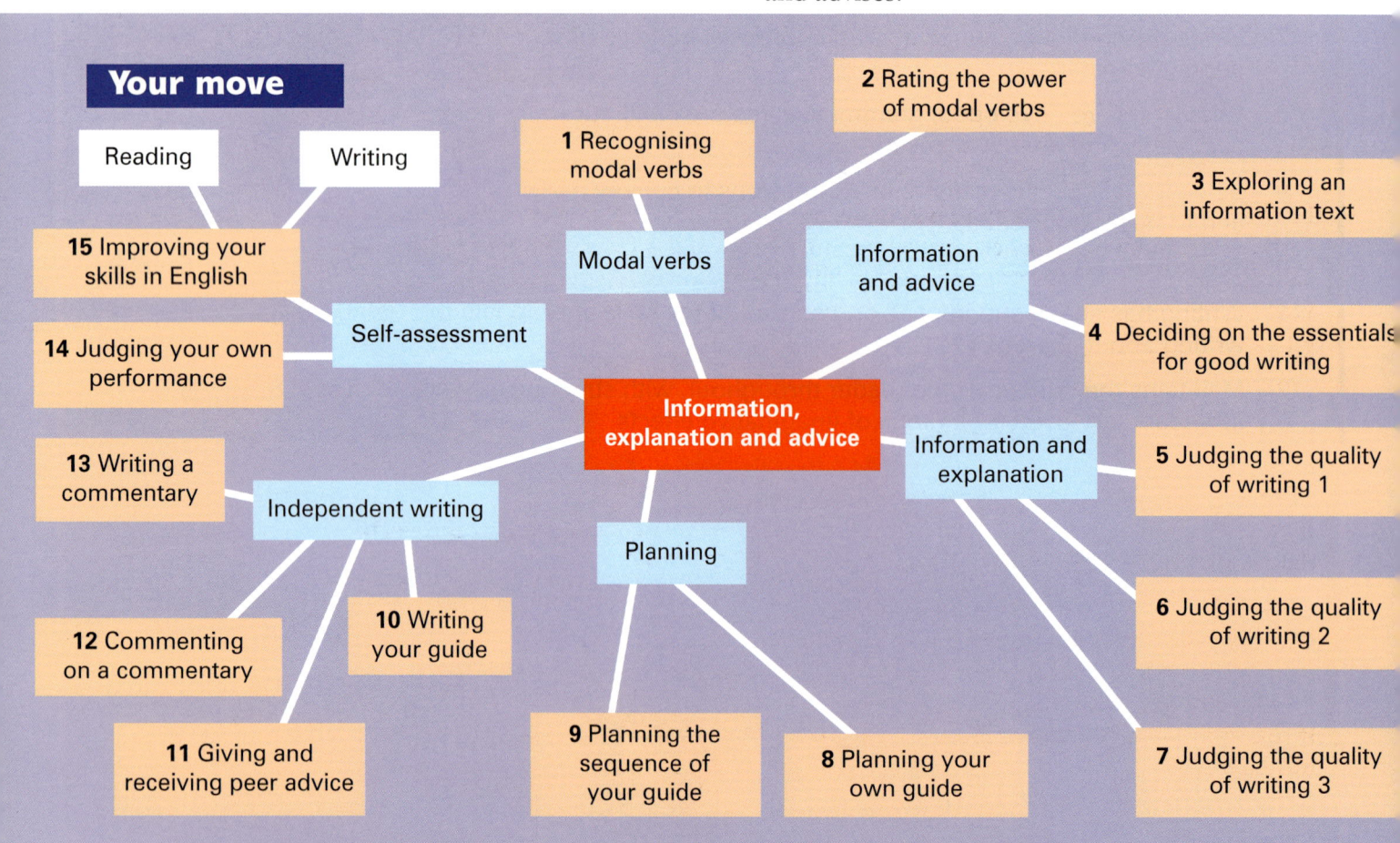

Your move

- Reading
- Writing

- 15 Improving your skills in English
- 14 Judging your own performance
- 13 Writing a commentary
- 12 Commenting on a commentary
- 11 Giving and receiving peer advice

- Self-assessment
- Independent writing

- 1 Recognising modal verbs
- 2 Rating the power of modal verbs
- Modal verbs

- 10 Writing your guide
- 9 Planning the sequence of your guide
- Planning
- 8 Planning your own guide

Information, explanation and advice

- Information and advice
  - 3 Exploring an information text
  - 4 Deciding on the essentials for good writing

- Information and explanation
  - 5 Judging the quality of writing 1
  - 6 Judging the quality of writing 2
  - 7 Judging the quality of writing 3

Unit 1 focused on writing about places, and included activities in which you wrote informatively and persuasively about places. Unit 4 also involves writing informatively, not in this case about a place, but on a topic of your choice. This unit also deals with writing *explanations* and writing *advice*.

Planning ahead

Towards the end of this unit you will be writing a guide to a sport/activity/topic that you know about – preferably one that you know more about than your teacher or others in the class.

This may or may not be an easy decision for you. To help you choose if there's any doubt, here is an A to Z of possibilities. Even if you don't choose one of these, they may start you thinking about other possibilities:

abseiling	judo	soccer
basketball	kick boxing	tennis
canoeing	life saving	under-age laws
dance	make-up	virtual reality
electric guitar	nutrition	weight training
fishing	orchestra	xylophone
go-karting	paintball	yachting
hockey	quilting	Zen
ice-skating	rowing	

Modal verbs

1 Recognising modal verbs

In your writing for this unit you will be using 'modal verbs'. You probably use these verbs every day, without necessarily knowing or remembering that's what they are called. The first activities are designed to improve your understanding of how modal verbs work, and how you can use them effectively in your own writing.

Is it a modal verb?

Check 1:
Is there an 's' at the end of the third person singular of the verb?
▶ Try this for: I can, I could, I eat, I may, I might, I move, I must, I ought to, I read, I shall, I should, I swim, I talk, I will, I would.
If you found there was **no 's' at the end of the third person singular of the verb**, that shows **the verb is a modal verb**.

Check 2:
Can you turn the verb into the infinitive by adding 'to' in front?
▶ Try this for: ask, borrow, can, could, jump, may, might, must, see, shall, should, swim, will, worry, would, yell.
If you found you **could not form an infinitive** in this way, that shows **the verb is a modal verb**.

ADVICE

▲ Different people find different ways to remember things. Decide which of the two methods of checking you have been given works best for you.

INFORMATION, EXPLANATION AND ADVICE

2 Rating the power of modal verbs

If one person wants to advise or instruct another person about what they should do, different degrees of persuasion can be given.

▶ Rate the following according to how strongly they are advising a person to go and do something: low, medium, strong.

▶ Use a table like the one below.

ADVICE

▲ It may help to imagine/act out *who* might be saying it, what *tone of voice* they might use, and *how they might continue* the sentence.

▲ There is no exact correct rating – decide in your group what rating you think works best, and which you can defend if challenged.

Choices of modal verb	Low	Medium	Strong
You **can** go ...			
You **could** go ...			
You **may** go ...			
You **might** go ...			
You **must** go ...			
You **need to** go ...			
You **ought to** go ...			
You **should** go ...			
You **will** go ...			
You **would** go ...			

Study the photos below and opposite.

▶ Rank them according to how strongly you think the message is being put across.

A

Parking here could cost a child's life

B

Drivers MUST give way at Zebra Crossings
THE HIGHWAY CODE 1999 Rule 171

64

Info A–Z

C

THIS BRIDGE IS:
"Clare Road 170m 57c SWM"

If you witness a vehicle striking this bridge contact

RAILTRACK on
01793 515410

as quickly as possible. The safety of trains may be affected

D

ONLY FOOD PURCHASED FROM MASONS ARMS MAY BE CONSUMED AT THESE TABLES

E

DO NOT ENTER HOPPER

F

PRIVATE CAR PARK

NO PARKING
— AT ANY TIME —

CARS PARKED HERE WITHOUT AUTHORISATION WILL BE **CLAMPED**
RELEASE FEE £75

G

Passengers must not cross the line
Except by means of the footbridge

Warning

Do not trespass on the Railway

INFORMATION, EXPLANATION AND ADVICE

ScotRail Outlook: just the ticket

Over recent years, a common complaint is that the range of tickets is now more confusing than ever. With more than 20 Train Operators running services in the UK, each providing tickets to suit their customers needs, maybe this is understandable.

But it is simpler than you think! All rail tickets sold in the UK fall into one of just a few ticket types. Understanding these will help you decide just exactly which ticket provides the best value.

This guide to tickets available in Scotland should help. Decide which ticket type suits you best, then take a look at the range of ScotRail tickets.

You can buy full price, fully flexible tickets at any time (item 1), with no limits on travel during the period they are valid. All other ticket types shown offer either reduced prices or include extra value items, so long as you accept some limits on when you can travel.

1 Buy any time, travel any time

Open Singles or Returns, Savers or Day Return tickets. Available Standard Class on all routes, and First Class/Business Class on appropriate routes.

2 Buy any time, travel restricted

For off-peak travel, Cheap Day Returns or SuperSavers are available on most routes (Standard Class).

Midweek Movers are available between Dundee and Glasgow/Edinburgh/Aberdeen, and small family groups travelling on a Sunday can save money with Family Funday Sunday tickets (all Standard Class) or with GroupSave.

3 Buy in advance, specified trains

Available on many routes, most advance purchase tickets include free seat reservations, but are only available in limited numbers, at certain times or on specified trains. Early booking is advisable to ensure availability.

This Standard Class ticket type includes APEX tickets, Friends Fares, and Rail/Sail tickets to Ireland.

4 Multi-journey tickets

Unlimited travel on certain routes or in certain areas. Multi-journey leisure tickets occasionally include a restriction on some peak-hour services.

This ticket type includes Season tickets, Zonecards (in Strathclyde) and Flexipass tickets, all with no restrictions.

You can also get Rover tickets (Freedom of Scotland Travelpass, Central Scotland Rover and Highland Rover), which include some peak-hour restrictions.

5 Special Tickets

During the year, ScotRail have other bargain tickets, each specially designed for major events or visitor attractions. These can offer reduced fares, or extra value such as reduced or free entry.

This ticket type includes tickets to tourist attractions such as the Seabird Centre (North Berwick), Royal Yacht Britannia (Leith) and Our Dynamic Earth (Edinburgh).

6 Railcards

You may be entitled to buy a Railcard, which can offer further savings on many of the fares shown, especially for leisure travel. Railcards are available for
- Senior Citizens (over 60)
- Families (adults travelling with children)
- Young Persons (16-25)
- Disabled Persons
- A special local Railcard is also available for West and North Highland residents only.

7 Railbus tickets

A railbus scheme, run by ScotRail and some of Scotland's leading bus operators, allows you to add on a bus ticket to your rail fare when travelling to certain parts of Scotland. Pick up a railbus guide at any staffed ScotRail station.

For information

For information on ticket types and prices, you can ask at
- any staffed ScotRail station
- National Rail Enquiries on 08457 484950
- any travel agent displaying the National Rail symbol
- visit our website at www.scotrail.co.uk

To buy your ticket

You can buy your ScotRail ticket from
- any staffed ScotRail station
- ScotRail Telesales on 08457 55 00 33
- ScotRail's internet site: www.scotrail.co.uk (enhanced ticketing service will soon be available)
- any travel agent displaying the National Rail symbol

All fares and ticket information included was applicable for the period from April to June 2001. Outlook is published by IPM Limited, Glasgow on behalf of ScotRail. © 2001 In Position Media Limited. For further copyright information visit www.inpositionmedia.co.uk/legal.html

---

WORDS

▲ **just the ticket** *colloquial* exactly what is required, proper or best.

many *adjective* (*comparative* **more**, *superlative* **most**) consisting of a large number, numerous.

▲ **pun** *noun* a form of joke consisting of the use of a word or phrase that can be understood in two different ways, especially one where an association is created between words of similar sound but different meaning.

▲ **ticket** *noun* a printed piece of paper or card which shows that the holder has paid a fare, e.g. for travel on a bus or train, or for admission, e.g. to a theatre or a cinema, or has the right to use certain services, e.g. a library.

Information and advice

3 Exploring an information text

One page of a rail information booklet is printed on page 66.
- Rank these words in order from the smallest proportion suggested to the largest proportion suggested:

    all, many, more, most, none, some

- Why are these words so important in an information text like this?
- Explain why the title is a pun.
- Why do you think some of the text is in bold and has a purple background colour?
- Why are there seven numbered sections?
- Why do you think 'bullet points' are used in section 6 and the last two sections?
- What modal verbs can you find in sections 5 and 6?
- Why is it important for a reader who is interested in this information to take notice of the modal verbs here?
- What modifiers can you find in sections 3 and 4 which increase the attraction of the offer?
- What modifiers can you find in sections 3 and 4 which reduce the attraction of the offer by laying down extra conditions?
- Find one imperative in section 7, 'Railbus tickets', and one imperative in the 'For information' section.
- Why do you think the author uses imperatives here? What do you think the author wants a reader to do?
- Overall, do you think this text is appropriately written, considering the topic (railway tickets), the audience (the general public) and the purpose (to inform)?

> **WORDS**
>
> ▲ **modifier** *noun grammar* a word or phrase that modifies or qualifies the sense of another word, e.g. **many** routes – here *many* is a modifier of the noun 'routes'.

4 Deciding on the essentials for good writing

You have probably had experiences at various points in your life when you had difficulty understanding information or advice. For example, you may have found booklets provided with computers or other electronic equipment hard to follow, or had problems assembling DIY furniture.
- Develop a set of guidelines of the essentials if information and advice are going to be clear and easy to follow.
- Try to write one guideline on each of the following.
  - layout
  - readability
  - technical terms
  - the audience aimed at
  - the style of writing
  - what order is chosen.

INFORMATION, EXPLANATION AND ADVICE

Information and explanation

5 Judging the quality of writing 1

Two pages from a booklet on the technology of sound have been printed on page 69.
- In your group, rate it as a piece of information and explanation writing, and prepare to explain your decisions.
- Use a table like the one below.

*0 = lowest (worst) rating, 3 = highest (best) rating

> **ADVICE**
> ▲ In judging the 'difficult terms' etc. (point 3) you must think of the typical non-expert, not someone who is familiar with the subject.
> ▲ In judging if the style is helpful without being patronising (point 9) you will need first to decide what age group you think the text is suitable for.
> ▲ Remember that this is just an extract from a much longer text.

Criteria for judging information and explanation	Rating: 0–3*	Note of your reasons, with examples to prove your point
1 Are any diagrams clearly labelled/captioned?		
2 Are any diagrams helpful?		
3 Are any difficult terms explained?		
4 Are any headings clear and appropriate?		
5 Are the illustrations well chosen?		
6 Is colour used effectively?		
7 Is it written in plain English?		
8 Is the layout clear and uncluttered?		
9 Is the style right, i.e. informative without being patronising?		
10 Is the text (choice of font design and size) easy to read and appropriate?		

- Write down one piece of advice you would give the author/designer on how to improve the pages.
- In the report-back session, make a note of any points you think are worth remembering – these could help you make a success of your own information and explanation writing.
- Overall, do you think this text is appropriately written, considering the topic (lasers), the audience (the general public) and the purpose (to inform and explain)?
- Now write five bullet points – the top five essentials you will need to remember when writing your own information and explanation text.

> **WORDS**
> ▲ **patronise** *verb* to act in a superior way, to treat someone condescendingly, as if looking down on them.

THE LASER REVOLUTION

When the laser was invented in 1960, it seemed to be little more than a scientific oddity. The first lasers were large, delicate and dangerous pieces of laboratory equipment. Now, almost every home has a laser. If you have a CD player or a DVD player, or your home computer has a CD-ROM drive or DVD drive, then you use a laser. Playing a disc by shining a laser on it is better than using a needle or stylus in a grooved disc in two ways. First, the laser beam is far narrower than any needle or stylus could be, so a laser disc can hold much more information. Second, because a laser disc is played without anything actually touching it, it doesn't wear out.

HOW A CD RECORDS

Music is recorded on a CD as a spiral of microscopic pits. When a CD is played, a laser beam shines on it. A light-sensitive cell picks up the reflections that bounce back. The mirrored disc surface reflects the beam but the pits do not. The player then changes these flashing reflections into sound.

Enlarged view of CD
Pit does not reflect beam
Lens
Prism
Lens
Laser
Photo sensor
No electrical signal produced
Mirrored surface reflects beam
Reflections are changed into electric currents

THE CD

The most popular laser disc in use today is the CD (compact disc). Each disc is 12 cm across and 1.2 mm thick. An audio CD can hold up to about an hour of high quality music. A CD-ROM (compact disc read only memory) is an identical disc designed to hold computer data instead of music.

CD PLAYERS

CD players can now be made almost as small as the CDs they play. The first battery-powered portable CD players had to be kept very still or their laser would jump out of position and the music would stop. Portable CD players are now designed to keep playing even when they are bumped or jogged.

THE MINI DISC

The mini disc is a miniature recordable disc. The discs are only 64 mm across, but they can hold 74 minutes of music. Unlike a CD, which is covered with microscopic pits, a mini disc uses magnetic spots. To make a recording, a laser heats each spot on the spinning disc to more than 200 °C and a magnetic recording head magnetizes it.

DVD: THE FUTURE

A new type of laser disc is now growing rapidly in popularity. The digital versatile disc (DVD) looks identical to a CD in size, but it can hold a whole feature film — both pictures and sound. DVD players can play existing CDs and CD-ROMs as well as the new multimedia DVDs. DVD players can be made almost as small as CD players. A portable DVD player looks like a CD player with a flip-up screen.

INFORMATION, EXPLANATION AND ADVICE

6 Judging the quality of writing 2

Extracts from a book called *Bulging Brains* have been printed on pages 71–72.

▶ In your group, rate it as a piece of information and explanation writing and prepare to explain your decisions. Use a table like the one below.

*0 = lowest (worst) rating, 3 = highest (best) rating

ADVICE

▲ In judging the 'difficult terms' etc. (point 3) you must think of the typical non-expert, not someone who is familiar with the subject.
▲ In judging if the style is helpful without being patronising (point 9) you will need first to decide what age group you think the text is suitable for.
▲ Remember that this is just an extract from a much longer text.

Criteria for judging information and explanation	Rating: 0–3*	Note of your reasons, with examples to prove your point
1 Are any diagrams clearly labelled/captioned?		
2 Are any diagrams helpful?		
3 Are any difficult terms explained?		
4 Are any headings clear and appropriate?		
5 Is it written in plain English?		
6 Is the layout clear and uncluttered?		
7 Are any explanations clearly written?		
8 Does the way it is written help you take in the information?		
9 Is the style right, i.e. helpful without being patronising?		
10 Is the text (choice of font design and size) easy to read and appropriate?		

▶ Write down one piece of advice you would give the author/designer on how to improve the pages.
▶ In the report-back session, make a note of any points you think are worth remembering – these could help you make a success of your own information and explanation writing.
▶ Overall, do you think this text is appropriately written, considering the topic (the way the brain works), the audience (young people?) and the purpose (to inform and explain)?
▶ Now add to or change your five bullet points – the essentials you will need to remember when writing your own information and explanation text.

Bulging brain secrets

Psst – wanna know a brain secret? There's more to your brain than water. For example, your brain's made up of millions of cells and each one is so small you need a microscope to see it. (No, these aren't cells that people get locked up in.) Read on, your brain might learn something...

Bulging fact file

NAME: The brain

BASIC FACTS: The brain is made up of three main parts:

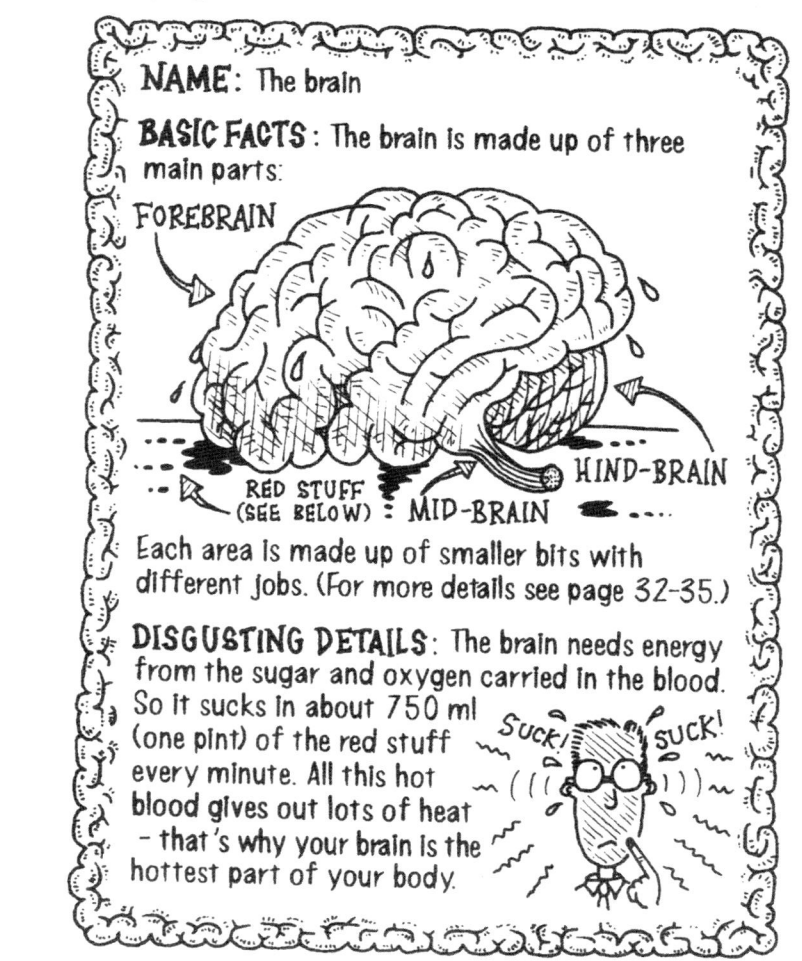

FOREBRAIN
MID-BRAIN
HIND-BRAIN
RED STUFF (SEE BELOW)

Each area is made up of smaller bits with different jobs. (For more details see page 32–35.)

DISGUSTING DETAILS: The brain needs energy from the sugar and oxygen carried in the blood. So it sucks in about 750 ml (one pint) of the red stuff every minute. All this hot blood gives out lots of heat – that's why your brain is the hottest part of your body.

Suck! Suck!

BULGING BRAIN BASICS

Bet you never knew!

Your brain weighs less than 1.3 kg – that's a little less than the weight of a large bag of sugar or the weight of all the germs swarming in your guts. In fact, the brain is only one-fiftieth the weight of a grown-up man and it's far lighter than your guts, your blood, your skin or your bones.

What's your brain for?

The brain is the part of your body that tells you what's going on around you. You can use your brain to order your body around and even to order everybody else around. But there's much more to your brain. Much, much more.

Inside your brain are your precious memories, your dreams, your hopes for the future and the knowledge of everything you love and care about. In your brain you can sense lovely smells and tastes and colours. Your brain helps you feel great and happy about life and that's the good side. But your brain also creates horrible fears and worries that can make you miserable.

Your brain makes the thoughts and feelings that make your personality. Your brain turns your body from a living object into *you* the person. Without a brain you'd be as dead as a dodo's tombstone, so it's good to know that you've got your very own bulging brain right now between your ears ... hopefully.

IT MAKES YOU THINK, DOESN'T IT?

71

BRAIN SURGERY FOR BEGINNERS

Chapter 1: Brain bits and pieces

Cerebrum (ser-ree-brum)
This is the largest bit of the brain – it's so big it makes up 85 per cent of the brain. This area is REALLY important because its wrinkly surface is the cortex, where thinking takes place. The cerebrum is divided into two halves (no one knows the reason for the split). The halves are linked by a bridge at the base made of millions of nerves cells.

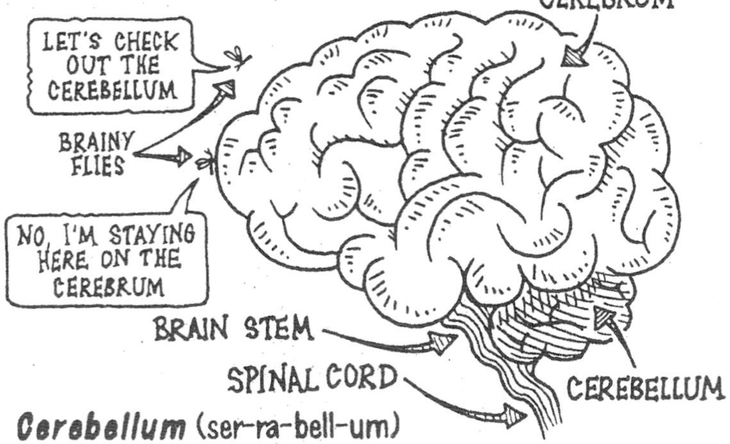

LET'S CHECK OUT THE CEREBELLUM

NO I'M STAYING HERE ON THE CEREBRUM

BRAINY FLIES

BRAIN STEM
SPINAL CORD
CEREBRUM
CEREBELLUM

Cerebellum (ser-ra-bell-um)
The name means "little brain" in Latin – because it looks a bit like a little brain. This pear-sized blob has two halves – one for each side of the brain. Both sides help the brain balance and control its body's movements.

Bet you never knew!
When you learn a skill such as riding a bike you think about what you're doing. Well, hopefully – otherwise you'd fall off. But after a while you happily pedal around without thinking. Oh, so you knew that? Well, when you stop thinking about what you're doing your cerebellum takes over from your thinking cortex and tells your body what to do. Scientists have found that with the cerebellum in charge you can move faster and less clumsily. (For more details on what the cerebellum can do check out pages 74 and 100.)

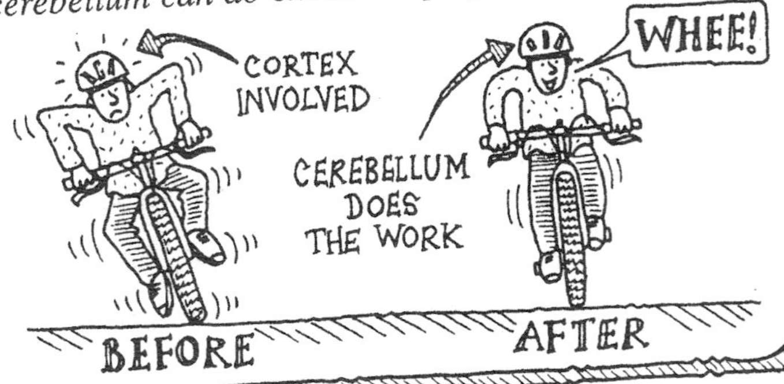

BEFORE — CORTEX INVOLVED
AFTER — CEREBELLUM DOES THE WORK
WHEE!

Spinal cord
This is a bundle of nerves 45 cm (18 inches) long and as thick as a thumb. Although it's not technically part of the brain, as a brain surgeon you need to know what it does. It actually takes signals to and from the brain.

Brain stem
This bit links the brain with the spinal cord. It's useful for helping the brain to go to sleep. And it's also useful for waking up the brain to danger or something interesting.

Info A–Z

7 Judging the quality of writing 3

Three pages from one pupil's response to this unit have been printed on pages 74–76.
▶ In your group, rate it as a piece of information, explanation and advice prepare to explain your decisions.
▶ Use a table like the one below.

*0 = lowest (worst) rating, 3 = highest (best) rating

ADVICE

▲ In judging the 'difficult terms' etc. (point 2) you must think of the typical non-expert, not someone who is familiar with the subject.
▲ In judging if the style is helpful without being patronising (point 8) you will need first to decide what age group you think the text is suitable for.

Criteria for judging information, explanation and advice	Rating: 0–3*	Note of your reasons, with examples to prove your point
1 Are any pictures well chosen with clear captions?		
2 Are any difficult terms explained?		
3 Are any headings clear and appropriate?		
4 Is it written in plain English?		
5 Is the layout clear and uncluttered?		
6 Are any explanations clearly written?		
7 Is any advice helpful and clear?		
8 Is the style right, i.e. helpful without being patronising?		
9 Is the text (choice of font design and size) easy to read and appropriate?		
10 Would this be a useful guide to someone considering taking up canoeing/kayaking?		

▶ Write down one piece of advice you would give the author on how to improve the pages.
▶ In the report-back session, make a note of any points you think are worth remembering – these could help you make a success of your own information and explanation writing.
▶ Overall, do you think this text is appropriately written, considering the topic (canoeing), the audience (anyone who might be interested in canoeing) and the purpose (to inform and explain)?
▶ Now add to or change your bullet points – the essentials you will need to remember when writing your own information and explanation text.

73

INFORMATION, EXPLANATION AND ADVICE

ALL YOU NEED TO START CANOEING

The starter's guide to canoeing/kayaking

Canoeing has been around for quite a long time. The boats were created in different forms, by many tribes, within several countries. Some were made of hollowed out trees, while others were made of reeds, weaved together. Today they are usually either made of wooden planks, fibreglass, or plastic. There are two main types of canoeing. Each has its advantages and disadvantages:

(1) **Canadian Canoeing:** this is where there are two people or more to a boat, which does not usually have a covered cockpit, although ones like this are available from special boat builders. They quite often have a wooden frame, with wooden planks to sit on or kneel by. You have to have a good sense of balance to use these boats as they can and will capsize (tip over) quite easily. The people paddling have one paddle each. The person in the front uses the shorter paddle, while the person at the rear has a longer paddle.

(2) **Kayaking:** this is the other main type of canoeing, and it is in my view the easier and more enjoyable one. These canoes, unlike Canadian Canoes, have a covered cockpit (the only hole in the canoe is where you sit). The most common type is the one-person kayak, but two-person ones are available. Whereas on the other canoe you would have had two different paddles, on this one you have one paddle with two blades on it, one on each end. These paddles are set at right angles to each other. These canoes are the ones generally favoured for their balance and handling, as they are able to turn quite quickly. For this reason they are very good for racing, or to compete in slalom courses. As you can probably see from the picture alongside, the covered cockpit enables large volumes of water to pass over the boat without it sinking.

INFORMATION, EXPLANATION AND ADVICE

How to start canoeing as a hobby

➔ Decide whether you are really going to be able to commit yourself to going to lessons or club meetings.

➔ Find out about some of your local groups or places where you are able to get lessons. Libraries are usually good places to look, as local groups can advertise there. If you are willing to travel to Swansea every Monday evening, the Leisure Centre there runs canoeing lessons.

➔ If after you have been for six months or so you are really enjoying it, you might find it better to buy your own wetsuit, and later on a canoe, helmet, paddle, and life jacket.

➔ It is best not to get a new canoe at first, as they are quite expensive. You can pick up a decent canoe from the "buy & sell" section in most newspapers for under £90. Failing this, you should ask the other members of the group whether they or anyone they know are going to be selling their boat in the near future. You should not have to wait long.

➔ For more information visit the website of the British Canoe Union at
http://www.bcu.org.uk/

Helpful Tips – Canadian Canoeing

▶ Remember that these boats can capsize very easily, so you should either sit very low on the bottom of the boat or kneel.

▶ Always try to hold the paddle by the handle at the top of the pole, as this will give you greater power.

▶ If there is shallow water or there are rocks on the bottom of the river, dock or sea, you must always wear a helmet.

▶ Never paddle alternately. This means that when you are on the water you should always put your paddle in, pull it back, and take it out, at the same time as the other person is paddling. This helps to ensure that the canoe does not capsize.

Helpful Tips - Kayaking

▶ When holding your paddle you should always grip and turn it with the hand that you write with, and let the other hand turn freely on the paddle. It should only be there to push or pull the paddle.

▶ Remember that the closer you have your hands to the centre of the paddle (as you are paddling) the more power you have; but also, the more the canoe will turn and the harder it will be to go in a straight line.

▶ Do not try to get out of your kayak if you capsize. Always wait until you are completely over/submerged.

▶ If there is shallow water or there are rocks on the bottom of the river, dock or sea, you must always wear a helmet.

Info A–Z

Information and explanation

These examples are taken from the guide to canoeing, printed on pages 74–76.
▶ Identify the words in each section which suggest to you that it is:
- information writing – left-hand column
- explanation writing – right-hand column.

Example of information writing	Example of explanation writing
Canoeing has been around for quite a long time. The boats were created in different forms, by many tribes within several countries. Some were made of hollowed out trees, while others were made of reeds, weaved together.	You have to have a good sense of balance to use these boats, as they can and will capsize (tip over) quite easily. These canoes are the ones generally favoured for their balance and handling, as they are able to turn quite quickly. For this reason they are very good for racing, or to compete in slalom courses.

Planning

8 Planning your own guide

▶ You will be writing a guide to the topic you have chosen.
▶ The way you write your guide will obviously depend on the topic you have chosen. You must include *advice* as well as *information* and *explanation* in your guide.
▶ For each idea about content in the left-hand column of the table on page 78, decide if you think that section of your guide will be mainly *information* writing, *explanation* writing or *advice*.
▶ Use a table like the one on page 78 and write notes on these points and/or any others you think are relevant to your topic.
▶ Give headings to help you organise your ideas.

WORDS

▲ **guide** *noun* a text that instructs or explains the fundamentals of a subject or skill.

WORDS

▲ **advice** *noun* recommendation as to appropriate course of action.
▲ **explanation** *noun* the act or process of making something understood, e.g. by giving a clear and detailed account of the relevant structure, operation, surrounding circumstances, etc.
▲ **information** *noun* knowledge gained or given; facts; news.

ADVICE

▲ *Note:* some sections will contain more than one of these three.

ADVICE

▲ The suggested sections on page 78 may need to be adapted by you to suit your topic – but the points should give you an idea of the types of issues you could include.

77

INFORMATION, EXPLANATION AND ADVICE

Possible content/sections of your guide	Information, explanation or advice?
✔ ideas based on your own experience: what to avoid, what to ensure ... and why	
✔ any ways your reader could prepare in advance/decide if it suits them	
✔ how easy it is to start up ...	
✔ how long it takes to get started ...	
✔ how much it costs to buy clothing/equipment/components ...	
✔ how parents may react ... and why	
✔ how to carry out a basic skill, e.g. pass a ball in football	
✔ safety points ... and why they are needed	
✔ where to find out information – internet, library, local contact, etc.	
✔ where to go to buy things/take part/meet up with others ...	
✔ why something works the way it does/is organised in a particular way	

9 Planning the sequence of your guide

▶ Using the headings you gave to your notes from Activity 8, decide on the most logical order for your guide. For example, it may help to think of the order someone might follow if they actively wanted to take up your sport etc. after reading your guide.
▶ Number your headings, and add headings for any other sections you now realise will be needed. Do not use numbering in your final draft.

Independent writing

10 Writing your guide

▶ Make clear your target audience. This could be:
  • everyone from a specified age upwards
  • only your own age group – state the youngest and oldest in your target range
  • another target audience which you define.

You should also decide which *technical terms* you need to explain. If you are familiar with a topic it is hard to understand that some other people may never use that word and have very little idea about what it means. If in doubt, check with two or three people who do not share the interest you are writing about.
▶ Do you simply need a definition?
▶ Do you need to explain the word more fully?
▶ Would it be easier to give an example and discuss how you use the word?

ADVICE

▲ Avoid 'rules of the game'.
▲ Concentrate on the most interesting aspects of your topic.

ADVICE

▲ Include a variety of the modal verbs you explored in this unit:
• essential safety advice – use a modal verb you ranked near the top, such as *must*
• something you would strongly advise – use a modal verb you ranked in the middle, such as *should*
• for something the reader has a choice about – think about using *could*, *may*, *might*.

78

11 Giving and receiving peer advice

10-point checklist for improving information, explanation and advice

▶ Give advice to your writing partner about how to improve the first draft.
▶ Select a maximum of five points – the ones you think will make the most difference in improving the writing.

Elements of a good information/ explanation/ advice text	Questions to consider
1 Accuracy	Are the details precise and accurate? If someone follows up the information/tries to follow the advice, will they succeed? Is the information correct? Does the information clearly state details such as days of the week businesses are open, hours of business, accurate costs, etc.?
2 Matching language to target audience	Can the words chosen be understood by the target audience? Are the sentence structures appropriate for the target audience? What alternative word choice or sentence structure might be more appropriate for the target audience?
3 Clarity	Is it written in plain English? Are explanations easy to follow? Can the meaning be made clearer by deleting any words? Can the meaning be made clearer by adding any words? Can the meaning be made clearer by changing any words?
4 Appropriate tone	Has the text been written in a way that is straightforward without being patronising? Does it seem aimed at a younger audience than the target audience?
5 Logical sequence	Are the sections put in the order that makes the most sense? Could the sequence be re-arranged for greater clarity and logic? Are the points within each section in the most helpful and logical order?
6 Appropriate connectives	Have connectives been used to help link different parts of the text? Have words such as *first*, *second*, *finally* been used in the advice part of the text? Have words such as *because*, *so that*, *as* been used in any explanation?
7 Appropriate modals/ imperatives	Have modal verbs been used appropriately? Have they been chosen to match the degree of persuasion required? Could any modal verbs be exchanged for a more appropriate one? Have imperatives been used appropriately? Have they been used without being 'bossy'?
8 Clear layout	Has the most appropriate layout been chosen? Have diagrams, cartoons, etc. been used, if appropriate? Has the information been presented in the best possible form, e.g. bar chart, pie diagram, flow chart? Have appropriate headings and subheadings been provided? Have bullet points been used if appropriate? Have clear captions etc. been provided?
9 Sentence patterns	Could the sentence patterns be more varied, e.g. changing the word order? Have some imperatives been used at the start of sentences in an advice section?
10 Clear and appropriate presentation	Is the handwriting clearly legible? If printed, is the font size and design well chosen for readability? Are there too many words in too small a space? Is the text too spread out for ease of reading? Does the size of font etc. match the audience?

INFORMATION, EXPLANATION AND ADVICE

⑫ Commenting on a commentary

The following is the commentary written by the pupil who wrote the text on canoeing.
▶ Decide how far you think it is effective in explaining the choices made.

Appreciation of techniques used in the guide to canoeing
I used **bold writing** and **underlining** for the **heading** and **subheadings** to draw attention to them and to split items into sections.
I used **a picture** on the first page to show some of the different things I explained, whilst also to draw attention to the leaflet and to make it attractive to look at.
I have used the **list** of two numbers to split up the two types of canoeing.
The picture at the bottom of the page is **aligned to the right-hand side** because it is illustrating what is meant by the text next to it on the left.
I used **bullet points** on the last page to separate each piece of advice or each tip.
I have used **imperatives** such as 'Decide', 'Find out', and 'Visit' to suggest to the reader what he or she should do.
I have used a **different style of bullet point** in the last two sections as they now give rules or tips instead of step-by-step advice.

⑬ Writing a commentary

▶ Write a commentary up to a maximum of half a side of A4 paper on the decisions you made in writing your guide, and why you made them.

ADVICE

▲ You could use some of the headings from the 10-point checklist, and use the 'Questions to consider' as a starting point for explaining your decisions.
▲ You could start by explaining how you attempted to match the choice of language and layout to your chosen audience.

Self-assessment

14 Judging your own performance

▶ From the list below:
   a select three points on which you feel you have made the most progress
   b select one point on which you most need to improve.
I can recognise a modal verb by ...
I can judge how strong a modal verb is in a given context.
I understand how significant modal verbs can be in information texts.
I can use appropriate modal verbs in my own writing, such as ...
I can judge how effective a piece of information and explanation is, and justify my opinion.
I appreciate how non-fiction texts can convey information and ideas in amusing or entertaining ways.
I can identify key features of information and explanation writing.
I can write a guide which includes information, explanation and advice appropriately.
I can write a guide which helps someone new to the topic to understand it.
I can use an impersonal style to give my advice authority.
I can use technical terms and explain them in a way that can be easily understood.
I can comment on my choice of words/sentences/layout, etc. and explain why I have made the most significant choices.

15 Improving your skills in English

▶ Select one or two skills you need to concentrate on to improve your skills in reading. Then do the same for your writing skills. (The descriptions of levels are a guide only.)

	Reading skill	From	To
1	Show understanding of significant ideas, beginning to use inference and deduction	Level 3	Level 4
2	Refer to the text when explaining views. Locate and use ideas and information	Level 3	Level 4
3	Select essential points and use inference and deduction where appropriate	Level 4	Level 5
4	Identify key features and select sentences, phrases and relevant information to support views	Level 4	Level 5
5	Identify different layers of meaning and comment on their significance and effect	Level 5	Level 6
6	Summarise a range of information from a variety of sources	Level 5	Level 6
7	Show understanding of the ways in which meaning and information are conveyed in a range of texts	Level 6	Level 7
8	Select and synthesise a range of information from a variety of sources	Level 6	Level 7
9	Show appreciation of, and comment on, a range of texts, evaluating how authors achieve their effects through the use of linguistic, structural and presentational devices	Level 7	Level 8

INFORMATION, EXPLANATION AND ADVICE

10	Select and analyse information and ideas, and comment on how these are conveyed in different texts	Level 7	Level 8
11	Confidently sustain responses to a demanding range of texts, developing ideas and referring in detail to aspects of language, structure and presentation	Level 8	E.P.
12	Make apt and careful comparison between texts, including consideration of audience, purpose and form	Level 8	E.P.

	Writing skill	From	To
1	Ideas are organised appropriately for a guide	Level 3	Level 4
2	Writing is thoughtful, and ideas are sustained and developed in interesting ways	Level 3	Level 4
3	Writing conveys meaning clearly, using an appropriate style	Level 4	Level 5
4	Vocabulary choices are imaginative and words are used precisely	Level 4	Level 5
5	Uses a style appropriate for a guide	Level 5	Level 6
6	Pupils use a range of sentence structures and varied vocabulary to create effects	Level 5	Level 6
7	Writing is confident and shows an appropriate choice of style for a guide	Level 6	Level 7
8	Ideas are organised and coherent, with grammatical features and vocabulary accurately and effectively used	Level 6	Level 7
9	Writing is coherent and gives a clear point of view	Level 7	Level 8
10	The use of vocabulary and grammar enables fine distinctions to be made or emphasis achieved	Level 7	Level 8
11	Writing has shape and impact, and control of the style appropriate for a guide	Level 8	E.P.
12	The guide is coherent and reasoned	Level 8	E.P.

5 Poetry to persuade
Mental Fight

Your focus

The content of this unit is designed to:
- improve your skills in reading and writing poetry
- improve your skills in commenting on poetry.

Your target

By the end of this unit you should be more able to:
- recognise different types of poem
- understand some of the techniques poets use
- comment on the way authors create particular effects
- read and perform poems effectively.

Your move

- Speaking and listening
- Reading
- Self-assessment
- Comparing poems by one author
- Exploring individual poems
- Comparing poems on a theme

Poetry to persuade

1 Exploring We Are the Cherokee
2 Exploring The British
3 Responding to 'He loved light, freedom and animals'
4 Exploring The Unknown Citizen
5 Preparing to read The Unknown Citizen aloud
6 Exploring To Daffodils
7 Exploring Nothing Gold Can Stay
8 Comparing two poems 1
9 Exploring Ballad of the Sad Astronaut
10 Exploring 'Do you think we'll ever get to see Earth, sir?'
11 Comparing two poems 2
12 Exploring three poems from a sequence
13 Taking a closer look at And because ...
14 Finding common techniques, approaches and themes
15 Judging your own performance
16 Improving your skills in English

83

5 POETRY TO PERSUADE

We Are the Cherokee

We made sacred fires
As instructed
By our ancestors.

We farmed beans
And corn
In harmony
With our surroundings,
We knew the sun well.

We learnt to count
Each drop of rain,
And when we had their number
We thanked the sky
For each drop of rain.

We were so in love
That each one of us
Gave ourselves
And married the Earth.

We are the Cherokee.

Then there came a time
When the land beneath us
Was taken from us.
Even those of us who were not born then
Remember that time.

It was a time of great sadness,
The time of countless tears.

In the state now known as Texas
In the land now known as America
We taught ourselves
To avoid evil thoughts,
And welcome strangers.

Soon after welcoming the strangers
We found we had no land
To welcome strangers.
We learnt the language of the strangers
And tried talk,
Using the language of survival
We tried food,
Then in a desperate bid to save ourselves
We tried self-defence.

Now we live on the land
That we farmed and loved,
On this same piece of land
In a foreign country.

We are the Cherokee

We can make for you
Beautiful baskets
To carry your dreams.

We can speak to you
In a language
That is older than the country
That contains us.

We can sing you songs
That were taught to us by big buffalo
And running bears,
To music that we gather
From the wind.

The cowboys were not that good
And we were not that bad.
All we wanted was
Our ways
Our names
Ourselves
And peace.

We are the Cherokee.

Benjamin Zephaniah

WORDS

▲ **Cherokee** *noun* a member of the Native American people formerly living in and around the Appalachian Mountains, now mostly in Oklahoma.

Mental Fight

Exploring individual poems

The poems in this unit are all making a point of some kind, perhaps trying to persuade you to a particular point of view. For this reason, you may find you react strongly to what the poet is saying. If you disagree with a point of view, be prepared to say why. But also be prepared to recognise skills and techniques that are used effectively even in poems with which you disagree.

1 Exploring We Are the Cherokee

- ▶ What line is repeated? How many times?
- ▶ Why do you think this line is repeated?

- ▶ What are the key words indicating the passing of time?
- ▶ What different stages does the poem suggest the Cherokee have lived through?
- ▶ Look at the verb tenses used at different points in the poem. Why do you think the author uses each tense change?

- ▶ What is special about the layout – the way the poem is presented on the page?
- ▶ Try to come up with a logical reason for any aspects of layout you identify.

- ▶ What word in the first section (lines 1–18) do you think best describes the relationship between the Cherokee and the environment? Be prepared to justify your choice.

- ▶ What word in the second section (lines 19–39) do you think best describes the feelings of the Cherokee at this stage of history? Be prepared to justify your choice.

- ▶ What do you think is the most important word in the third section (lines 40–44)?

- ▶ Who do you think the second person pronoun 'you' refers to in the last section (lines 45–64)?
- ▶ Why do you think Benjamin Zephaniah, who is not a Cherokee, uses the first person plural 'we' in the poem?

- ▶ This poem is intended to help the reader understand and appreciate the Cherokees' point of view. Do you think it is effective in doing this? Be ready to justify your answer.

Tracking elements of persuasive poems

Use a table like the following to keep a record of each poem in this unit.

Whose point of view is being expressed?	
In whose voice is the poem written?	
What opinion is being expressed?	
Who is being addressed?	

Cherokee Eagle Dance

85

The British
Serves 60 million

Take some Picts, Celts and Silures
And let them settle,
Then overrun them with Roman conquerors.

Remove the Romans after approximately four hundred years
Add lots of Norman French to some
Angles, Saxons, Jutes and Vikings, then stir vigorously.

Mix some hot Chileans, cool Jamaicans, Dominicans,
Trinidadians and Bajans with some Ethiopians,
Chinese, Vietnamese and Sudanese.

Then take a blend of Somalians, Sri Lankans, Nigerians
And Pakistanis,
Combine with some Guyanese
And turn up the heat.

Sprinkle some fresh Indians, Malaysians, Bosnians,
Iraqis and Bangladeshis together with some
Afghans, Spanish, Turkish, Kurdish, Japanese
And Palestinians
Then add to the melting pot.

Leave the ingredients to simmer.

As they mix and blend allow their languages to flourish
Binding them together with English.

Allow time to cool.

Add some unity, understanding and respect for the future
Serve with justice
And enjoy.

Note: All the ingredients are equally important. Treating one ingredient better than another will leave a bitter, unpleasant taste.

Warning: An unequal spread of justice will damage the people and cause pain.

Benjamin Zephaniah

WORDS
▲ **chile/chilli** *noun* small red hot-tasting pod of a type of pepper (capsicum).
▲ **melting-pot** *noun* **1** a place or situation in which varying beliefs, ideas, cultures, etc. come together. **2** a vessel for melting something (e.g. metal) in. **3** an uncertain situation.

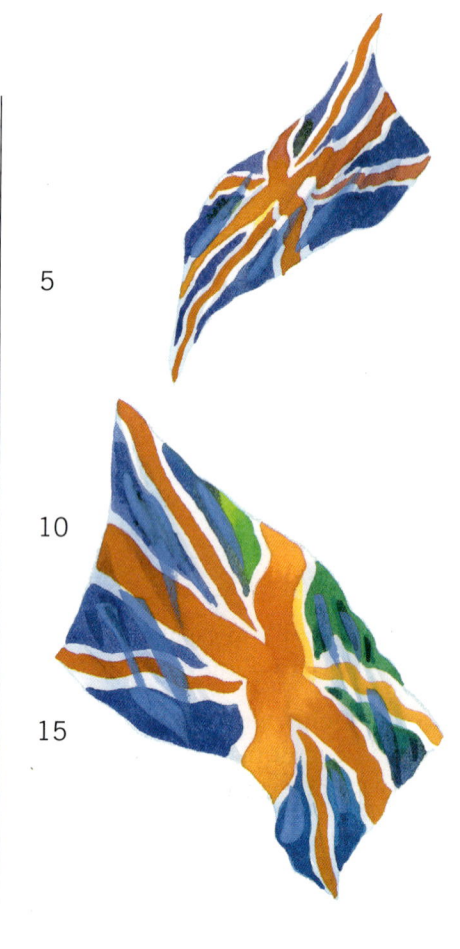

Mental Fight

2 Exploring The British

- What words typically found in recipes are used in this poem?
- Which of these words are *imperatives*?
- What reasons can you think of for Benjamin Zephaniah writing the poem in this way?

- Choose five of the words taken from cookery that Benjamin Zephaniah uses in the poem. Explain the connection between the way that word is used in a recipe, and the way that word is used in the poem. Use a table like the one below.

Word	Meaning when used in recipe	Meaning when used in this poem

- What abstract nouns does Benjamin Zephaniah use in the last stanza of the poem? Do these words have anything else in common?
- This poem puts forward a particular point of view. Do you think it is effective in doing this? Be ready to justify your answer.

Tracking elements of persuasive poems

- Use a table like the following:

Whose point of view is being expressed?	
In whose voice is the poem written?	
What opinion is being expressed?	
Who is being addressed?	

WORDS

▲ **abstract noun** *noun* denoting a quality, condition or action rather than a physical thing.

87

5 POETRY TO PERSUADE

'He loved light, freedom and animals'

No grave could contain him.
He will always be young
in the classroom
waving an answer
like a greeting.   5

Buried alive –
alive he is
by the river
skimming stones down
the path of the sun.   10

When the tumour on the hillside
burst and the black blood
of coal drowned him,
he ran forever
with his sheepdog leaping   15
for sticks, tumbling together
in windblown abandon.

I gulp back tears
because of a notion of manliness.
After the October rain   20
the slag-heap sagged
its greedy belly.
He drew a picture of a wren,
his favourite bird for frailty
and determination. His eyes gleamed   25
as gorse-flowers do now
above the village.

His scream was stopped mid-flight.
Black and blemished
with the hill's sickness   30
he must have been,
like a child collier, dragged
out of one of Bute's mines.

There he is, climbing a tree,
mimicking an ape, calling out names   35
at classmates. Laughs springing
down the slope: my wife hears them,
ears attuned as a ewe's in lambing
and I try to foster the inscription,
away from its stubborn stone.   40

Mike Jenkins

WORDS

▲ **'He loved light, freedom and animals'**: inscription on the grave of a boy killed in October 1966 when a slag heap at Aberfan in South Wales became unstable after rain and engulfed a school below. 144 people, including 116 children, were killed.

Mike Jenkins comments: 'I was visiting the cemetery in Aberfan with my family – a lot of the inscriptions really moved me. This one really moved me: it's so personal. At the time myself and my wife were thinking of having children. The presence of the kid was strong in the cemetery – it was almost as if his presence came out at me from the gravestone.'

> **WORDS**
>
> ▲ **blemish** *verb* to stain or spoil the beauty of something.
> ▲ **collier** *noun* a coal miner.
> ▲ **Bute** the Marquess of Bute (1793–1848), principal landowner in the Rhondda valley, who received royalties on minerals found beneath the soil of his estates.
> ▲ **foster** *verb* to encourage the development of ideas, feelings, etc.
> ▲ **inscription** *noun* words written, printed or engraved, e.g. as a dedication in the front of a book or as an epitaph on a gravestone.

3 Responding to 'He loved light, freedom and animals'

▶ Before tackling any of the questions below, write down your first reaction to the poem after first reading it or hearing it read. Simply note down as honestly as you can your personal reaction.

▶ Make a note of any words in the poem that have a positive association for you.

▶ From these, select the five that have the most positive associations in the poem. Be prepared to justify your choice.

▶ Make a note of any words in the poem that have a negative association for you.

▶ From these, select the five that have the most negative associations in the poem. Be prepared to justify your choice.

▶ What is the effect for you of repeating the word *alive* in the second stanza?

▶ Discuss in your group what you think these two lines suggest:
I gulp back tears
because of a notion of manliness.

▶ What do you think the last two lines could mean?

▶ What impression of the boy does Mike Jenkins (the poet) leave you with?

▶ Choose the two or three details that create the strongest impression on you, and explain how you think this impression is created.

Tracking elements of persuasive poems

▶ Use a table like the one below.

Whose point of view is being expressed?	
In whose voice is the poem written?	
What opinion is being expressed?	

5 POETRY TO PERSUADE

The Unknown Citizen

(To JS/07/M/378
This Marble Monument
Is Erected by the State)

He was found by the Bureau of Statistics to be
One against whom there was no official complaint,
And all the reports on his conduct agree
That, in the modern sense of an old-fashioned word, he was a saint,
For in everything he did he served the Greater Community. 5
Except for the War till the day he retired
He worked in a factory and never got fired,
But satisfied his employers, Fudge Motors Inc.
Yet he wasn't a scab or odd in his views,
For his Union reports that he paid his dues, 10
(Our report on his Union shows it was sound)
And our Social Psychology workers found
That he was popular with his mates and liked a drink.
The Press are convinced that he bought a paper every day
And that his reactions to advertisements were normal in every way. 15
Policies taken out in his name prove that he was fully insured,
And his Health-card shows he was once in hospital but left it cured.
Both Producers Research and High-Grade Living declare
He was fully sensible to the advantages of the Instalment Plan
And had everything necessary to the Modern Man, 20
A phonograph, a radio, a car and a frigidaire.
Our researchers into Public Opinion are content
That he held the proper opinions for the time of year;
When there was peace, he was for peace; when there was war, he went.
He was married and added five children to the population, 25
Which our Eugenist says was the right number for a parent of his generation,
And our teachers report that he never interfered with their education.
Was he free? Was he happy? The question is absurd:
Had anything been wrong, we should certainly have heard.

W. H. Auden, March 1939

WORDS

▲ **Unknown Soldier** and **Unknown Warrior** *noun* unidentified soldier, representative of the members of a country's armed forces who have been killed in war, for whom a tomb is established to serve as a memorial.
▲ **monument** *noun* something (e.g. a statue) built to preserve the memory of a person or event.
▲ **Inc.** *abbreviation, especially US* Incorporated: said of a company, etc. forming or formed into a legal corporation.
▲ **instalment** *noun* one of a series of parts into which a debt is divided for payment, e.g. *to be paid in six monthly instalments*.
▲ **phonograph** *noun, North America, old use* a record-player.
▲ **eugenics** *singular noun* the principle or practice, now largely discredited, of improving the human race by selective breeding from individuals who are regarded as strong, healthy, intelligent, etc.

Mental Fight

4 Exploring the Unknown Citizen

▶ What do you think might be suggested by the fact that the monument is made out of marble?

▶ Why do you think a Marble Monument is being 'Erected by the State'?

▶ The second line of the title refers to *JS/07/M/378*. Why do you think Auden does not give the man a name?

▶ Suggest possible reasons why W. H. Auden might have chosen the title 'The Unknown Citizen'.

▶ What words used in the poem suggest that it is was not written recently?

▶ What words suggest that the setting might be based on the USA?

▶ Look at lines 6 and 7; 9 and 10; 16 and 17; 28 and 29.

▶ Count up the number of syllables in each pair of lines.

▶ What else do you notice about the pairs of lines?

▶ How might you expect this line to end?
When there was peace, he was for peace; when there was war, he ...

▶ What is the effect of the actual ending of the line?

▶ Look again at line 27: *And our teachers report that he never interfered with their [his children's] education*.

▶ Do you think Auden is suggesting there is anything wrong with this attitude? If so, how?

▶ Decide which of these words most accurately reflects the type of language used in the poem:
businesslike; *comic*; *formal*; *informal*; *serious*.

▶ Does the word you have chosen fit the poem all the way through?

▶ Is any part of the poem not suitable for engraving on a monument? Explain why you choose any particular lines as inappropriate for a monument.

▶ If you find any, decide if you think it is a mistake by Auden.

▶ Rate the statements in the table below according to how far you think they match W. H. Auden's opinion in this poem:

*0 = not at all in line with W. H. Auden's view; 3 = totally in line with W. H. Auden's view.

Statement	Rating 0–3*
The Unknown Citizen was unknown because he fitted in to society so well, and he should be praised for this.	
The Unknown Citizen was the perfect citizen.	
The Unknown Citizen is being mocked for being such a conformist.	
If you fit in too well you lose all sense of identity.	
A perfect citizen is one who doesn't make a fuss.	
Auden is mainly criticising the society that praises (and creates) a man like this.	

> **WORDS**
>
> ▲ **conformist** *noun* person who behaves, dresses, etc. in obedience to some standard considered normal by the majority.
>
> ▲ **satire** *noun* a literary composition, originally in verse, which holds up follies and vices for criticism, ridicule and scorn.

5 POETRY TO PERSUADE

5 Preparing to read The Unknown Citizen aloud

▶ Your aim should be to make the meaning of the poem clear to an audience, but most of the time still keeping to the formal tone of an official announcement.

▶ Some of these choices could be considered:
- changing the speaker at particular points in the poem
- using a single voice for some parts of the poem, using more than one voice at others
- changing the pace, tone of voice, rhythm and intonation to match particular parts of the poem
- using male and female voices where possible, separately or together.

▶ In particular, think carefully about the appropriate tone of voice for:
- the couplets, for example lines 6–7; 9–10
- the word *normal* in line 15
- the word *proper* in line 23
- the word *interfered* in line 27

and the appropriate pace, rhythm and intonation for:
- line 21: *A phonograph, a radio, a car and a frigidaire.*
- line 24: *When there was peace, he was for peace; when there was war, he went.*

▶ Having heard all the groups 'perform' the poem, decide which version best captured the tone of the poem and why.

ADVICE

▲ Each choice must be made for a definite reason: it must help the audience appreciate the poem in some way that you have planned for and can explain.

▲ For example, you could choose to use the person in your group whose voice sounds most authoritative for the sections that sound most official and serious.

Rhyme

Stephen Sondheim, who wrote the lyrics for 'West Side Story', comments on the use of rhyme:

> Not enough people think about what rhyme is for and it is so useful to help an audience understand. And that seems to me its major function. It's to help the ear follow what you're doing – not only necessarily the clever ones, but just the grace of the language.
>
> It's such fun in English when words match, and also it enhances the thought. You can tell a very mediocre joke and if you rhyme it you'll get a big laugh. It **is** funnier. It's funnier like a limerick which may have a very mediocre joke gets a bigger laugh at the end because the accumulation of the rhyme gives you the extra delight that you miss in the thought. It's the delight to the ear and the road map for the ear.

▶ Do you think any of this description fits any part of 'The Unknown Citizen'?

Tracking elements of persuasive poems

Whose point of view is being expressed?	
In whose voice is the poem written?	
What opinion is being expressed?	
Who is being addressed?	

Comparing poems on a theme

To Daffodils

Fair daffodils, we weep to see
    You haste away so soon;
As yet the early-rising sun
    Has not attain'd his noon.
       Stay, stay,
      Until the hasting day
         Has run
      But to the evensong;
And having pray'd together, we
    Will go with you along.

We have short time to stay, as you,
    We have as short a spring;
As quick a growth to meet decay,
    As you, or any thing.
      We die,
    As your hours do, and dry
        Away,
      Like to the summer's rain;
Or as the pearls of morning's dew,
    Ne'er to be found again.

Robert Herrick

6 Exploring To Daffodils

▶ Find as many lexical sets as you can in 'To Daffodils', using a table like the one below.

WORDS

▲ **lexical set** a group of words linked by some common theme or idea.

Linking idea	Words that match this linking idea in some way
Time	
Speed (fast or slow)	
Religion	
Water	
Seasons	
Death and decay	

▶ Choose one of these lexical sets.
▶ Select two words within that set that you think help you understand some aspect of the poem.
▶ Be prepared to explain to the other groups what these words reveal about the poem and its themes.
▶ Work out how many syllables there are to each stanza. Fill in a table like the one below.

Line	1	2	3	4	5	6	7	8	9	10
Stanza 1										
Stanza 2										

5 POETRY TO PERSUADE

▶ Choose one of the lines to argue a case about why you think the length of that particular line is appropriate.

ADVICE

▲ You could think about:
- what types of line are longer (6 or 8 syllables)
- what types of line are short (2 syllables)
- what impact the length of line has
- if the choice of words matches the choice of line length – and if so how this works.

WORDS

▲ **apostrophe** *noun rhetoric* a passage in a speech, poem, etc. that addresses a person or thing.

▲ **personification** *noun* in art or literature: the representation of an idea or quality as a person or human figure.

▶ Work out the rhyme scheme of the poem 'To Daffodils'.
▶ Can you think of any reasons why the rhyme scheme forms the pattern it does?

Tracking elements of persuasive poems

▶ Use a table like the one below.

Whose point of view is being expressed?	
In whose voice is the poem written?	
What opinion is being expressed?	
Who is being addressed?	

Nothing Gold Can Stay

Nature's first green is gold,
Her hardest hue to hold.
Her early leaf's a flower;
But only so an hour.
Then leaf subsides to leaf.
So Eden sank to grief,
So dawn goes down to day.
Nothing gold can stay.

Robert Frost

7 Exploring Nothing Gold Can Stay

▶ Work out the number of syllables to the line in this poem.
▶ Use a table like the one below.

1	2	3	4	5	6	7	8

▶ Work out the rhyme scheme of the poem.
▶ Write out the poem, underlining in one colour anything that suggests a positive feeling or hope, and in a second colour anything that suggests a negative feeling or depression.
▶ What can you tell about the way the poem is structured as a result of this activity?

▶ Make a note of one thing that you notice about the rhyme and its effect on the meaning of the poem. Refer to some specific detail in the poem and be prepared to explain your point to the other groups.

▶ Make a note of one thing that you notice about the rhythm of the poem and its effect on the meaning of the poem. Refer to some specific detail in the poem and be prepared to explain your point to the other groups.

Tracking elements of persuasive poems

▶ Use a table like the one below.

Whose point of view is being expressed?	
In whose voice is the poem written?	
What opinion is being expressed?	
Who is being addressed?	

8 Comparing two poems 1

It is sometimes easier to comment on a particular poem when you compare it with another poem. If you just look at one poem you may feel it could not have been written any other way, and find little to say about it. However, by comparing it with another poem, the choices made in each case may become clearer.

▶ Use a table like the one below to compare 'To Daffodils' and 'Nothing Gold Can Stay'.

▶ Choose at least five of the features in the left-hand column to explore.

Feature	'To Daffodils'	'Nothing Gold Can Stay'	Similar or different?
Words connected with nature			
Words connected with time passing			
Words connected with new life			
Words connected with death or decay			
Words connected with religion			
Point of view			
How realistically time is represented			
Words used in both poems			
Opposites used close to each other			
Structure			
Theme			

5 POETRY TO PERSUADE

Ballad of the Sad Astronaut

Why are you weeping, child of the future,
For what are you grieving, son of the earth?
Acorns of autumn and white woods of winter,
Song-thrush of spring in the land of my birth.

You have a new life, child of the future,
Drifting through stars to a land of your own.
With Sirius to guide you, Orion beside you
Wandering the heavens you are free from earth's harm.

I have a new life, the speckled skies' beauty,
Left far behind me the dark cries of earth;
Oh, but I long for the soft rains of April,
Ice-ferned Decembers and suns of the south.

What was I dreaming, to drift with Orion,
To leave for cold Neptune my home and my hearth?
Stars in their millions stretch endless, remind me
Far far behind lies my blue-marbled earth.

Here on the hillside the dawn is just rising,
Buttercups dew-fill, all silken and gold.
Well you may weep, sad child of the future,
Well may you yearn for your beautiful world.

Judith Nicholls

WORDS

▲ **ballad** *noun* a poem or song with short verses, which tells a popular story.
▲ **Sirius** *noun astronomy* the brightest star in the night sky.
▲ **Orion** *noun astronomy* a large brilliant constellation that is visible in both hemispheres.
▲ **Neptune** *noun* planet which circles the same sun as the Earth; the eighth planet from the sun.
▲ **hearth** *noun* **1** the floor of a fireplace, or the area surrounding it. **2** the home.
▲ **marbled** *adjective* mottled, or having irregular streaks of different colours, like marble.

9 Exploring Ballad of the Sad Astronaut

▶ Decide why some of the poem is written in italics and some is not.
▶ In your group, work out a clear idea of the feelings expressed in each part of the poem (the italic part and the non-italic part).

ADVICE

▲ You could think about:
- how the different parts of the poem connect with each other
- the use of repetition of *far* and *my*
- any use of contrast
- which words best express the feelings at each point in the poem.

Mental Fight

Tracking elements of persuasive poems

▶ Use a table like the one below, for the poem 'Ballad of the Sad Astronaut'.

Whose point of view is being expressed?	
In whose voice is the poem written?	
What opinion is being expressed?	
Who is being addressed?	

WORDS

▲ **toxic** *adjective* poisonous.
▲ **damascene** *verb* to decorate (especially steel) by inlaying or encrusting.
▲ **iridescence** *noun* quality of having many bright rainbow-like colours which seem to shimmer and change constantly.

'Do you think we'll ever get to see Earth, sir?'
I hear they're hoping to run trips
one day, for the young and fit, of course.
I don't see much use in it myself;
there'll be any number of places
you can't land, because they're still toxic,　　5
and even in the relatively safe bits
you won't see what it was; what it could be.
I can't fancy a tour through the ruins
of my home with a party of twenty-five
and a guide to tell me what to see.　　10
But if you should see some beautiful thing,
some leaf, say, damascened with frost,
some iridescence on a pigeon's neck,
some stone, some curve, some clear water;
look at it as if you were made of eyes,　　15
as if you were nothing but an eye, lidless
and tender, to be probed and scorched
by extreme light. Look at it with your skin,
with the small hairs on the back of your neck.
If it is well-shaped, look at it with your hands;　　20
if it has fragrance, breathe it into yourself;
if it tastes sweet, put your tongue to it.
Look at it as a happening, a moment;
let nothing of it go unrecorded,
map it as if it were already passing.　　25
Look at it with the inside of your head,
look at it for later, look at it for ever,
and look at it once for me.

Sheenagh Pugh

This is one of a series of poems written by Sheenagh Pugh about a future in which the Earth has become uninhabitable, and pupils of a generation who have never seen the Earth learn about the Earth from their teachers.

5 POETRY TO PERSUADE

10 Exploring 'Do you think we'll ever get to see Earth, sir?'

- Who is speaking in the title of the poem, and who is speaking in the rest of the poem?
- What do you think is suggested about the way you would look if *you were made of eyes*?
- What do you think is suggested about the way you would 'look' if you looked with *the small hairs on the back of your neck*?
- What do you think is suggested about the way you would 'look' if you *look at it with your hands*?
- What do you think is suggested by *map it as if it were already passing*?
  Be prepared to explain your reasoning in each case.
- Why do you think the speaker says *I don't see much use in it myself*, but then goes on to give detailed advice to anyone who might go?
- What impression do you get of the character of the speaker?

Tracking elements of persuasive poems

- Use a table like the one below.

Whose point of view is being expressed?	
In whose voice is the poem written?	
What opinion is being expressed?	
Who is being addressed?	

11 Comparing two poems 2

- Use a table like the one below to compare 'Ballad of the Sad Astronaut' and 'Do you think we'll ever get to see Earth, sir?'
- Make notes under as many 'Features' mentioned in the left-hand column as you can.

Feature	Ballad of the Sad Astronaut	'Do you think we'll ever get to see Earth, sir?'	Similar or different?
Time poem is set			
What is happening on Earth			
The narrator/persona of the poem			
What is seen as the most negative thing by the narrator/persona			
What is seen as the most positive thing by the narrator/persona			
The structure of the poem			
Use of rhyme			
Who is being spoken to			
Overall tone of the poem – bitter, angry, sad, yearning, hopeful, regretful, cynical ...			
Underlying theme			

Mental Fight

Comparing poems by one author

12 Exploring three poems from a sequence

The final poems in this unit come from a book by the Nigerian poet Ben Okri: *Mental Fight: an anti-spell for the twenty-first century*. All the poems in this book are linked, and you will be exploring three poems from different sections of the book.

▶ Before looking at the poems' techniques, make a note of your immediate personal reaction to each poem.
▶ Identify any examples you can find of the following in any of the three poems:
- alliteration
- use of the first person – I/we/our, etc.
- imagery
- imperatives
- repetition/patterning/opposites.

The first poem comes from the section headed 'Time to be real'.

> **WORDS**
> ▲ **patterning** *noun* an arrangement of repeated or related words for deliberate effect.

VI

Everyone loves a Spring cleaning.
Let's have a humanity cleaning.
Open up history's chamber of horrors
And clear out the skeletons behind the mirrors,
Put our breeding nightmares to flight　　　　5
Transform our monsters with our light.
Clear out the stables
In our celebrated fables
A giant cleaning
Is no mean undertaking.　　　　　　　　　10
A cleaning of pogroms and fears
Of genocide and tears
Of torture and slavery
Hatred and brutality.
Let's turn around and face them　　　　　15
Let's turn around and face them
The bullies that our pasts have become
Let's turn around and face them
Let's make this clearing-out moment
A legendary material atonement.　　　　　20

Ben Okri

> **WORDS**
> ▲ **breed** *verb* (**bred, breeding**) make or produce (usually something bad).
> ▲ **pogrom** *noun* an organised persecution or massacre of a particular group of people, originally that of Jews in 19th-century Russia.
> ▲ **genocide** *noun* the deliberate killing of a whole nation or people.
> ▲ **material** *adjective* important, significant.
> ▲ **atonement** *noun* an act of making amends for, making up for, or paying for a wrongdoing, crime, sin, etc. from earlier *at onement*, meaning 'in harmony'.

5 POETRY TO PERSUADE

The second of Ben Okri's poems comes from Section 7 headed 'No one is a loser'.

II

We must not think ourselves victims,
Disadvantaged, held back –
Because of race, colour, creed,
Education, class, gender,
Religion, height, or age.
The world is not made of labels.
The world, from now on,
Will be made through the mind.
Through great dreaming, great loving
And masterly application.
Those who transcend their apparent limitations
Are greater than those who apparently
Have little to transcend.
Our handicaps can be the seed of our glories.
We shouldn't deny them.
We should embrace them,
Embrace our marginalisation,
Our invisibility, our powerlessness.
Embrace our handicaps, and use them,
And go beyond them,
For they could well be the key
To some of the most beautiful energies
That we have been given.
Accept no limitations to our human potential.
We have the power of solar systems
In our minds.
Our rage is powerful.
Our love is mighty.
Our desire to survive is awesome.
Our quest for freedom is noble, and great.
And just as astonishing is the knowledge
That we are, more or less,
The makers of the future.
We create what time will frame.
And a beautiful dream, shaped
And realised by a beautiful mind,
Is one of the greatest gifts
We can make to our fellow beings.

Ben Okri

WORDS

▲ **label** *noun* a word or short phrase that is used to describe a person, movement or school of thought.
▲ **transcend** *verb* overcome, go beyond, surpass.
▲ **seed** *noun* a source or origin.
▲ **marginalisation** *noun* the act of pushing something or someone to the edge of anything (especially society or one's consciousness) in order to reduce its or their effect, relevance, significance, etc.
▲ **key** *noun* a means of achievement.

Mental Fight

The third poem from the sequence of poems is from Section 8 'Turn on your light'.

IV

And because we have too much information,
And no clear direction;
Too many facts,
And not enough faith;
Too much confusion, 5
And crave clear vision;
Too many fears,
And not enough light –
I whisper to myself modest maxims
As thought-friends for a new age. 10
   See clearly, think clearly.
   Face pleasant and unpleasant truths;
   Face reality.
   Free the past.
   Catch up with ourselves. 15
   Never cease from upward striving.
   We are better than we think.
   Don't be afraid to love, or be loved.
   As within, so without.
   We owe life abundant happiness. 20

Ben Okri

> **WORDS**
>
> ▲ **crave** *verb* (**craved, craving**) (often **crave for** or **after something**) to long for it; to desire it overwhelmingly.
> ▲ **maxim** *noun* **1** a saying that expresses a general truth. **2** a general rule or principle.

13 Taking a closer look at And because…

- Explore the structure of the poem by working out:
  - why certain lines are indented and others are not
  - how many sentences there are in each section.
- What patterns/repetition can you find in the poem?
- Look at the following pairs of lines:
  - 1 and 2
  - 3 and 4
  - 5 and 6
  - 7 and 8.
- How does the author, Ben Okri, connect the two lines in each case?
  Think about:
  - use of alliteration
  - use of contrast
  - use of rhyme.
- What do you think the author might mean by the term *thought-friends*?
- In your group, decide on one or two lines that you will try to explain or comment on to the other groups. Discuss:
  - what you think the meaning is
  - if and how it connects with your own experience
  - how the way it is written helps to convey that meaning.

> **WORDS**
>
> ▲ **indent** *verb, printing, typing* to begin (a line or paragraph) further in from the margin than the main body of the text.

5 POETRY TO PERSUADE

14 Finding the common techniques, approaches and themes

The three poems by Ben Okri come from a single book.
- Identify any connections, such as in terms of:
  - techniques
  - approaches or
  - themes

  that you find in more than one of the poems.
- Sum up in your group what you have found out about the techniques, approaches and themes in these poems as a result of these activities and your discussion.

Self-assessment

15 Judging your own performance

- From the list below:
  a select three points on which you feel you have made the most progress
  b select one point on which you most need to improve.
  I can identify and comment on techniques used by poets to achieve particular effects.
  I can give logical reasons why some poems have a particular layout on the page.
  I can identify the point of view and the voice of a poem.
  I can comment effectively on an author's choice of words in a poem.
  I can contribute effectively to the planning for a group reading of a poem.
  I can use pace, pitch, volume and intonation appropriately in bringing out the meaning of a poem.
  I can identify lexical sets in a poem.
  I can make effective comparisons between two poems.
  I can write an essay effectively comparing two poems.
  I can identify common techniques, approaches and themes in a set of linked poems.

16 Improving your skills in English

- Select one or two skills you need to concentrate on to improve your skills in speaking and listening. Then do the same for your reading skills. (The descriptions of levels are a guide only.)

	Speaking and listening skill	From	To
1	Talk and listen with confidence in an increasing range of contexts	Level 3	Level 4
2	Listen carefully, making contributions and asking questions that are responsive to others' ideas and views	Level 3	Level 4
3	Talk and listen confidently in a wide range of contexts	Level 4	Level 5
4	Pay close attention to what others say, ask questions to develop ideas and make contributions that take account of others' views	Level 4	Level 5
5	Adapt talk to the demands of different contexts with increasing confidence	Level 5	Level 6
6	Take an active part in discussion, showing understanding of ideas and sensitivity to others	Level 5	Level 6

		From	To
7	Confident in matching talk to demands of different contexts	Level 6	Level 7
8	Make significant contributions, evaluating others' ideas and varying how and when they participate	Level 6	Level 7
9	Maintain and develop talk in a range of contexts, using appropriate intonation and emphasis	Level 7	Level 8
10	Make a range of contributions which show that they have listened perceptively and are sensitive to the development of discussion	Level 7	Level 8
11	Vary vocabulary and expression confidently for a range of purposes	Level 8	E.P.
12	Initiate and sustain discussion through the sensitive use of a variety of contributions, take a leading role in discussion	Level 8	E.P.

	Reading skill	From	To
1	Show understanding of significant ideas and themes, beginning to use inference and deduction	Level 3	Level 4
2	Refer to the text when explaining views, locating and using ideas and information	Level 3	Level 4
3	Select essential points, using inference and deduction where appropriate	Level 4	Level 5
4	Identify key features and themes, and select sentences, phrases and relevant information to support views	Level 4	Level 5
5	Identify different layers of meaning and comment on their significance and effect	Level 5	Level 6
6	Give a personal response to texts, referring to aspects of language, structure and themes in justifying views	Level 5	Level 6
7	Articulate personal and critical responses to poems	Level 6	Level 7
8	Show awareness of thematic, structural and linguistic features	Level 6	Level 7
9	Appreciate and comment on a range of texts	Level 7	Level 8
10	Evaluate how authors achieve their effects through the use of linguistic, structural and presentational devices	Level 7	Level 8
11	Sustain responses to a demanding range of texts, developing ideas and referring in detail to aspects of language, structure and presentation	Level 8	E.P.
12	Make apt and careful comparison between poems, including consideration of form	Level 8	E.P.

6 Persuasive writing
Hooked

Your focus
The content of this unit is designed to:
- improve your skills in analysing persuasive writing
- improve your skills in writing persuasively.

Your target
By the end of this unit you should be more able to:
- recognise the techniques writers use in persuasion texts
- explore the effects of the techniques writers use in persuasion texts
- use these techniques in your own writing to present a case persuasively.

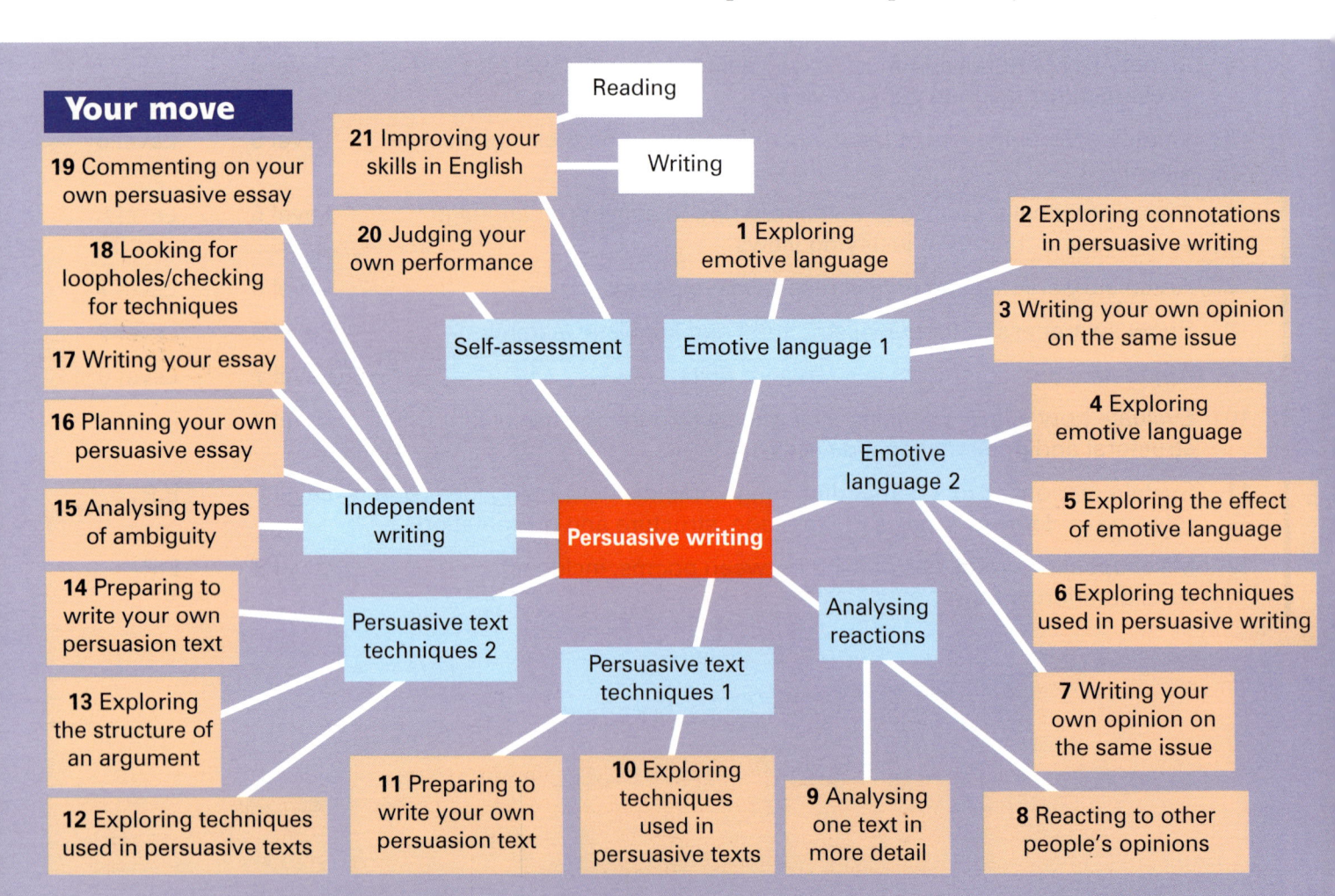

Your move

- **19** Commenting on your own persuasive essay
- **18** Looking for loopholes/checking for techniques
- **17** Writing your essay
- **16** Planning your own persuasive essay
- **15** Analysing types of ambiguity
- **14** Preparing to write your own persuasion text
- **13** Exploring the structure of an argument
- **12** Exploring techniques used in persuasive texts
- **21** Improving your skills in English
- **20** Judging your own performance
- Reading
- Writing
- Self-assessment
- Independent writing
- Persuasive text techniques 2
- **11** Preparing to write your own persuasion text
- **10** Exploring techniques used in persuasive texts
- Persuasive text techniques 1
- **Persuasive writing**
- **1** Exploring emotive language
- Emotive language 1
- Emotive language 2
- Analysing reactions
- **9** Analysing one text in more detail
- **2** Exploring connotations in persuasive writing
- **3** Writing your own opinion on the same issue
- **4** Exploring emotive language
- **5** Exploring the effect of emotive language
- **6** Exploring techniques used in persuasive writing
- **7** Writing your own opinion on the same issue
- **8** Reacting to other people's opinions

Emotive language 1

1 Exploring emotive language

The following extract is taken from a book by Michael Rosen called *Just Kids*.
- As you read it, be aware of when you are agreeing or disagreeing. You may feel that some of your own views are being challenged in some way.
- Track your feelings as you read the extract so that you can explain your changing reactions to others in your group afterwards. There may well be a mixture of reactions.

Clothes

I will begin with the most sensitive: shoes. I will betray my un-hip, un-clued-up approach to life when I describe a scene of some nine years ago. My oldest son and I are in a shoe shop to buy some trainers. He is twelve, I am forty. In my usual sickeningly matter-of-fact and brutal way, I tell my son what the upper limit on price is and he can choose from there. The assistant starts to proffer sample items. One of them is too small, one of them is the wrong colour but then we find a pair that fit and they are the colour that he said he was looking for.

'Put the other one on,' I say.

His face loses muscular tone. His arms hang limply by his side. He doesn't move.

'Put the other one on,' I say.

In a dull mechanical way, he puts on the other trainer.

'Walk around in them.'

He shuffles across the shop and back.

'They fit OK? Right. They're the ones. OK?'

He bursts into tears.

So I say to the assistant that we seem to have a little problem on our hands, smile grimly and retreat. Outside the shop I try to get to the bottom of it.

'What was the matter with the shoes?'

'Nothing.'

'There must have been something wrong with them. You burst into tears when I said that I was going to buy them for you. What exactly is the problem with them?'

'Nothing.'

'Is it because one of your mates has got exactly the same shoes, or something?'

'No.'

'What is it then?'

'They were Dunlops.'

'They were Dunlops? What's wrong with them being Dunlops? They make shoes don't they? Why does putting on a pair of Dunlops make you burst into tears?'

Silence.

'Oh I get it. It's the wrong label. It doesn't matter whether the shoe is any good or not. It's just the wrong label to be seen in. Dunlops are wally-label shoes, and you don't want to be seen in wally-label shoes, is that it?'

'Yep.'

'So why didn't you say? How was I supposed to know that there are some shoes you can't wear. What happens at school if you turn up with wally-label shoes? All the other kids stand round and jeer? And you've been one of the kids who do the jeering so if you turn up at school with wally-label shoes they'll really go for you. Hmmm. I get the picture.'

6 PERSUASIVE WRITING

Some parents cottoned on to this crisis in clothes about ten years earlier than me but once I realized I was no problem as a parent. I still give upper limits on prices which may well mean that this eliminates the ultra-hip, most desirable item. But that's just tough. I'm not going to be so much of a sucker for style that I have to succumb entirely. But I can face the reality of my kids not wanting to be nerds. Yes, I know I am conspiring with the style tyrants. I am bowing to their dictates. I am putty in their hands. They say: 'THIS MONTH IT WILL BE BLACK NIKES!!!' And I just roll over and say, 'OK, I am giving my son the money now, straightaway. He will just do as you say, Mr Nike. He will wear black Nikes this month. Please tell me what shoes he should wear next month and I will do my best to get them.'

'DOING YOUR BEST IS NOT GOOD ENOUGH. GET WHAT I SAY, OR DIE!!!'

'Yes, of course.'

And these trainers are truly amazing. They say they are 'engineered'. Millions of pounds are spent developing them. And they fall apart when you look at them. One game of football and all you've got on your feet is a bit of tyre tread. Another fifty quid gone. The most robust thing about these trainers are the laces. And at the time of writing, my kids are going through a phase of not doing them up. Untied laces are cool. When I was at school it was always some poor unfortunate nerd who walked about with his laces not tied up and one of the playground helpers was always tying them up for him. Now it's cool. A few weeks ago I said to one of my kids that they're designing some great new trainers with built-in windscreen wipers on them … AND HE BELIEVED ME!

It was a great relief when those big heavy leather boots started to become fashionable. Suddenly Dad was cool too. My old hiking boots were safe, man. Smart. Wikkid. Bad. My old hiking boots, for goodness sake.

Michael Rosen, from Just Kids

WORDS

▲ **bad** *slang* very good.
▲ **nerd** *noun, derogatory, slang* someone who is foolish or annoying, often because they are so wrapped up in something that isn't thought worthy of such interest.
▲ **poor** *adjective* used in expressing pity or sympathy.
▲ **robust** *adjective* strongly built or constructed.
▲ **succumb** *verb* give in to (e.g. pressure, temptation, desire, etc.)
▲ **wally** *noun* (**wallies**) *British colloquial* an ineffectual, stupid or foolish person.
▲ **wicked** *adjective, slang* excellent or cool, admirable.

Hooked

2 Exploring connotations in persuasive writing

▶ For each of the words listed below, decide if that word has a **positive** connotation in the passage (a 'purr' word) or a **negative** connotation in the passage (a 'snarl' word).
▶ Make brief notes on the effect of each word, saying who is being praised or criticised.
▶ Look at how the words are used in the passage before you decide.
▶ Use a table like the one below.

Line	Word from passage	Positive or negative connotation?	Who or what is being praised or criticised, and why?
1, 4	un-hip/un-clued-up/ sickeningly/brutal		
6, 20, 27, 30	wrong (label/colour)		
11 13	dull/mechanical/ shuffles		
16–17	(smile) grimly		
31, 32	wally-label		
41, 42	ultra-hip/desirable		
42	sucker		
44	nerds		
44	tyrants		
53	amazing		
56	robust		
59	poor/unfortunate		
65, 66	cool/safe/ Smart/Wikkid		

3 Writing your own opinion on the same issue

▶ Write between 5 and 10 lines giving your opinion on 'style tyrants'.
▶ As you hear some of these short opinion pieces read out, decide which has the most impact on you – and then try to work out why it has that impact.

ADVICE

▲ You could consider some of the following issues:

- Who puts pressure on you to buy certain shoes or clothes?
- Do you go along with the 'style tyrants' or do you decide for yourself what to wear?
- What pressure is put on those who do not conform?
- Do you think there is too much pressure on young people to buy certain items?

6 PERSUASIVE WRITING

Emotive language 2

4 Exploring emotive language

The following extract is taken from a book by Bill Bryson called *Notes from a Big Country*.
▶ As you read it, or hear it read, be alert to emotive words that may be influencing your opinion.

Junk Food Heaven

I decided to clean out the fridge the other day. There I was, down on my knees unwrapping pieces of foil and peering cautiously into Tupperware containers, when I came across an interesting product called a breakfast pizza.

Some weeks ago I announced to my wife that I was going to the supermarket with her next time. Here we were living in a paradise of junk food – the country that gave the world cheese in a spray can – and she kept bringing home healthy stuff like fresh broccoli and packets of Ryvita.

It was because she was English, of course. She didn't really understand the rich, unrivalled possibilities for greasiness and goo that the American diet offers. I longed for artificial bacon bits, melted cheese in a shade of yellow unknown to nature, and creamy chocolate fillings, sometimes all in the same product. I wanted food that squirts when you bite into it or plops onto your shirt front in such gross quantities that you have to rise carefully from the table and limbo over to the sink to clean yourself up. So I accompanied her to the supermarket and while she was off squeezing melons I made for the junk food section – which was essentially all the rest of the store. Well, it was heaven.

The breakfast cereals alone could have occupied me for most of the afternoon. There must have been 200 types, and I am not exaggerating. Every possible substance that could be dried, puffed and coated with sugar was there. The most immediately arresting was a cereal called Cookie Crisp, which tried to pretend it was a nutritious breakfast but was really just chocolate chip cookies that you put in a bowl and ate with milk. Brilliant.

Also of note were cereals called Peanut Butter Crunch, Cinnamon Mini Buns, Count Chocula ('with Monster Marshmallows'), and a particular offering called Cookie Blast Oat Meal, which contained *four* kinds of cookies. I grabbed one of each of the cereals and two of the oatmeal – how often I've said that you shouldn't start the day without a big steaming bowl of cookies – and sprinted with them back to the trolley.

'What's that?' my wife asked in that special tone of voice.

I didn't have time to explain. 'Breakfast for the next six months,' I panted as I dashed past, ' and don't even think about putting any of it back and getting muesli.'

You really cannot believe the bounteous variety of non-nutritious foods available to the American shopper these days or the quantities in which they are consumed. I recently read that the average American eats 17.8 *pounds* of pretzels every year.

Aisle seven ('Food for the Seriously Obese') was especially productive. It had a whole section devoted exclusively to a product called Toaster Pastries, which included, among much else, eight different types of toaster strudel. And what exactly is a toaster strudel? Who cares? It was coated in sugar and looked drippy. I grabbed an armload.

I admit I got a little carried away – but there was so much and I had been away so long.

It was the breakfast pizza that finally made my wife snap. She looked at the box and said, 'No.'

'I beg your pardon, my sweet?'

'You are not bringing home something called breakfast pizza. I will let you have' – she reached into the trolley for some specimen samples – 'root beer buttons and toaster strudel and …' She lifted out a packet she hadn't noticed before. 'What's this?'

I looked over her shoulder. 'Microwave pancakes,' I said.

'Microwave pancakes,' she repeated, but with less enthusiasm.

'Isn't science wonderful?'

'You're going to eat it all,' she said. 'Every bit of everything that you don't put back on the shelves now. You do understand that?'

'Of course,' I said in my sincerest voice.

And do you know she actually made me eat it. I spent weeks working my way through a symphony of American junk food, and it was all awful. Every bit of it. I don't know whether American junk food has got worse or whether my taste buds have matured, but even the treats I'd grown up with now seemed disgustingly sickly.

The most awful of all was the breakfast pizza. I tried it three or four times, baked in the oven or zapped with microwaves. Eventually I gave up altogether and hid the box in the Tupperware graveyard on the bottom shelf of the fridge.

Which is why, when I came across it again the other day, I regarded it with mixed feelings. I started to chuck it out, then hesitated and opened the lid. It didn't smell bad – I expect it was pumped so full of chemicals that there wasn't any room for bacteria – and I thought about keeping it a while longer as a reminder of my folly, but in the end I discarded it. And then, feeling peckish, I went off to the larder to see if I couldn't find myself a nice plain piece of Ryvita and maybe a stick of celery.

From Bill Bryson Notes from a Big Country

WORDS

▲ **junk food** *noun* food that is low in nutritional value, often highly processed or ready-prepared, and eaten instead of or in addition to well-balanced meals.

5 Exploring the effect of emotive language

Look back to lines 58–62.
- Select the three most emotive words you can find in these lines.
- For each word you choose, try to explain the effect on the reader you think Bill Bryson would like to achieve.

6 PERSUASIVE WRITING

6 Exploring techniques used in persuasive writing

▶ Match the quotations to the techniques and the effect of those techniques.

5	paradise
9	greasiness and goo
13	gross
19	200 types
20	dried, puffed and coated with sugar
23	Brilliant.
29	sprinted
36–37	the average American eats 17.8 *pounds* of pretzels every year
59	awful
62	disgustingly sickly
71	folly
73	Ryvita/celery

Techniques:
- Choice of noun
- Choice of adjective
- Choice of adjective
- Choice of verb
- Choice of noun
- Use of alliteration
- Use of contrast
- Use of modifiers (adverb + adjective)
- Use of statistics
- Use of one-word sentence
- Use of statistics
- Use of italics
- Use of tripling

Effects:
- Emphasises just how 'wonderful' he thinks this idea is
- Creates the impression of almost unlimited choice of breakfast cereal
- Makes the food sound particularly nasty
- Draws attention to the two words – either to encourage the reader/eater or to discourage them
- Ends this section of text by humorously mentioning food that is as different as possible from junk food
- Suggests it's like living in heaven to have the choice of food they have
- Makes the food sound revoltingly sweet and unpleasant
- Suggests he can't wait to get back home to try out these 'offerings'
- Shows the author is now admitting that he had been behaving foolishly
- Makes the quantities sound excessive
- Suggests the same three steps are taken whatever the original 'substance'
- Makes the amount eaten seem quite shocking, and emphasises just how much is actually eaten on average

110

Hooked

7. Writing your own opinion on the same issue

▶ Write between 5 and 10 lines giving your opinion on 'junk food'.
▶ As you hear some of these short opinion pieces from other pupils read out, decide which has the most impact on you – and then try to work out why it has that impact.

slow food

Slow Food is a rebellion against the fast food culture in which we live, against mass-market, high-yield-but-low-taste production of goods and against the creeping safe-but-boring standardisation which threatens today's small producers. If you actually like all this kind of thing, well, then Slow Food is not for you (and nor, probably, are we).

http://www.thecafe.org.uk/slow_food.htm

ADVICE

▲ You could consider some of the following issues:
- Do you consider all fast food is junk food?
- Do you think 'junk food' is a fair label?
- Do you eat 'fast food' or 'slow food' and why?
- Do you think there is too much pressure on young people to eat certain products?
- Is more pressure put on you by *advertisers* or *your peer group* to eat certain products?

Analysing reactions

8. Reacting to other people's opinions

This section contains short opinion pieces from various writers. It includes writing by authors whose work has been used in the *Level Best* books and who have written comments especially for this unit on topics they feel strongly about.

▶ As you read them, or hear them read, make a note of your reactions. You may react in many ways, for example: agreement; disagreement; agreement/disagreement with part of the argument; anger over the issue raised; anger with the line of argument taken...
▶ Be prepared to comment on how you reacted and why you reacted this way in your discussion afterwards.

Malorie Blackman on 'intolerance'

Don't believe everything we so-called grown-ups tell you. Why? Because far too many of us grow old without growing wise. After all, you know better. You wouldn't stand, hurling abuse and bombs and anything else you could get your hands on at girls aged 11 or under, just because their religion is different to yours, would you? You wouldn't hate people of another colour, religion or nationality just because some bigoted wrinklies told you that you should, would you? You wouldn't assume that every man, woman and child fleeing intolerable conditions and persecution in their own country only wanted to come to our country to scrounge, would you? What's happened to 'live and let live'? What's happened to 'treat others as you'd like them to treat you'? We seem to be losing all respect for the differences in others which make us all interesting and unique. I truly hope that newer generations will have more sense than us oldies. Because you wouldn't believe that when it comes to anyone in any way different from yourself, they should die for that difference, would you? *Would you?*

WORDS

▲ **bigot** someone who is persistently prejudiced, especially about religion or politics, and refuses to tolerate the opinions of others. **bigoted** adjective
▲ **wrinkly** noun (usually **wrinklies**) derogatory an elderly person.

6 PERSUASIVE WRITING

Jamila Gavin on 'childhood'

What is childhood? The word often used in association with childhood is 'innocence'. But innocent of what? I think adults often assume an innocence in children, and think of childhood as a state of bliss, in which children know only what they are told by adults; that they are nurtured like flowers, grow and blossom and somehow, through a state of innocence, achieve wise maturity and the right to knowledge. I challenge this.

What is true, is that children can be innocent of consequences. This is one of the core themes of *Coram Boy*. Adults can also fail to consider consequences, but in their case I would more often use the word 'ignorant' or 'dis-regarding' or 'irresponsible'.

The vast majority of children round the world are having to fight to survive on equal terms with adults almost as soon as they can walk. Barely a hundred years ago the same situation existed here in Britain. Perhaps we treat children here as infants far beyond their actual infancy. Perhaps if we respected the quality of their wisdom, and enabled them to play a more responsible role in society, we might have less cynicism, disenchantment and discontent.

> **WORDS**
> ▲ **innocent** *adjective*
> 1 free from sin; pure.
> 2 trusting, not able or willing to trick or deceive.
> ▲ **nurture** *verb* to feed or support; to educate or train.
> ▲ **cynicism** *noun* attitude of believing the worst about people or the outcome of events.

Jan Mark on 'voting'

People are happy to vote for favourite films, favourite singers, favourite books; when it comes to choosing who runs the country, too many of them can't be bothered. When I was at school I used to go canvassing, asking people to vote Labour at the General Election. A lot of women would answer the door nervously and mutter, 'I'll have to ask my husband.' I wanted to yell, 'No, you don't! It's a secret ballot. Vote for who you like.'

My neighbour comes from a country with a poor record on democracy and women's rights. She never misses an election. 'Everyone should vote if they can,' she says, 'especially women'.

> **WORDS**
> ▲ **canvass** *verb* to ask for votes or support for someone.
> ▲ **democracy** *noun* a form of government in which the people govern themselves or elect representatives to govern them.

Thich Nhat Hanh on 'television'

We are what we feel and perceive. If we are angry, we are the anger. If we are in love, we are the love. If we look at a snowy mountain peak, we are the mountain. Watching a bad TV program, we are the TV program. While dreaming, we are the dream. We can be anything we want, even without a magic wand. So why do we open our windows to bad movies and TV programs, movies made by sensationalist producers in search of easy money, movies which make our hearts pound, our fists tighten, and send us back into the streets exhausted. Who allows such movies and TV programs to be made? Especially for the very young. We do! We are too undemanding, too ready to watch whatever is on the screen, too lonely, lazy, or bored to create our own lives. We turn on the TV and leave it on, allowing someone else to guide us, shape us, and destroy us. Losing ourselves in this way is leaving our fate in the hands of others who may not be acting responsibly. We must be aware of what kinds of programs do harm to our nervous systems, our minds, and our hearts, and which programs and films benefit us.

Translated from the Vietnamese by Anh Huong Nguyen, Elin Sand, and Annabel Laity

> **WORDS**
> ▲ **sensationalist** *noun* someone who aims to make something more exciting or shocking than it really is.
> ▲ **programme** or (*North America*) **program** *noun* a scheduled radio or TV presentation.

9 Analysing one text in more detail

Writers indicate approval or disapproval of people's attitudes by choosing particular vocabulary. The passages in Activity 8 include these words:

Indicating approval/praise	Indicating disapproval/blame
interesting	bigoted
responsible	can't be bothered
sense	irresponsible
unique	lazy
wisdom	sensationalist
benefit	undemanding

- In your group, select **one** of the texts from Activity 8 that you react to strongly. Discuss in your group:
  - how you react to the argument being presented
  - the ways in which the author tries to persuade you
  - how far the writer is trying to influence you through emotions (the 'heart') and how far through reason (the 'head')
  - how far you think the author has succeeded in shifting your personal opinion at all.
- Be prepared to explain *why* you reacted in the way you did when you report back to the other groups.

Persuasive text techniques 1

You will now look at two longer texts written for an adult audience. Your aim is to identify some of the techniques writers use, and select the techniques that will be most effective in your own opinion writing.

10 Exploring techniques used in persuasive texts – A

We're all hooked by woolly thinking
NATASHA WALTER

'There must be a way to enter the debate about animal welfare without pretending that a fish is a dog and a dog is a person'

AT LEAST the People for the Ethical Treatment of Animals (Peta) has the virtue of consistency. It knows where it stands: for animals, any animals, against the hunters, the chompers, the fishers, the farmers. Its new campaign against angling in Britain has kicked off with a nasty-looking advertisement showing a dog with a sharp metal hook stuck through its cheek. Poor pup! But the caption takes it further: 'If you wouldn't do this to a dog, why do you do it to a fish? Fishing hurts.'

Peta is much better known for its campaigns against fur, including that old advertisement, 'I'd rather go naked than wear fur', starring supermodels in peek-a-boo poses, which pushed fur to the fringes of fashion for a few seasons.

6 PERSUASIVE WRITING

This new campaign is a lot less likely to be successful. It isn't just against the sport of angling, since Peta has taken a stand against all killing and eating of, as it puts it, sea animals. But a generation which happily shrugged off its furs will be less likely to give up its tuna carpaccio.

I don't agree with a word that Peta says but I love it. I love it because its ferocity brilliantly exposes the woolly thinking of most people who delicately pretend to have animal welfare at heart. Almost everyone else who talks about the poor, suffering animals draws themselves arbitrary lines for their own comfort, while preening themselves on their moral superiority. Hypocrisy rules!

There are people who are vegetarians because they pity the poor cows, but who happily chomp away on cheese produced by cows who are, yes, warehoused together with as much indignity as beef cattle and killed with the same carelessness. There are the people who won't eat chicken from battery farms but who eagerly order salmon from fish farms where the fish are crammed together at higher density than battery chickens. There are people who condemn the dog-eating Chinese, but do dogs feel more pain at being made into chops than pigs do? There are all the people who can't eat a bit of an animal that looks like an animal – an ear, a tongue, a head – but who munch away at reconstituted burgers. And there are the people who wept over the pictures of cows culled for foot-and-mouth, when those same cows, if not shot by MAFF, would have been shot the following month at the abattoir.

The almost unbroken silence over angling, as opposed to the furore over fox hunting, has always shown up this woolly thinking perfectly. British town dwellers get so hot under the collar about fox hunting because they don't like the people who hunt and they think that foxes have rather sweet faces. But they are never going to rise up against angling, because – well, ordinary people do it, don't they, and fish are slippery creatures. But if you don't like the idea of foxes being torn apart by hounds for sport, how can you approve of fish being speared by metal hooks for sport? Especially when Peta has brought you some research purporting to show that even if fish don't scream, boy, can they hurt.

But logic hardly ever gets a look-in when it comes to animal welfare. That's because we don't rely on arguments about animals, we rely on feelings and habits. And those feelings and habits go way back. We grow up steeped in sentimentality about animals. Now that I have a child myself, I spend days plunged back into the themes and visions of early childhood. And what do you know, it's all about the cuddly bears, and the enthusiastic tigers, and the intelligent foxes. My daughter sleeps surrounded by animals keeping guard over her, wild carnivores recast by the toy makers into fluffy bundles. Every book she opens plunges her into a world where the animals, from ducks to caterpillars to rabbits, are chatting away to her, inviting her into their jolly worlds.

Indeed, although I'd like to be absolutely unsentimental about animal welfare, I'm still affected by my own childhood training. Over the past few years I've realised that although I've munched through dozens of lambs and calves in my time, I still couldn't force down a mouthful of rabbit or horse, because, well, they might come from Watership Down or be friends with Black Beauty. Uh-oh, how absurd. The only statement I can make in my defence is that I know it's absurd, and I won't be trying to force anyone else to stop eating rabbit because I once cried when Bigwig took his stand against General Woundwort.

I wish we could lay this sentimentality about animals aside, without losing all admiration for non-human life. There must be a way to enter the debate about animal welfare without pretending that a fish is a dog and a dog is a person. Instead of trying to argue that all life has independent value (an argument that gets beached long before the bacteria, usually around the rights of rats and wasps), let's remind ourselves that animals don't have rights, but they have beauty. And if we want to retain that beauty, we'll have to build a world where animals can just be animals. And that means letting them live their own lives, even if those lives end, as they always will, in sudden death.

For instance, I can't help thinking that the fox who snuffles around woods and fields, pouncing on chickens and running through gardens at night, mating and breeding when it likes, who dies after just one day of fear and pain, has a better life than the cow who is brought up in a concrete barn, standing in rows to be milked by a machine twice a day, separated from her calf a day after its birth. It's typical of our sentimentality about animals that the few dozen foxes which get killed every year should command such acres of newsprint and aeons of government time. But if we wanted a world in which animals could be animals, we might be less worried about hunting, and more worried about the lives of farmed animals and the wider effects that a degraded environment has on animal habitats.

And when Peta's angling campaign has, thankfully, faded from our minds, we might still try to keep alive some anger at the farmed fish industry. After all, a carp that has lived its life in a great clean lake, flashing in and out of weeds and warm shallows, chasing the little fish and whisking through the moonlit waters, must have lived a better life than the farmed salmon, caged in with half a million other fish, eating antibiotics and colourants to turn his flesh fat and pink, unable to swim to clear water. As Peta might have it, free the Orkney millions!

From The Independent *Wednesday 1 August 2001*

▶ Try to find examples in the passage of the techniques listed below.
  They are listed in the order in which they occur in the passage.
▶ Discuss in your group the effect of each of the techniques you identify, and be prepared to report back your findings to the other groups.
▶ Make a note of the line numbers so that other people can find your examples easily.

1 Use of a pun	7 Use of first person plural pronoun
2 Use of exclamation	8 Use of personal experience
3 Use of contrast or contradiction	9 Use of non-standard English
4 Use of rhetorical question	10 Evaluating alternatives
5 Use of second person pronoun	11 Use of emotive language
6 Use of evidence from named source	12 Use of imperative

6 PERSUASIVE WRITING

If you wouldn't do this to a dog, why do it to a fish?
PeTA FishingHurts.com

11 Preparing to write your own persuasive text

▶ Make a note of some of the sentence patterns, connectives and other vocabulary you could use in your own argument writing on a topic that you choose:

Use of 'if' plus suggested consequences:
If you don't like the idea of *foxes being torn apart by hounds for sport, how can you approve of fish being speared by metal hooks for sport*?
If you don't like (one thing), *how can you approve of* (a similar thing)?

Use of 'yes' – insistence that this statement is in fact correct (even if the reader may doubt it or not want to believe it): cows who are, *yes*, warehoused together with as much dignity as beef cattle…

Patterning of sentences: That's because *we don't rely on arguments* about animals, *we rely on feelings and habits*.

Tripling, using dashes to separate the three examples: There are all the people who can't eat a bit of an animal that looks like an animal – *an ear*, *a tongue*, *a head* – but who munch away at reconstituted burgers.

Tripling, using commas to separate the three examples: …has a better life than the cow *who is brought up in a concrete barn*, *standing in rows to be milked by a machine twice a day*, *separated from her calf a day after its birth*.

Deliberate use of unexpected word for effect: *the chompers* (line 3), *chomp away*, *chops* (do dogs feel any more pain at being made into *chops* than pigs do?), munch (*munch* away at reconstituted burgers), speared, metal hooks (fish being *speared* by *metal hooks* for sport). Here there is also the deliberate use of the word 'sport', as if to force the reader to ask if this is a 'sport'.

Use of lively, non-pompous style: *boy*, can they hurt; *Uh-oh*.

Use of hyperbole (exaggeration): The few dozen foxes that get killed command such *acres* of newsprint and *aeons* of government time.

Connectives used in passage: *at least, but* (12), *since, because* (6), *while, if* (2), *as opposed to, even if* (2), *especially, indeed, although* (2), *still, instead of, for instance, after all*.

WORDS

▲ **reconstituted burgers** burgers made from parts of different animals, reassembled.
▲ **MAFF** Ministry of Fisheries and Food (until 2001).
▲ **furore** *noun* a general outburst of excitement or indignation in reaction to something.
▲ **hot under the collar** *colloquial* angry or flustered.
▲ **purport** *verb* claim.
▲ **to be steeped in something** to be closely familiar with it.
▲ **sentimentality** *noun* tendency to be over-emotional, especially showing pity in large measure and without subtlety.
▲ **carnivore** *noun* an animal that feeds mainly on the flesh of other animals.
▲ **aeon** *noun* an endless or immeasurable period of time.
▲ **degrade** *verb* to reduce the quality of something.

Persuasive text techniques 2

12 Exploring techniques used in persuasive texts – B

We have to realise that it's wrong to drop litter

The Government must get tough with slovenly Britons or we will be lost under a mountain of rubbish, believes Rupert Christiansen

Blazing sunshine greeted my return from a wonderful holiday abroad. The stock market was up a bit, the Gatwick Express was only 20 minutes late – my spirits were high. But not for long. When I cut through the station alley near my home, I saw a sleek, plump, furry creature slinking away from the same black plastic bag, splurging its rotted contents over the pavement, which I had tripped over when leaving for the airport a week ago. No, all was not well after all: the depressing mess reminded me that I live in what must be the dirtiest country in Europe. Or am I becoming over-sensitive to the plague of litter?

I admit to the habit of picking offending items off the street and furiously stuffing them into their proper receptacles. Perhaps that's a wee bit excessive. I suppose I risk being lynched when I politely hand empty crisp packets back to children who airily drop them on to the pavement (needless to say, they remain totally undaunted). Even fag ends and apple cores set me twitching for a dustpan and brush. I could always emigrate to squeaky-clean Singapore, as kind friends have gently suggested.

But litter has become a real problem – a serious national problem, and one which we only evade by blaming inefficient public services. I live in the London Borough of Lambeth and, aside from that rogue plastic bag, I cannot fault its efforts on the score of refuse collection: we have wheelie bins with flip-top lids, the recycling boxes are collected once a week, pavements are regularly brushed.

Yes, there are areas in which local government could try harder. Yet the problem is ultimately not one of equipment – it's one of underlying social attitude. We simply can't be bothered to take responsibility for what we consume: when a personal item becomes a momentary inconvenience, we flick it into the public arena for the state to take care of. Inasmuch as we think at all when we drop a wrapper or a fast-food box, we justify ourselves by claiming that there will always be somebody waiting to pick it up afterwards.

Nor should we comfortably assume that dropping litter is a sin of the stressed urban working class. People who should know better evidently don't. On pleasant country roads, I frequently see the windows of sleek Volvos being rolled down and cartons casually hurled out. I would dearly like to name and shame the former presenter of a long-running quiz show whom I witnessed flinging his interval ice-cream box into the gutter outside the Royal Opera House.

To the young, there's even an aura of glamour about a littered landscape – just watch MTV for half an hour, and take in its taste for abandon and release from the world of the neat and tidy. I daresay that 99 per cent of the audience at a rock concert would claim to be profoundly concerned with the future of the environment, but not to the extent of taking their rubbish home with them.

6 PERSUASIVE WRITING

Mess is not just something for other people to clear up; mess is intrinsically cool.

What can be done? Parents can teach their children that not creating litter is as civil as saying please and thank you, but the situation requires tactics more immediately effective than that. I'm surprised that the present government hasn't taken stronger initiatives, because the great hypocrisy is that none of us likes other people's litter and any clean-up crusade would be popular with the electorate and the press. (Margaret Thatcher had a go, of course, but her campaign never went much further than the formation of a committee and she wasn't prepared to invest any money in it.)

The difficulty lies in establishing what sort of practical measures would be effective against individual culprits. Talk of zero tolerance is all very well, but with levels of street crime running so high, it's hard to see the 'bobby on the beat' finding the time or motivation to write out tickets or on-the-spot fines, and in any case it ought to be a matter of self-respect rather than the courts. Perhaps the German idea of making us all legally responsible for litter surrounding our property might have some limited usefulness, but I'm not convinced.

What might make a difference is the addition of a little more stick to attempts to advertise the virtues of the bin. In America you see slogans along the lines of 'Littering is dirty and disgusting, so don't do it' – much more effective than the current variations on 'Keep Britain tidy', when Britain clearly isn't tidy in the first place. The newly shaped Environment Department could win itself some badly needed friends by taking an imaginative lead.

From The Daily Telegraph *Thursday 2 August 2001*

WORDS

▲ **slovenly** *adjective* careless or untidy in habits or methods of working.
▲ **splurge** *verb informal* to use or display something in large amounts or in order to attract attention.
▲ **receptacle** *noun* anything that receives, stores or holds something; a container.
▲ **undaunted** *adjective* not discouraged or put off.
▲ **evade** *verb* to avoid answering (a question).

▶ Try to find examples of the following in the passage. In most cases the techniques are listed in the order they occur in the passage.
▶ Discuss in your group the effect of each of the techniques you identify, and be prepared to report back your findings to the other groups.
▶ Make a note of the line numbers so that other people can find your examples easily.

1 Use of hyperbole (exaggeration)	6 Use of superlative
2 Use of contrast	7 Questioning of own beliefs
3 Use of short sentence	8 Use of first person plural pronoun
4 Use of evidence from personal experience	9 Tackling readers' possible assumptions
5 Use of emotive language	10 Evaluating alternatives

Hooked

13 Exploring the structure of an argument

Use these headings to label the nine paragraphs of the litter article:

A Attitudes of the young
B Attitudes of different classes
C Conclusion
D Introduction
E Personal attitudes of the writer
F Problems with some 'solutions'
G Real (underlying) problem
H What is to be done
I Who/what is not to blame

14 Preparing to write your own persuasive text

▶ Make a note of some of the sentence patterns, connectives and other vocabulary you could use in your own argument writing on your chosen topic:

Use of insistence that something must be done, or else…:
The Government *must* get tough… *or we will be lost under a mountain of rubbish.*
(Somebody) *must* (do something) *or* (people will suffer the consequences).
Contradicting what was stated earlier: *No, (all was not well…)*
Admitting exceptions to the rule: *Yes, (there are areas in which local government could try harder).*
Tripling, using a colon to introduce the three examples: *I cannot fault (Lambeth) on the score of refuse collection: we have wheelie-bins with flip-top lids, the recycling boxes are collected once a week, pavements are regularly brushed.*
Patterning of sentence: *Mess is not just something for other people to clear up; mess is intrinsically cool.*
Use of lively, non-pompous style: *furry creature slinking away from the … plastic bag, splurging its rotted contents…*
Connectives used in passage: *but* (7), *after all, or, yet, because, in any case, perhaps.*
Other useful vocabulary: *stick* (vs *carrot*), *zero tolerance*.

Independent writing

15 Analysing types of ambiguity

▶ Study the following arguments. In your group, decide what is unclear or ambiguous about the way the points have been expressed.

1	30% of people were worried about how the food they ate was produced, and 50% had decided to become vegetarian.	6	The hospital helped 1,500 people back to a healthy lifestyle.
2	Every year, some eight billion carrier bags are buried in landfill sites or left to litter the streets, and scientists estimate that each one takes at least a century to rot.	7	There was considerable anger at the school.
3	They built an amazing 10,000 houses.	8	The review was very good.
4	The death rate among smokers is much higher than among non-smokers.	9	When I was on holiday in France, there were recycling collection points with more bins than we have in the UK.
5	80% of people prefer coffee.	10	This phone-line is the most popular in Britain.

WORDS

▲ **carrot** *noun colloquial* something offered as an incentive.
▲ **stick** *noun* the threat of punishment as a means of obtaining compliance.
▲ **zero tolerance** *noun* a policy of total strictness in law enforcement in which not even the most minor offences are overlooked.

ADVICE

▲ You could think about:
- Who or what is being referred to exactly.
- What time period is being referred to.
- What country/countries, etc. are covered by the comment.

119

6 PERSUASIVE WRITING

16 Planning your own persuasive essay

▶ Choose a topic about which you have plenty of ideas and if possible some background material, e.g. leaflets, letters to magazines or newspapers.

- Age limits on drinking/driving/films/getting a job/voting, etc.
- An issue causing debate in your local area at the moment, perhaps reflected in the letter column of your local newspaper
- Animal rights issues
- Being a meat eater/vegetarian
- Being expected to baby-sit/look after Gran/Granddad, etc.
- Being pressured to wear brand name clothes/footwear, etc.
- Bullying
- Conforming to peer group pressure
- 'Crime and punishment' at home and at school
- Environmental issues, e.g. waste disposal
- Equality between the sexes, e.g. at school/in sport/in choices available/access to equipment, etc.
- Favouritism at home/school, etc.
- Not being able to have the kind of party you want
- Not being allowed your favourite clothes/food/music, etc. at home/school, etc.
- The influence of television
- Young people and democracy – what votes young people should have and why

ADVICE

▲ You could consider adapting one of the following, or choosing your own topic. If you want to choose your own topic, discuss your proposal with your teacher first.

ADVICE

▲ Your aim should be to present your argument persuasively enough to gain the attention and influence the attitudes of your target audience.
▲ The most obvious structure for an opinion piece would be the following, using a separate paragraph for each:
1 Introduction to the topic, e.g. why it is topical now/why you are interested in it.
2 Your opinion on the topic and why you hold this view, with evidence.
3 What those who disagree with you say and why, with evidence.
4 Why you think these arguments are wrong; show up weaknesses in their arguments.
5 Summary, stating your point of view.

17 Writing your essay

▶ Write your own essay on the topic of your choice.
- **Key words you may find helpful:**
  Look at the kinds of words in the two columns in Activity 9 for examples of positive lexis and negative lexis.
- **Key words and phrases you may find helpful:**
  But, Evidence from... shows..., In my opinion, In most/some cases, On the other hand, Some people argue..., Statistics show...
- **Useful sentence patterns for opinion writing:**
  Look back to the notes you made based on the sentence types used in the 'fish' and 'litter' articles (Activities 11 and 14). Decide which ones you can use effectively in your own writing.

ADVICE

▲ Use any of the writing you have done during the course of this unit, if they fit your topic (e.g. Activities 3 and 7). But decide where these fit best, if at all, in the overall structure of your argument.
▲ In your planning, give a clear title to each paragraph, but do not include these titles in your final draft.

Hooked

> **ADVICE**
>
> ▲ Techniques you can choose from:
> - undermining the opposition case by showing up weaknesses in their argument
> - use of comparison – to link what you support to a positive image and what you attack to a negative image
> - use of examples – to make the argument sound stronger and less vague
> - use of experts – to show that what you say is supported by someone in the know
> - use of humour – to lighten up the argument/suggest you are not pompous or opinionated
> - use of individuals – to suggest how real people are affected
> - use of statistics – to impress the reader
> - use of well-known personalities – to encourage people to support your argument if they admire/respect/trust that person
> - use of words to influence people, such as **positive**, **negative** and **non-emotive** words.

> **ADVICE**
>
> ▲ Don't try to use all of these! Select the techniques that have the most impact for your particular choice of topic.

> **WORDS**
>
> ▲ **opinionated** *adjective* holding obstinately and unreasonably to one's own opinion; dogmatic.

18 Looking for loopholes/checking for techniques

▶ After you have written the first draft of your own opinion piece, exchange your essay with a partner and see if you can find any loopholes in the argument. Are all statements clear and unambiguous?

▶ See if you can find any of the following techniques, or if you can suggest where any of these techniques might be effective.

> **WORDS**
>
> ▲ **loophole** *noun* a means of escape; *especially* an ambiguity or omission in a text through which its intent may be evaded.

> **ADVICE**
>
> ▲ Think particularly of the types of ambiguity you explored in Activity 15.

20 techniques for use in persuasive writing – to be used selectively and appropriately

1 Anticipating objections and answering them	11 Questions
2 Comparison (e.g. dogs *vs* pigs)	12 Short sentences for effect and impact
3 Connectives used to link sentences and paragraphs	13 Spotting contradictions in opponents' argument
4 Emotive language	14 Statistics
5 Evaluation of alternative solutions – which is better/best?	15 Superlatives
6 Exclamations	16 Tripling
7 Hyperbole (exaggeration)	17 Use of first person plural pronoun to suggest a shared problem/solution
8 Named sources	18 Use of lively, non-pompous style
9 Patterning of sentences	19 Use of second person pronoun to challenge, etc.
10 Personal experience	20 Using conditional: if... then...

6 PERSUASIVE WRITING

19 Commenting on your own persuasive essay

▶ Write a maximum of half a side of A4 paper explaining the following:
- who you were most trying to influence – your target audience
- what techniques you have used, giving the technical term where possible, with an example of each technique from your essay
- how far you think you have succeeded in writing a persuasive essay
- what you would try to do differently next time, if anything.

Self-assessment

20 Judging your own performance

▶ From the list below:
  a select three points on which you feel you have made the most progress
  b select one point on which you most need to improve.
  I can identify techniques used by authors in persuasive writing.
  I can use some of these techniques in my own writing.
  I can recognise when an author is using emotive language and comment on the effect it has.
  I can identify the structure of a piece of persuasive writing.
  I can work out why a statement is ambiguous and avoid ambiguity in my own writing.
  I can organise my persuasive writing in appropriate paragraphs.
  I can use evidence of different types to back up my argument.
  I can show up weaknesses in opposition views and offer alternatives.
  I can write an argument persuasively enough to gain the attention of the target audience.
  I can write an argument persuasively enough to influence the opinions of the target audience.

21 Improving your skills in English

▶ Select one or two skills you need to concentrate on to improve your skills in reading. Then do the same for your writing skills. (The descriptions of levels are a guide only.)

	Reading skill	From	To
1	Show understanding of significant ideas, beginning to use inference and deduction	Level 3	Level 4
2	Refer to the text when explaining views, locating and using ideas and information	Level 3	Level 4
3	Select essential points and use inference and deduction where appropriate	Level 4	Level 5
4	Identify key features and select sentences, phrases and relevant information to support views	Level 4	Level 5
5	Identify different layers of meaning in a range of texts	Level 5	Level 6
6	Comment on the significance and effect of word choice	Level 5	Level 6
7	Show understanding of the ways in which meaning and information are conveyed in a range of texts	Level 6	Level 7
8	Select and synthesise a range of information from a variety of sources	Level 6	Level 7

		From	To
9	Evaluate how authors achieve their effects through the use of linguistic, structural and presentational devices	Level 7	Level 8
10	Select and analyse information and ideas, and comment on how these are conveyed in different texts	Level 7	Level 8
11	Develop ideas, referring in detail to aspects of language, structure and presentation	Level 8	E.P.
12	Identify and analyse argument, opinion and alternative interpretations, making cross-references where appropriate	Level 8	E.P.

	Writing skill	From	To
1	Ideas are organised appropriately for a piece of persuasive writing	Level 3	Level 4
2	Writing is thoughtful, and ideas are sustained and developed in interesting ways	Level 3	Level 4
3	Writing is varied and interesting, conveying meaning clearly in a form appropriate for persuasive writing	Level 4	Level 5
4	Vocabulary choices are imaginative and words are used precisely	Level 4	Level 5
5	Writing engages and sustains the reader's interest, showing some use of style appropriate to persuasive writing	Level 5	Level 6
6	Use a range of sentence structures and varied vocabulary to create effects	Level 5	Level 6
7	Writing is confident, and shows an appropriate choice of style for persuasive writing	Level 6	Level 7
8	Ideas are organised and coherent, with grammatical features and vocabulary accurately and effectively used	Level 6	Level 7
9	Writing is coherent and gives clear points of view	Level 7	Level 8
10	The use of vocabulary and grammar enables fine distinctions to be made or emphasis achieved	Level 7	Level 8
11	Writing has shape and impact, and control of the style appropriate for persuasive writing	Level 8	E.P.
12	The written text is coherent, reasoned and persuasive	Level 8	E.P.

7 Creating drama
Frankenstein's monster

Your focus
The content of this unit is designed to:
- develop your skills in appreciating the differences between prose and drama.

Your target
By the end of this unit you should be more able to:
- read a playscript with appropriate expression
- understand some of the choices playwrights make
- identify features that make a play in performance dramatic
- identify features of spoken and written English, and apply these in your own writing.

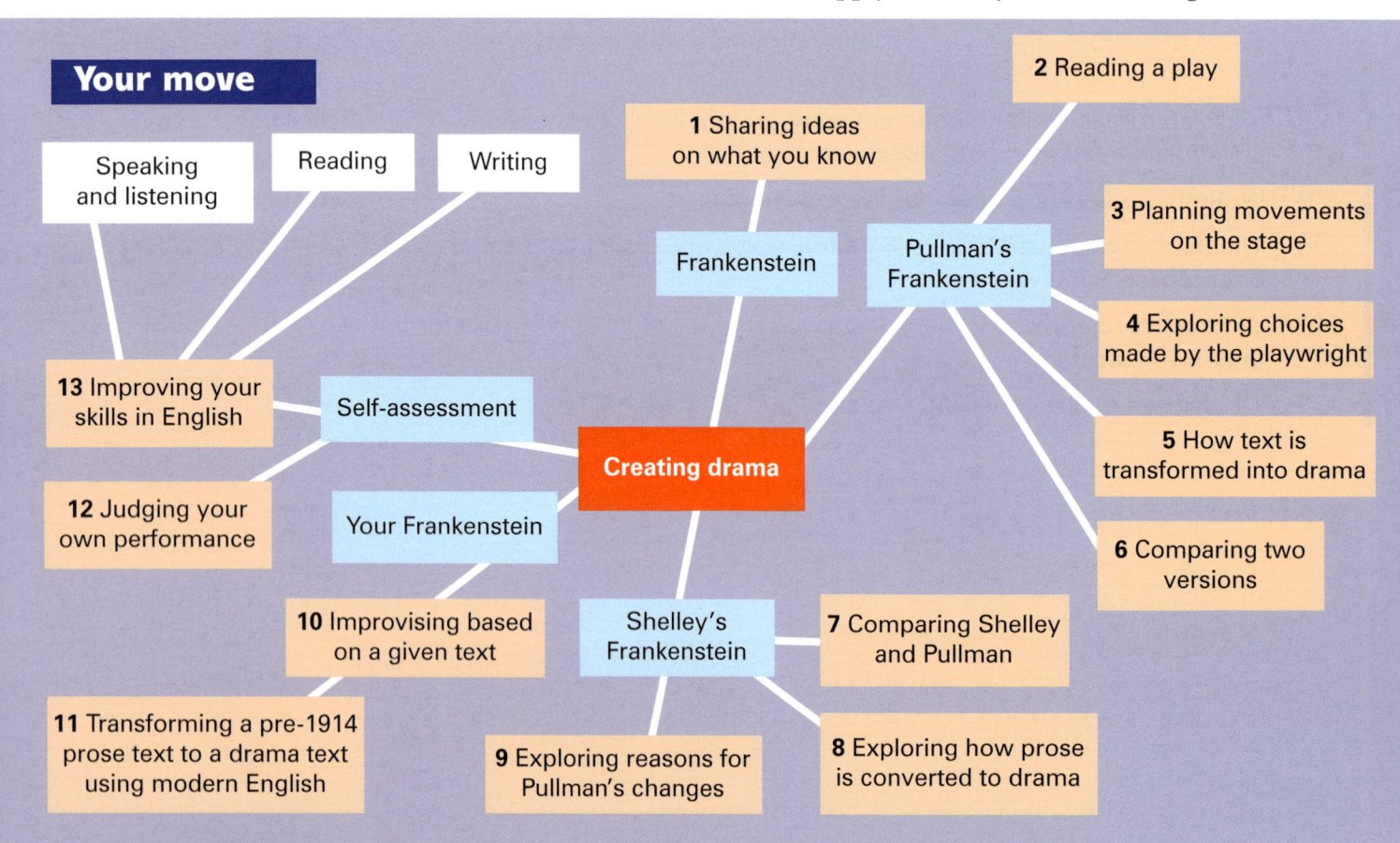

Your move

- Speaking and listening
- Reading
- Writing

Creating drama

- Frankenstein
  - 1 Sharing ideas on what you know
  - 2 Reading a play
- Pullman's Frankenstein
  - 3 Planning movements on the stage
  - 4 Exploring choices made by the playwright
  - 5 How text is transformed into drama
  - 6 Comparing two versions
- Shelley's Frankenstein
  - 7 Comparing Shelley and Pullman
  - 8 Exploring how prose is converted to drama
  - 9 Exploring reasons for Pullman's changes
- Your Frankenstein
  - 10 Improvising based on a given text
  - 11 Transforming a pre-1914 prose text to a drama text using modern English
- Self-assessment
  - 12 Judging your own performance
  - 13 Improving your skills in English

Frankenstein

1 Sharing ideas on what you know

▶ In your group, decide how much you know about the story of Frankenstein under each of these headings:
  ● what you definitely know
  ● what you are fairly sure about
  ● what you think may be true but are not at all sure about.
▶ Can you remember where the information came from?
▶ In the report-back session, see if the whole class can come to some definite conclusions without looking up any references.

Pullman's Frankenstein

2 Reading a play

▶ If you are taking a part in the play, use your skills in pace, pitch, volume and intonation to make the words come alive for your audience and make that particular speech sound natural.
▶ If you are listening to others read the play, decide what helps to make the play **dramatic** (dictionary definitions 2 and 3).

Mary Shelley's Frankenstein, adapted as a play by Philip Pullman

In this unit, you will be exploring Act 2 of this version. The plot so far: Frankenstein has created a man out of the parts of the bodies of dead humans, and then brought him to life. As soon as he has brought the 'man' to life, he is so horrified at the appearance of this 'monster' that he rejects his own creation.

WORDS

▲ **pace** *noun* rate of walking, running, speaking etc. *at a fast pace, at a slow pace*.
▲ **pitch** *noun* the degree of highness or lowness of a sound *high pitch, low pitch*.
▲ **volume** *noun* loudness of sound.
▲ **intonation** *noun* the rise and fall of the pitch of the voice in speech.
▲ **dramatic** *adjective* **1** belonging or relating to plays, the theatre or acting in general. **2** exciting. **3** sudden and striking; drastic.

Notes on the characters written by Philip Pullman:

The Monster	It is important that he should look hideous. He is made of corpses, after all. But in the novel he is shown as being very strong and agile, and although when he first comes to life he cannot move easily, it makes him much more impressive in the later Acts if he is graceful and powerful and does not lurch about clumsily. His voice should be impressive.
Felix	Young, quick-tempered, fiery. He and Agathe are political refugees.
Agathe	Although she is blind, she should move about the room as easily as a sighted person. She knows it well, knows where everything is. It is when she first becomes aware that something is wrong that she begins to look vulnerable.

7 CREATING DRAMA

Act Two

Inside a simple cottage in the forest. A rough table, a couple of rough chairs, a simple fireplace, a window overlooking some trees. It is neat and clean, but very simply furnished. On the table, the remains of a meal – some bread, an apple, a piece of cheese. Sunlight is streaming in through the window, and through the door upstage, through which we see more trees. To one side there is another door. Birds can be heard singing.

In the distance, there is the furious barking of dogs – like hounds in a hunt. It lasts for a short while and then dies away.

Suddenly the light is blocked in the doorway. The **Monster** is standing there, panting. It is hard to tell what his expression is, though anger and fear seem to mingle in it. He is wearing a torn white shirt which is too small for him, and his hands and arms are torn and bloody.

He stands there nervously for a moment, then makes up his mind and steps in, looking around as if for any threat.

Then he sees the food on the table and seizes it, devouring it ravenously, cramming the bread and cheese into his mouth and sniffing at the apple. His feet are clearly badly torn.

Hearing something, the **Monster** freezes. It is a young man's voice, and a young girl's. During their exchange the **Monster** looks around desperately – sees the other door – makes for it – and gets through, shutting it behind him, just before **Felix** and **Agathe** enter.

Felix	(*Outside*) Not far now. Mind that stone.	
Agathe	(*Outside*) Heavens above, Felix, I know there's a stone there. I know every inch of the path…	
Felix	You ought to carry a stick. I don't know why you don't.	
Agathe	What, and go tap-tapping everywhere? I need my hands to carry things in. I'm more agile than you are. And I bet I could find my way back to the cottage from anywhere in these woods, I know them so well…	5
	*They appear in the doorway, just as the **Monster** closes the other door.*	
	*They are young and simply dressed. **Felix** is carrying a musket and a dead rabbit, **Agathe** a basket of mushrooms. Although blind, she knows her surroundings so well that she moves around with great freedom.*	
	***Felix** stands the musket in the corner –*	
Felix	There. I'll clean that this evening. Time I made some more bullets…	10
	– and puts the rabbit on the table, but carelessly: he does not notice that the food has been eaten. Agathe puts her basket there too and then sits down.	
Agathe	And I'll skin the rabbit in a minute. Shall I make a pie? Or would you like a stew?	
Felix	He's an old one – he'll be a bit tough. We'll have a stew, and put some of that wild garlic in.	
Agathe	And the mushrooms and a carrot or two…we're living quite well. Who'd have thought we could?	15
Felix	Not the judges who sent us here, that's for sure. They thought exile would kill us, as it killed father.	
Agathe	We'll survive. We'll do more than survive – we'll prosper.	

126

Felix	We haven't faced winter yet. That won't be so easy … look, I think I'll load the gun before I go. Just in case.	20
Agathe	If you must. But don't expect me to shoot anyone.	
	*During the discussion **Felix** loads his musket with powder and shot, while **Agathe** fetches and tunes a guitar from the corner of the room.*	
Felix	I don't like leaving you alone without any protection. Just point it roughly in the right direction and pull the trigger – that's all you have to do.	25
Agathe	I don't like the noise.	
Felix	All right, swing it round and hit 'em with it, I don't care. But I'll feel better if you have something to protect you, even if you're so brave and independent that you don't want it.	
	*ptfFelix** uses the musket's ramrod to check that the bullet is firmly in place.*	
Agathe	Who's going to attack me, Felix?	30
Felix	That's a silly question. This is a wild part of the country, Agathe – there are wolves and bears in the forest, even if the bandits are having a day off. And there's been some kind of trouble down in the town. Didn't you hear the dogs earlier on?	
Agathe	I thought the men were hunting …	35
Felix	The town dogs were barking too. You must have heard them.	
Agathe	Well, if it's down in the town, you'll need the musket more than I will. Oh, I'm not arguing – I know you're right. But I feel safe here.	
Felix	No harm in being prepared. If we didn't need more powder and lead I'd leave the rest of the stuff for a day or so, but I might as well get it all … what else was it? Flour?	40
Agathe	And soap, and salt. And if you can find some honey …	
Felix	We could set up a hive or two ourselves next year. I wonder if I can find anyone who could let me have a queen bee?	45
Agathe	We'll be living like kings!	
Felix	I suppose we could settle here … the people in the town are friendly enough, and I could get some kind of work on a farm, perhaps. But it's very lonely for you.	
Agathe	Better than prison. Have you loaded that thing yet?	50
Felix	Just about. It's here in the corner. Remember, you pull back the hammer two clicks. And hold it tight, or you'll hurt yourself.	
	He stands the gun in the corner and shoulders a canvas bag.	
Felix	I'll be back before sundown. D'you want some wood for the fire before I go?	55
Agathe	No, I'll do that. You go.	
	He kisses her.	
Felix	I should get that rabbit cooking soon, or it'll be like eating a boot.	
Agathe	Oh, stop fussing!	
	Laughing, he goes out.	
	She puts the guitar down and reaches on to the table for the apple. Feeling that it is not there, she frowns.	

7 CREATING DRAMA

Agathe Oh, you might have left me the apple ... that's a mean trick. 60
Her hand finds the loaf, torn and half-eaten.
She picks it up to feel it properly.
That's odd ... it was a fresh loaf.
She feels around for the cheese.
And where's the cheese? He hasn't taken that too? Felix, you greedy pig.
She gets up and goes to the door as if to call him back, but changes her mind.
Well, he's got a long way to go, and a lot to carry. But it's not 65
like him to take it without saying anything ...
She comes back and sits down, picking up the guitar.

Agathe Anyway, I'm not hungry.
She plucks a chord – then stops abruptly.
Supposing it wasn't Felix, though? ...
Head alert, listening, she 'looks' around.
Hello? Is anyone there?
Silence.
The door was open ... anyone could have come in ... no, I'm
being silly. This place is safe. 70
She begins to play a simple folk tune. A few bars into it, the **Monster** *silently appears. He merely stands and listens, as if he has never heard music before.*
She comes to the end of her short piece and puts the guitar down, sighing.
No ... that's too sad. Oh, Papa ...
She gets up and wanders towards the **Monster**, *who does not move, though he watches her carefully. Beside him on the wall is a picture: the portrait of an elderly man. She comes close and seems to be staring at it. The* **Monster** *is holding his breath, as if he is afraid of being discovered – and then he seems to realise that the girl cannot see him, and moves his hand slowly in front of her face, getting no reaction. A light dawns in his expression, but he does not move.*
Then she reaches up, takes the picture from the wall, and goes back to sit down. He stays where he is and listens.

Agathe Father, I expect it's silly talking to a picture I can't see – it's
silly talking to a picture anyway. But I can't worry Felix, and I
can't write a diary, and ... I'm just worried, Papa. Will we
survive here? Will we manage to find enough food? Will 75
Felix find work somewhere? – You're silent. You don't know
any more than I do. Are you watching over us, Papa? I'm sure
you would if you could. But we haven't done badly, have we?
We never had to lift a finger before. The servants did it all for
us. But we've lived here for six months now, and every so 80
often Felix shoots a rabbit or a couple of pigeons, and there's
the apple tree, and I know where the wild strawberries grow ...
I think you *are* looking after us, Papa. You wouldn't leave us on
our own ...

*During this speech the **Monster** silently moves towards the door and goes out.*
She presses the picture to her heart, bowing her head over it.
But it's very hard … I wish we'd said goodbye before they took you away. Though I don't know how I could have let you go …
*The **Monster** returns. His arms are full of logs. As she sits still with her head bowed, he puts them down very carefully, so as not to make a noise, in the hearth.*
Then he takes an apple from his pocket and puts it on the table – only to freeze and draw his hand back as she looks up at where he is standing. He stands still as she gets up slowly and goes to put the picture back on the wall. Then she picks up a little mirror from the shelf.

Agathe   Thank Heaven, I remember what you looked like, Papa … I can judge a real face with my hands now, but I can't judge the expression of a picture. And I can't see my own face any more … I used to be pretty. I *think* I was pretty. What I am now, only Felix knows …
*She looks in the mirror. The **Monster**, who has come up silently beside her, watches curiously, comparing her face with the image. Then she puts the mirror back.*

Agathe   It's no good. Everything's changed, there's no point in looking back.
She goes to the fireplace and tries to pick up the basket of logs – but finds it full, and feels them, surprised.
Oh! Felix, you've done it after all! But it's not like you to play tricks on me. Or – I wonder – the bread, the apple – *was* it Felix?
*She gets up swiftly and goes to stand in the doorway, as if she is nervous about remaining inside. She looks out, biting a nail. Meanwhile the **Monster**, unable to resist it, picks up the mirror, feeling his own face, and slowly brings the glass up and looks in it.*

Monster   Uggghhhh!
*He drops the mirror, which shatters. **Agathe** hears, and turns at once in fear.*
Who's that? Who's there?
He leaps to her and seizes her hand before she can run away.

Agathe   (Screams)
He puts his hand over her mouth. She struggles, but he is too strong.

Monster   No! No! Friend!
With one hand he holds her, and with the other he reaches to the table and picks up the apple, which he puts into her hands. As she feels it he says again –

Monster   Friend! Friend!
Agathe   You're giving me an apple – who are you? What do you want?
Seeing her relax a little, he releases her.
She steps away at once, still fearful.

Monster   I have come … a long way … help. Help me.
Agathe   It was you that ate the bread – and brought the logs in?

7 CREATING DRAMA

Monster	I will not hurt anyone. I am their friend. Friend of everyone. I give you …	105
	He reaches for her hands and folds them around the apple again.	
	Not hurt anyone. Not kill, not hurt. Friend.	
	She releases her hands gently and puts the apple on the table.	
Agathe	Let me … please, I'm blind, you see … may I feel your face? So I can tell what you look like?	
Monster	You see with hands?	
Agathe	It's the only way I can.	110
Monster	No. Not touch me. No.	
	He backs away as she reaches for him.	
Agathe	But you can see what I look like.	
	He shakes his head, turning away, as her hands reach up to his face.	
Monster	No – not good, not good –	
	Her hands are on his cheeks, his eyes, his mouth. Suddenly she pulls them away and steps back.	
Agathe	I'm sorry …	
Monster	I said *not good*.	115
Agathe	You poor man!	
	He is puzzled.	
Monster	Man?	
Agathe	You must have suffered … What's your name?	
Monster	No name. Please – you listen. I come a long way. I look for friends. I have no home. Men see me, they hurt me – dogs – they shout, they throw stones. But I am *good*. I want to love them, not hurt, not kill. I come here – I see house – I was hungry, I take food. Pardon. Forgive me. Everywhere I go, they hate me. Am I not good? I look bad. But I am good, I want to help and love – I help you? Bring you food, bring you wood? Please! My heart is unhappy – I stay here? You tell the man?	120

125 |

Felix	*(Calling)* Agathe – are you there?	
Agathe	*(Calling)* Felix! Oh, Felix, listen to me –	
	*Felix runs in, sees the **Monster** apparently attacking her and **Agathe** apparently struggling to be free, and without hesitation seizes the musket.*	
Felix	Dear God! He's here –	130
Agathe	No, Felix! Don't! Don't shoot –	
Monster	Tell him!	
Agathe	Don't, Felix.	
Felix	Out of the way – Agathe, get *down* –	
	*But she turns to the **Monster** and clings to him, trying to shield him.*	
Agathe	Felix, listen –	135
	*The **Monster**, far stronger than she is, pushes her aside, and as she falls **Felix** shoots.*	
	*The roar of the musket fills the stage – the **Monster** staggers and cries out –*	
Monster	AAAAGGGGHHHHHHH!	
	– and clutching his breast, he staggers to the door, where he clings to the frame.	
Agathe	Felix! What have you done?	
Felix	Are you hurt? What's he done to you?	
	*He runs to **Agathe** and helps her to sit up – she pushes him away and feels for the **Monster**.*	
Agathe	Oh, where are you? Where have you gone?	
Felix	Agathe! What are you doing? For God's sake, keep away from him –	140
	*She reaches the **Monster** and seizes his hand, but he thrusts her away.*	
Monster	You *want* me bad! All of you – everyone – you all *want* me bad!	
Agathe	No – no –	
	*Felix runs to hold her and keep her back from the **Monster**, who pulls himself up and looks at them both with a face twisted with hatred.*	
Monster	Evil? Evil – you *want* evil – then I shall be evil! I shall be terror and hatred and revenge – *revenge*!	145
	With a mighty howl of anger, he runs off.	
Agathe	Oh, Felix! What have you done?	
Felix	You didn't see him, Agathe – and you don't know what he's done already! The villagers have been hunting him for days –	
Agathe	*We* should have understood him, Felix. He was an outcast just like us. We could have helped him – he begged for it! What have you done to him now? Have you made him evil for ever? *She pulls herself away from him and runs out. **Felix** makes as if to follow, but stops and sits down in baffled defeat. A long way off we hear:*	150
Monster	*(Howling faintly)* Revenge! Revenge!	

7 CREATING DRAMA

3 Planning movements on the stage

- Draw a diagram of the layout of the stage. Use just the stage directions before any speeches in Act 2.
- Show the positions of each character at a maximum of six moments up to line 71.
- Use up to six planning frames (see below), giving a line reference for each.

ADVICE

▲ You only need to show the full details of layout in your first diagram.

Front of stage	Front of stage
Front of stage	Front of stage
Front of stage	Front of stage

- What details included by the playwright up to line 10 could add to the drama (tension) of this section?

ADVICE

▲ You need to read the stage directions carefully.

WORDS

▲ **stage directions** *plural noun* the instructions that relate to actors' movements (e.g. when they should enter and exit the stage), sound and lighting effects, placement of props, etc. all of which are written as part of the script of a play.
▲ **upstage** *adverb* on, at or towards the back of a theatre stage.

4 Exploring choices made by the playwright

- Felix and Agathe have not appeared in Act 1. Make a note of the line numbers where Philip Pullman lets the audience know the names of the two characters.
- Why do you think there is a reference to dogs barking in both the stage directions at the start of Act 2 and also at lines 34–36?
- Suggest possible reasons for Philip Pullman writing … at the end of some speeches.
- After line 67 the stage directions read:
  Head alert, listening, she 'looks' around.
  Explain the reason for the quotation marks around the word 'looks'.
- The audience learns about the character of the Monster in various ways. What is suggested about the Monster at these points?
  - line 36
  - stage directions after line 70
  - stage directions after line 71
  - stage directions after line 86
  - stage directions after line 91
  - stage directions after line 96 and the Monster's reaction
  - line 111
  - line 117
  - lines 142–143
- Look at the Monster's speech in lines 119–127.
  - In what way is the speech different from standard English?
  - What reasons could there be for Philip Pullman representing the Monster's speech in this way?

Investigating point of view

Taking the three characters Agathe, Felix and the Monster:
- Do you think Philip Pullman encourages us to take sides with all these characters?
- Rate how sympathetic you are to each character, putting a 1 for the character you most sympathise with and a 3 for the character you least sympathise with.
- Then try to explain what it is about the way Philip Pullman has written the play (or any other reason) that produces these reactions.

Investigating theme

Agathe says: **We should have understood him, Felix.** (line 150)
- Why does she think they should have understood the Monster?
- Think of any other individuals or groups the Monster could represent/make an audience think of.
- What is the connection between the individual or group you have chosen, and the Monster?
- When you have heard the suggestions from the other groups, decide which ones you think are most closely connected with the themes of the play, and why.

7 CREATING DRAMA

5. How text is transformed into drama

▶ Tom Stoppard, a playwright, has said:
'Plays are events rather than texts. They're written to happen, not to be read.'
Imagine Act 2 of Philip Pullman's adaptation of Mary Shelley's *Frankenstein* performed on a stage.

▶ Find the most interesting or dramatic examples for each of the features listed.

Feature of performance	How this is indicated in the text	Line reference
Costume		
Make-up		
Props		
Sounds from the performers other than words		
Using actions of performers – acting together		
Using body language of performers to express their feelings		
Using the sense of hearing, and not just for speech: sound effects		
Using the sense of sight – allowing the audience to see events occurring		
Using the tone of voice of performers. How is this suggested to a performer?		
What people do as well as what people say		

WORDS

▲ **costume** *noun* set of clothes, especially of a particular historical period, worn in a play by an actor, or at a fancy dress party, etc.

▲ **make-up** *noun* cosmetics worn by actors to give the required appearance for a part.

134

Frankenstein's monster

In Act 3 of Philip Pullman's adaptation of the play, the Monster tells Frankenstein about the events covered in Act 2:

Monster   Ah, yes. I went down into the town, and they called out their dogs. Creatures full of beauty, with soft fur and bright eyes – I wanted to kneel down and pet them and play with them, but they tore at me with their teeth, and then I knew fear for the first time. I ran to the forest, where it was quiet, where there was cool water to bathe my flesh. The moon came up – oh, Frankenstein, to see the moon for the first time! And I found out what sadness was, and loneliness. Those other beings like myself – they stood upright, like me – they'd thrown stones, and shouted harsh words at me, but they had companions, fellows, friends. Couldn't I find a friend? So I began to look ...

Frankenstein   Where? Where did you look? And how did you learn to speak?

Monster   By listening. By hiding, and listening, and practising by myself. I found a cottage in the forest where a girl and her brother were living – a blind girl, the only piece of luck I ever had. She couldn't see me. We spoke together; oh, I would have been her slave, I would have helped them and worked for them, I would have done anything if they'd only accepted me – but her brother shot me with his musket as if I were a wild beast. It broke my arm. The bullet's still in my shoulder. That was when I found out what pain was really like. All alone in the icy mountains, weeping, crying with rage and loneliness – Frankenstein, you can't imagine how I suffered. If you could imagine it, you'd be on your knees praying to your God for forgiveness.

> **WORDS**
>
> ▲ **ah** *exclamation* expressing surprise, sympathy, admiration, pleasure, etc. according to the intonation of the speaker's voice.
> ▲ **oh** *exclamation* expressing surprise, admiration, pleasure, anger or fear, etc.

6 Comparing two versions

▶ Is your impression of the Monster here the same as the one you had from reading Act 2?
▶ Discuss in your group if and why your reaction is the same or different.
▶ What reasons might Philip Pullman have for including the same events told in two different ways?

135

7 CREATING DRAMA

Shelley's Frankenstein

7 Comparing Shelley and Pullman

▶ Compare the extract from Act 3 on page 135 with Mary Shelley's version of the same events in the first few lines of the extract printed below. Both authors intend to represent speech, but Philip Pullman also knows his version will be spoken rather than just read.
▶ What are the main differences between the language used in each version?
▶ What do you think makes Philip Pullman's version easier to read aloud?

Way Philip Pullman has written his text	Example from extract on page 135
Length of sentences	
Repetition	
Suggestion of a natural pause in speech	
Use of exclamations	
Use of exclamation mark	
Use of interruption to speech	
Use of minor sentences – without main verb	
Use of question to indicate feelings	
Use of questions as part of a dialogue between two people	
Use of second person pronoun	

Extracts from *Frankenstein* by Mary Shelley

Many months after the events described in Act 2 of the play version, the 'monster' finds Frankenstein, and insists that Frankenstein should listen to his story.

Treatment by the villagers   Finding the cottage   Taking bread

… at sunset I arrived at a village. How miraculous did this appear! the huts, the neater cottages, and stately houses engaged my admiration by turns. The vegetables in the gardens, the milk and cheese that I saw placed at the windows of some of the cottages, allured my appetite. One of the best of these I entered; but I had hardly placed my foot within the door before the children shrieked,   5
and one of the women fainted. The whole village was roused; some fled, some attacked me, until, grievously bruised by stones and many other kinds of missile weapons, I escaped to the open country and fearfully took refuge in a low hovel, quite bare, and making a wretched appearance after the palaces I had beheld in the village. This hovel, however, joined a cottage of a neat and   10
pleasant appearance; but, after my late and dearly bought experience, I dared not enter it.

   Here then I retreated, and lay down happy to have found a shelter, however miserable, from the inclemency of the season, and still more from the barbarity of man.   15

Having arranged my dwelling and carpeted it with clean straw, I retired; for I saw the figure of a man at a distance, and I remembered too well my treatment the night before, to trust myself in his power. I had first, however, provided for my sustenance for that day by a loaf of coarse bread, which I purloined, and a cup with which I could drink, more conveniently than from my hand, of the pure water which flowed by my retreat. The floor was a little raised, so that is was kept perfectly dry, and by its vicinity to the chimney of the cottage it was tolerably warm.

Hearing music

On examining my dwelling, I found that one of the windows of the cottage had formerly occupied a part of it, but the panes had been filled up with wood. In one of these was a small and almost imperceptible chink, through which the eye could just penetrate. Through this crevice a small room was visible, white-washed and clean, but very bare of furniture. In one corner, near a small fire, sat an old man, leaning his head on his hands in a disconsolate attitude. The young girl was occupied in arranging the cottage; but presently she took something out of a drawer, which employed her hands, and she sat down beside the old man, who, taking up an instrument, began to play, and to produce sounds sweeter than the voice of the thrush or the nightingale. It was a lovely sight, even to me, poor wretch! who had never beheld aught beautiful before.

Collecting wood   Hearing speech

I found that the youth spent a great part of each day in collecting wood for the family fire; and, during the night I often took his tools, the use of which I quickly discovered, and brought home firing sufficient for the consumption of several days.

I remember, the first time I did this, the young woman, when she opened the door in the morning, appeared greatly astonished on seeing a great pile of wood on the outside. She uttered some words in a loud voice, and the youth joined her, who also expressed surprise. I observed, with pleasure, that he did not go to the forest that day, but spent it in repairing the cottage and cultivating the garden.

By degrees I made a discovery of still greater moment. I found that these people possessed a method of communicating their experience and feelings to one another by articulate sounds. I perceived that the words they spoke sometimes produced pleasure or pain, smiles or sadness, in the minds and countenances of the hearers. This was indeed a godlike science, and I ardently desired to become acquainted with it. But I was baffled in every attempt I made for this purpose. Their pronunciation was quick; and the words they uttered, not having any apparent connection with visible objects, I was unable to discover any clue by which I could unravel the mystery of their reference. By great application, however, and after having remained during the space of several revolutions of the moon in my hovel, I discovered the names that were given to some of the most familiar objects of discourse; I learned and applied the words, 'fire', 'milk', 'bread', and 'wood'. I learned also the names of the cottagers themselves. The youth and his companion had each of them several names, but the old man had only one, which was 'father'. The girl was called 'sister', or 'Agatha', and the youth 'Felix', 'brother', or 'son'. I cannot describe the delight I felt when I learned the ideas appropriated to each of these sounds, and was able to pronounce them. I distinguished several other words without being able as yet to understand or apply them; such as 'good', 'dearest', 'unhappy'.

Reading   Seeing himself in a 'mirror'

This reading had puzzled me extremely at first; but, by degrees, I discovered that he uttered many of the same sounds when he read, as when he talked. I conjectured, therefore, that he found on the paper signs for speech which he understood, and I ardently longed to comprehend these also; but how was that possible when I did not even understand the sounds for which they stood as signs? I improved, however, sensible of this science, but not sufficiently to follow up any kind of conversation, although I applied my whole mind to the endeavour: for I easily perceived that, although I eagerly longed to discover myself to the cottagers, I ought not to make the attempt until I had first become master of their language; which knowledge might enable me to make them overlook the deformity of my figure; for with this also the contrast perpetually presented to my eyes had made me acquainted.

I had admired the perfect forms of my cottagers – their grace, beauty, and delicate complexions: but how was I terrified, when I viewed myself in a transparent pool! At first I started back, unable to believe that it was indeed I who was reflected in the mirror; and when I became fully convinced that I was in reality the monster that I am, I was filled with the bitterest sensations of despondence and mortification. Alas! I did not entirely know the fatal effects of this miserable deformity.

Finding out his own history

Soon after my arrival in the hovel, I discovered some papers in the pocket of the dress which I had taken from your laboratory. At first I had neglected them; but now that I was able to decipher the characters in which they were written, I began to study them with diligence. It was your journal of the four months that preceded my creation. You minutely described in these papers every step you took in the progress of your work; this history was mingled with accounts of domestic occurrences. You doubtless recollect these papers. Here they are. Every thing is related in them which bears reference to my accursed origin; the whole detail of that series of disgusting circumstances which produced it is set in view; the minutest description of my odious and loathsome person is given, in language which painted your own horrors and rendered mine indelible. I sickened as I read. 'Hateful day when I received life!' I exclaimed in agony. "Accursed creator! Why did you form a monster so hideous that even *you* turned from me in disgust? God, in pity, made man beautiful and alluring, after his own image; but my form is a filthy type of yours, more horrid even from the very resemblance. Satan had his companions, fellow-devils, to admire and encourage him; but I am solitary and abhorred.

These were the reflections of my hours of despondency and solitude; but when I contemplated the virtues of the cottagers, their amiable and benevolent dispositions, I persuaded myself that when they should become acquainted with my admiration of their virtues, they would compassionate me and overlook my personal deformity. Could they turn from their door one, however monstrous, who solicited their compassion and friendship? I resolved, at least, not to despair, but in every way to fit myself for an interview with them, which would decide my fate.

Frankenstein's monster

Making himself known to the cottagers (Safie is a friend of Felix)

One day, when the sun shone on the red leaves that strewed the ground, and diffused cheerfulness, although it denied warmth, Safie, Agatha, and Felix departed on a long country walk, and the old man, at his own desire, was left alone in the cottage. When his children had departed, he took up his guitar, and played several mournful but sweet airs, more sweet and mournful than I had ever heard him play before.

My heart beat quick; this was the hour and moment of trial, which would decide my hopes, or realise my fears. The servants were gone to a neighbouring fair. All was silent in and around the cottage: it was an excellent opportunity; yet, when I proceeded to execute my plan, my limbs failed me, and I sank to the ground. Again I rose; and, exerting all the firmness of which I was master, removed the planks which I had placed before my hovel to conceal my retreat. The fresh air revived me, and, with renewed determination, I approached the door of their cottage.

I knocked. 'Who is there?' said the old man – 'Come in.'

I entered; 'Pardon this intrusion', said I; 'I am a traveller in want of a little rest; you would greatly oblige me if you would allow me to remain a few minutes before the fire.'

'Enter,' said De Lacey, "and I will try in what manner I can to relieve your wants; but, unfortunately, my children are from home, and as I am blind, I am afraid I shall find it difficult to procure food for you."

'Do not trouble yourself, my kind host; I have food; it is warmth and rest only that I need.'

I sat down, and a silence ensued. I knew that every minute was precious to me, yet I remained irresolute in what manner to commence the interview; when the old man addressed me. 'By your language, stranger, I suppose you are my countryman; – are you French?'

'No; but I was educated by a French family, and understand that language only. I am now going to claim the protection of some friends, whom I sincerely love, and of whose favour I have some hopes.'

'Are they Germans?'

'No, they are French. But let us change the subject. I am an unfortunate and deserted creature; I look around, and I have no relation or friend upon earth. These amiable people to whom I go have never seen me, and know little of me. I am full of fears, for if I fail there, I am an outcast in the world forever.'

'Do not despair. To be friendless is indeed to be unfortunate; but the hearts of men, when unprejudiced by any obvious self-interest, are full of brotherly love and charity. Rely, therefore, on your hopes; and if these friends are good and amiable, do not despair.'

'They are kind – they are the most excellent creatures in the world; but unfortunately, they are prejudiced against me. I have good dispositions; my life has been hitherto harmless and in some degree beneficial; but a fatal prejudice clouds their eyes, and where they ought to see a feeling and kind friend, they behold only a detestable monster.'

'That is indeed unfortunate; but if you are really blameless, cannot you undeceive them?'

'I am about to undertake that task; and it is on that account that I feel so many overwhelming terrors. I tenderly love these friends; I have, unknown to them, been for many months in the habits of daily kindness towards them; but they believe that I wish to injure them, and it is that prejudice which I wish to overcome.'

'Where do these friends reside?'

'Near this spot.'

The old man paused and then continued, 'If you will unreservedly confide to me the particulars of your tale, I perhaps may be of use in undeceiving them. I am blind and cannot judge of your countenance, but there is something in your words which persuades me that you are sincere. I am poor and an exile, but it will afford me true pleasure to be in any way serviceable to a human creature.'

'Excellent man! I thank you and accept your generous offer. You raise me from the dust by this kindness; and I trust that, by your aid, I shall not be driven from the society and sympathy of your fellow-creatures.'

'Heaven forbid! Even if you were really criminal, for that can only drive you to desperation, and not instigate you to virtue. I also am unfortunate; I and my family have been condemned, although innocent; judge, therefore, if I do not feel for your misfortunes.'

'How can I thank you, my best and only benefactor? From your lips first have I heard the voice of kindness directed towards me; I shall be forever grateful; and your present humanity assures me of success with those friends whom I am on the point of meeting.'

'May I know the names and residence of those friends?'

I paused. This, I thought, was the moment of decision, which was to rob me of, or bestow happiness on me forever. I struggled vainly for firmness sufficient to answer him, but the effort destroyed all my remaining strength; I sank on the chair and sobbed aloud. At that moment I heard the steps of my younger protectors. I had not a moment to lose, but, seizing the hand of the old man, I cried, 'Now is the time! Save and protect me! You and your family are the friends whom I seek. Do not you desert me in the hour of trial!'

'Great God!' exclaimed the old man, 'who are you?'

At that instant the cottage door was opened, and Felix, Safie and Agatha entered. Who can describe their horror and consternation on beholding me? Agatha fainted, and Safie, unable to attend to her friend, rushed out of the cottage. Felix darted forward, and with supernatural force tore me from his father, to whose knees I clung: in a transport of fury, he dashed me to the ground and struck me violently with a stick. I could have torn him limb from limb, as the lion rends the antelope. But my heart sunk within me as with bitter sickness, and I refrained. I saw him on the point of repeating his blow, when, overcome by pain and anguish, I quitted the cottage, and in the general tumult escaped unperceived to my hovel.

Robert de Niro as the monster in Kenneth Branagh's *Mary Shelley's Frankenstein*.

Frankenstein's monster

8 Exploring how prose is converted to drama

▶ Match up at least five of the details from the Mary Shelley text with details from the Philip Pullman text on pages 126–131. Use a table like the one below.

Line	Detail in Mary Shelley text	How this detail is revealed to the audience of the play by Philip Pullman
6–7	The whole village was roused; some fled, some attacked me	
19–20	a loaf of coarse bread, which I purloined, and a cup with which I could drink	
32–33	the old man, who, taking up an instrument, began to play, and to produce sounds sweeter than the voice of the thrush or the nightingale	
36–39	'the youth spent a great part of each day in collecting wood for the family fire; and, during the night I … brought home firing sufficient for the consumption of several days.	
80–83	At first I started back, unable to believe that it was indeed I who was reflected in the mirror; and when I became fully convinced that I was in reality the monster that I am, I was filled with the bitterest sensations of despondence and mortification.	
164–166	'there is something in your words which persuades me that you are sincere. I am poor and an exile, but it will afford me true pleasure to be in any way serviceable to a human creature.'	
190–192	Felix darted forward, and with supernatural force tore me from his father, to whose knees I clung: in a transport of fury, he dashed me to the ground and struck me violently with a stick.	

▶ Select two of these changes, one mainly expressed by Philip Pullman in stage directions, and one mainly expressed in speech.
▶ Discuss the decisions Philip Pullman has taken in each case. Suggest reasons for presenting the original version in this particular way.

141

7 CREATING DRAMA

9 Exploring reasons for Pullman's changes

Philip Pullman has changed the text in some significant ways in turning Mary Shelley's prose into his drama version.

▶ Suggest how Philip Pullman has made the play more dramatic by making each of the following changes:

Significant differences Philip Pullman has made	In what way might the change make the play more dramatic?
Agathe blind rather than father	
Monster appears in room very soon after finding the cottage	
Time-scale reduced from several months to a single day	
Felix uses a gun rather than a stick to attack the monster	

One major change I made was to have the blind person, whom the Monster tries to befriend, a young woman instead of an old man. In the book, there are three people in the cottage: Felix, Agatha, and their blind father. You might feel that in making this change, I was being sexist, and wanting to exploit the contrast between a powerful male monster and a frail, helpless female. On the other hand, you might feel that I was providing a more interesting role for an actress in a story where women have otherwise very little to do. I know what I think I was doing.   **Philip Pullman**

Your Frankenstein

10 Improvising based on a given text

▶ In a novel, the reader tends to take sides with a particular person, usually the person telling the story. There is a clear *point of view*. In a play, unless there is a narrator or there are soliloquies, there is no single point of view, and the author allows characters to present their own thoughts and feelings in their own way. The way a performer acts in a particular part may well influence how much sympathy the audience feels for that character.

When taking part in an improvisation, think yourself into the character's thoughts and feelings. You may think Felix's behaviour is quite wrong, and yet from his perspective he is acting in a totally logical way.

Imagine the scene in the cottage after the Monster has left, at the end of Act 2.
▶ Act out the scene between Agathe and Felix.

How an improvisation is judged:
- Could the audience hear what you said?
- Did you keep up the flow of conversation?
- Was everything you said convincingly in character?
- Did you use pace, pitch, volume and intonation appropriately?
- Did you make use of details in the text to help you make this character convincing?
- Did you help the audience to see your character's point of view?

ADVICE

▲ When commenting on other improvisations, refer to the technique that you felt was effective or not effective, not the person performing.

WORDS

▲ **in character** typical of a person's nature; fitting in with what we already know about that character.

Frankenstein's monster

You should take into consideration:
- They are very close to each other, e.g. see stage direction after line 56.
- Agathe knows the Monster has provided them with food and wood.
- Agathe has not seen the Monster.
- Felix thought the Monster was attacking Agathe.
- Felix has not heard the Monster's side of the story.
- Agathe feels they all share the fact of being outsiders.
- Agathe fears for the consequences of Felix's actions.

Possible questions/reactions to get you started:

Agathe
Why did you have to shoot?
Did you know he's the person who's been getting all our logs?
You're just judging by the outside – that's prejudice.
We were outcasts too.
What have we/you started?

Felix
He/It looked dangerous.
He/It looked as if he/it was attacking you.
He/It looked like …
If you'd seen him/it, you'd …
I had to protect you.

11 Transforming a pre-1914 prose text to a drama text using modern English

▶ Use the techniques you have identified in Philip Pullman's adaptation to change the following extract from Mary Shelley's *Frankenstein* into a drama text.

ADVICE

▲ Include the setting at the beginning of your scene, and indicate stage directions.
▲ Set it out as a play, using **Monster** and **Frankenstein** in the margin opposite their speeches.
▲ Use a natural form of modern speech, such as that used by Philip Pullman in his adaptation. If in doubt, try reading it aloud.
▲ Consider including tone of voice directions to the performers.
▲ When writing Frankenstein's speech, get 'into the skin' of Frankenstein; when writing the Monster's speech, get 'into the skin' of the Monster.
▲ Aim to reduce the length of the original, so that your text is about one-quarter as long.

At this point in the story, the Monster has committed murder, including the murder of Frankenstein's younger brother. Frankenstein is telling the story of what happened, speaking to another character.

I suddenly beheld the figure of a man, at some distance, advancing towards me with superhuman speed. He bounded over the crevices in the ice, among which I had walked with caution; his stature, also, as he approached, seemed to exceed that of man. I was troubled: a mist came over my eyes, and I felt a faintness seize me; but I was quickly

143

7 CREATING DRAMA

restored by the cold gale of the mountains. I perceived, as the shape came nearer (sight tremendous and abhorred!) that it was the wretch whom I had created. I trembled with rage and horror, resolving to wait his approach, and then close with him in mortal combat. He approached; his countenance bespoke bitter anguish, combined with disdain and malignity, while its unearthly ugliness rendered it almost too horrible for human eyes. But I scarcely observed this; rage and hatred had at first deprived me of utterance, and I recovered only to overwhelm him with words expressive of furious detestation and contempt.

'Devil,' I exclaimed, 'do you dare approach me? and do not you fear the fierce vengeance of my arm wreaked on your miserable head? Begone, vile insect! or rather, stay, that I may trample you to dust! and, oh! that I could, with the extinction of your miserable existence, restore those victims whom you have so diabolically murdered!'

'I expected this reception,' said the daemon. 'All men hate the wretched; how, then, must I be hated, who am miserable beyond all living things! Yet you, my creator, detest and spurn me, thy creature, to whom thou art bound by ties only dissoluble by the annihilation of one of us. You purpose to kill me. How dare you sport thus with life? Do your duty towards me, and I will do mine towards you and the rest of mankind. If you will comply with my conditions, I will leave them and you at peace; but if you refuse, I will glut the maw of death, until it be satiated with the blood of your remaining friends.'

'Abhorred monster! fiend that thou art! the tortures of hell are too mild a vengeance for thy crimes. Wretched devil! you reproach me with your creation; come on, then, that I may extinguish the spark which I so negligently bestowed.'

My rage was without bounds; I sprang on him, impelled by all the feelings which can arm one being against the existence of another.

He easily eluded me, and said –

'Be calm! I intreat you to hear me, before you give vent to your hatred on my devoted head. Have I not suffered enough, that you seek to increase my misery? Life, although it may only be an accumulation of anguish, is dear to me, and I will defend it. Remember, thou hast made me more powerful than thyself; my height is superior to thine, my joints more supple. But I will not be tempted to set myself in opposition to thee. I am thy creature, and I will be even mild and docile to my natural lord and king, if thou wilt also perform thy part, the which thou owest me. Oh, Frankenstein, be not equitable to every other and trample upon me alone, to whom thy justice, and even thy clemency and affection, is most due. Remember, that I am thy creature; I ought to be thy Adam, but I am rather the fallen angel, whom thou drivest from joy for no misdeed. Everywhere I see bliss, from which I alone am irrevocably excluded. I was benevolent and good; misery made me a fiend. Make me happy, and I shall again be virtuous.'

'Begone! I will not hear you. There can be no community between you and me; we are enemies. Begone, or let us try our strength in a fight in which one must fall.'

▶ Write a commentary, comparing the way you have changed the Mary Shelley text with the changes you identified Philip Pullman making in Activity 7.
▶ Give some brief examples of how you have changed particular words, actions and movements, explaining your decisions.

Self-assessment

12 Judging your own performance

▶ From the list below:
   a select three points on which you feel you have made the most progress
   b select one point on which you most need to improve.
   I can read a part in a play varying pace, pitch, volume and intonation appropriately.

Frankenstein's monster

I can make constructive comments on how others read a part in a play.
I can imagine a play performed on a stage, suggest an appropriate set, and suggest an effective sequence of movements by performers.
I understand and can comment on some of the changes an author makes when converting prose to drama.
I understand and can comment on how an author presents a character to an audience in drama.
I understand and can comment on the way an author may introduce themes that have a wider significance outside the text.
I understand and can comment on the way a text is transformed when performed.
I can identify features which are typical of drama productions.
I can compare and comment on a single event presented in different ways.
I can identify and comment on features of a pre-1914 prose text.
I understand and can comment on the ways in which an author may make a text dramatic on stage.
I can improvise effectively and keep in character.
I can effectively adapt a pre-1914 prose text to a drama text in modern English.

13 Improving your skills in English

▶ Select one or two skills you need to concentrate on to improve your skills in speaking and listening. Then do the same for your reading and writing skills. (The descriptions of levels are a guide only.)

	Speaking and listening skill	From	To
1	Talk and listen with confidence in an increasing range of contexts, developing ideas thoughtfully	Level 3	Level 4
2	In discussion, listen carefully, making contributions and asking questions that are responsive to others' ideas and views	Level 3	Level 4
3	Talk and listen confidently in a wide range of contexts, varying expression and vocabulary	Level 4	Level 5
4	In discussion, pay close attention to what others say, ask questions and develop ideas and make contributions that take account of others' views	Level 4	Level 5
5	Adapt talk to demands of different contexts with increasing confidence	Level 5	Level 6
6	Take an active part in discussion, showing understanding of ideas and sensitivity to others	Level 5	Level 6
7	Confident in matching talk to the demands of different contexts	Level 6	Level 7
8	In discussion, make significant contributions, evaluate others' ideas and vary how and when to participate	Level 6	Level 7
9	Maintain and develop talk purposefully in a range of contexts, use appropriate intonation and emphasis	Level 7	Level 8
10	Make a range of contributions which show perceptive listening and sensitivity to the development of the discussion	Level 7	Level 8
11	Select and use structures, styles and registers appropriately in a range of contexts, varying vocabulary and expression confidently for a range of purposes	Level 8	E.P.
12	Make apt and careful comparison between texts, including consideration of audience, purpose and form	Level 8	E.P.

7 CREATING DRAMA

	Reading skill	From	To
1	Show understanding of significant ideas, themes, events and characters	Level 3	Level 4
2	Refer to the text when explaining views, locating and using ideas	Level 3	Level 4
3	Show understanding of a range of texts, selecting essential points and using inference and deduction where appropriate	Level 4	Level 5
4	Identify key features, themes and characters	Level 4	Level 5
5	Identify different layers of meaning; comment on significance/effect	Level 5	Level 6
6	Give personal responses to literary texts, referring to aspects of language, structure and themes in justifying views	Level 5	Level 6
7	Show understanding of the ways in which meaning and information are conveyed in a range of texts	Level 6	Level 7
8	Articulate personal and critical responses to prose and drama, showing awareness of their thematic, structural and linguistic features	Level 6	Level 7
9	Evaluate how authors achieve their effects through the use of linguistic, structural and presentational devices	Level 7	Level 8
10	Select and analyse information and ideas, and comment on how these are conveyed in different texts	Level 7	Level 8
11	Develop ideas; refer in detail to language/structure/presentation	Level 8	E.P.
12	Make apt and careful comparison between texts, including consideration of audience, purpose and form	Level 8	E.P.

	Writing skill	From	To
1	Ideas are organised appropriately for a drama text; vocabulary choices are often adventurous and words are used for effect	Level 3	Level 4
2	Writing is lively and thoughtful, and is sustained and developed in an interesting way	Level 3	Level 4
3	Writing is varied and interesting, and conveys meaning clearly in an appropriate form	Level 4	Level 5
4	Vocabulary choices are imaginative and words are used precisely	Level 4	Level 5
5	Writing often engages and sustains the audience's interest, showing some adaptation of style and register to a drama text	Level 5	Level 6
6	Use range of sentence structures and varied vocabulary to create effects	Level 5	Level 6
7	Writing is confident and shows appropriate choices of style for a drama text in modern English	Level 6	Level 7
8	Characters and settings are developed	Level 6	Level 7
9	Show selection of specific features or expressions to convey particular effects and to interest the audience	Level 7	Level 8
10	Show control of characters, events and settings, and variety in structure	Level 7	Level 8
11	Writing has shape and impact and shows control of style	Level 8	E.P.
12	Use structure as well as vocabulary for a range of imaginative effects	Level 8	E.P.

8 Report writing
Changing places

Your focus
The content of this unit is designed to:
- improve your skills in writing a report.

Your target
By the end of this unit you should be more able to:
- choose an appropriate formal style for a report
- plan an effective structure for a report
- edit and improve a report.

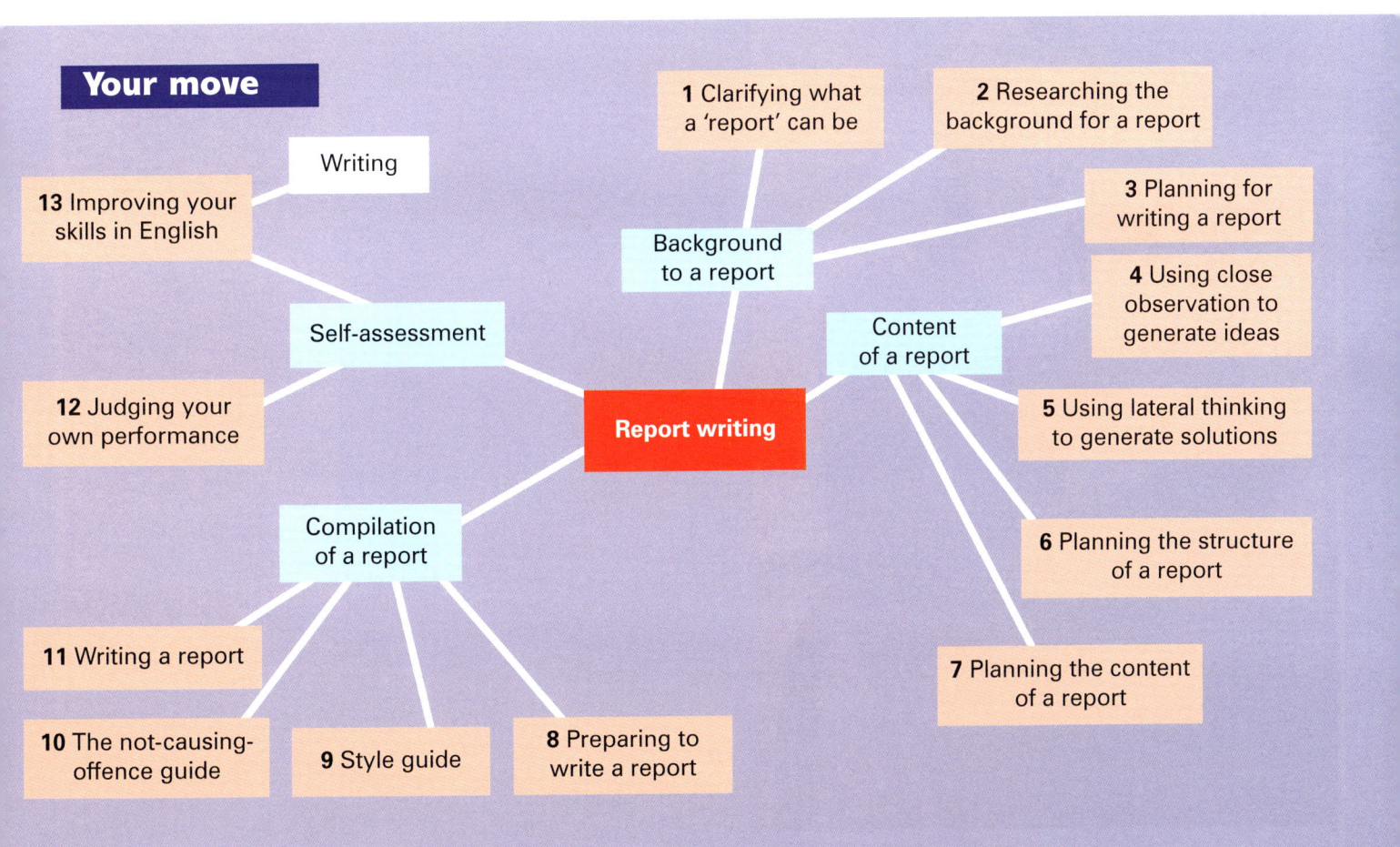

Your move

Report writing

- Background to a report
  - 1 Clarifying what a 'report' can be
  - 2 Researching the background for a report
- Content of a report
  - 3 Planning for writing a report
  - 4 Using close observation to generate ideas
  - 5 Using lateral thinking to generate solutions
  - 6 Planning the structure of a report
  - 7 Planning the content of a report
- Compilation of a report
  - 8 Preparing to write a report
  - 9 Style guide
  - 10 The not-causing-offence guide
  - 11 Writing a report
- Self-assessment
  - 12 Judging your own performance
- Writing
  - 13 Improving your skills in English

8 REPORT WRITING

The Ramp

'And in third place, Britain's best known Paralympian...'

That's me! Disbelief quickly gave way to an inane grin. Ever since I'd been a young girl, I'd dreamt of winning a BBC Sports Personality of the Year award and now that dream was a reality. But the issue that would dominate the papers the following morning was not the fact I'd become the first Paralympian to be honoured in such a way or the fulfilment of a lifelong ambition, but the simple lack of a ramp. An oversight by the BBC propelled disability sport into the headlines and ended up raising awareness in a way that any number of gold medals could never do.

It is traditional for the BBC award-winners to leave their seats and collect their trophies on the stage. But I quickly realised that there was nowhere for me to go. The only way I could have got on to the stage was by getting out of my wheelchair and crawling across the floor. I have no problem in doing that. You have to accept that, as a disabled person, you sometimes have to do things differently, but I knew that would embarrass people. So I sat there while Steve Redgrave and Denise Law, who came first and second, stood on the stage.

The lack of a ramp for me to join them did not bother me. I was just thrilled to get an award. No Paralympian had ever come close before and the most we had ever got in the past was a couple of film clips as they reviewed the year. It was only afterwards that I realised that there was an issue. Kelly Holmes, the runner, whom I know, came up to me at the post-awards party and told me she had been trying to drum up support to march down to where I was sitting and lift me on to the stage. Then a few other members of

Tanni Grey-Thompson also won the Welsh Woman of the Year 2001 award for her sporting achievements

WORDS

▲ **the Paralympics** noun an Olympic competition for people with physical disabilities, held at the same time as the traditional Olympic games; **paralympic** adjective 1950s: from *para*plegic + O*lympics*.

▲ **paraplegia** noun, medicine paralysis of the lower half of the body, usually caused by injury or disease to the spinal cord; from *para-* 'alongside' + *plege* 'blow'.

▲ **inane** adjective silly.

▲ **marginalise** verb to push something or someone to the edges of anything (especially of society or one's consciousness), in order to reduce its or their effect, relevance, significance.

▲ **aftermath** noun circumstances that follow and are a result of something, especially a great and terrible event.

▲ **mar** verb (**marred, marring**) to spoil something.

▲ **mundane** adjective ordinary, dull, everyday.

▲ **furore** noun a general outburst of excitement or indignation in reaction to something; from Latin *furor* 'frenzy'.

the Olympic team came up and asked me why I wasn't on the stage. So did Kate Hoey, the Minister for Sport. Steve Redgrave and Matthew Pinset admitted they had both considered how appropriate it would have been to carry me on to the stage. I was glad they didn't. It's not that I've got a problem with a couple of lads manhandling me but, if they had done that, there wouldn't have been the massive outcry that followed. Suddenly the ramp was a major issue. The BBC was flooded with complaints. *Points of View* had its biggest ever postbag that week and it made all the national papers.

I wasn't angry about the lack of a ramp at the time and I'm not angry now. It wasn't malicious on the part of the BBC. They just didn't think. I did an incredible number of interviews about it in the week or so afterwards and I said the same thing in each one. 'These things happen. It was an oversight, that's all.' The BBC thought they could get away with it but things had changed. Disabled athletes could no longer be marginalised and stuck away in a corner. That night at the BBC highlighted the shift in attitudes towards disabled sport in the aftermath of Sydney.

Afterwards, the BBC produced a thorough report detailing how they should treat disabled people. Now, when I reflect on what happened, I am so glad that there wasn't a ramp there. It was such a positive mistake. I got my letter of apology and I am absolutely convinced that the BBC will not make the same error again. But two years ago there would not have been the same reaction. It was exciting to see just how many people rang in to complain and the fact that a good proportion of them were non-disabled showed how much the Paralympics had moved on. Disability had been thrust into the spotlight and it was a huge boost for the overall picture as well as my own profile.

People expect me to be furious and bitter that my big night was marred, but I'm not. Instead, I was hugely encouraged that such a mundane thing could spark such an outcry. Winning the award and the furore that followed made me appreciate just how far I had come, but it had been a long, long road ...

From Prologue to Seize the Day: My Autobiography *by Tanni Grey-Thompson with Rick Broadbent*

▶ Read the Prologue to Tanni Grey-Thompson's autobiography on pages 148–149.

This unit is all about facilities in your area for people who are disabled, and how to write a report on the issue. You will notice that the BBC produced a **report** *after* the *Sports Personality of the Year* programme had been broadcast. Obviously it is preferable in this situation if a report can be written in advance, and then acted on, so that possible problems can be avoided.

Reports can be produced to anticipate and avoid problems, or they can be produced after things have gone wrong to make recommendations on how to avoid mistakes on other occasions.

In the case of the report you will be writing, facilities in your area for people who are disabled have probably been changing steadily over the years. For the purposes of this report, you will need to say what the situation is now, and suggest possible improvements.

8 REPORT WRITING

Background to a report

1 Clarifying what a 'report' can be

▶ The word **report** is sometimes used to describe entries in reference books. For example:
The nightingale is a bird of the species ...
However, you are more likely to find the word **report** used in these ways:
a In English lessons, the word **report** is used to describe the kind of writing you will be exploring in this unit: investigating and giving some facts about a situation for a particular audience and making a recommendation.
b In Science lessons, you might write a **report** on an experiment, and this will probably have a very different pattern and layout.
c The word **report** is also used for newspaper reports, especially for a topical news story, such as the story about Tanni Grey-Thompson at the *Sports Personality of the Year* award ceremony, which 'made all the national papers'. A less immediately topical item might be called a newspaper **article** – such as an article on the way children's use of English is changing (*Level Best 1*, Unit 8).
d Mention a school **report**, and a completely different kind of text comes to mind.

WORDS

▲ **report** *noun*
1 a detailed statement, description or account, especially one made after some form of investigation. **2** an account of some matter of news or a topical story.
3 a statement of a pupil's work and behaviour at school, usually made at the end of each school year or each term.

2 Researching the background for a report

▶ Find out enough to write a five-line entry in a biographical dictionary for *one* of the following:
- Jack Ashley
- David Blunkett
- Tanni Grey-Thompson
- Stephen Hawking
- Heather Mills
- Emma Nicholson
- Christopher Reeve
- Simon Weston

▶ Keep a record of where you find the information as well as what you find out.
▶ Prepare to give the information as a short presentation to the class.

You could use this example of a biographical entry as a model:

ADVICE

▲ The definition of 'report' that you should use for this unit is the first one. This mentions 'some form of investigation', and this is what you will be doing first.

ABBOTT, Diane Julie
(1953–   )
English politician. Educated at Harrow City Girls' School and Newnham College, Cambridge, she was an administration trainee in the civil service before working for the National Council for Civil Liberties, the Greater London Council (GLC) and Lambeth Borough Council. She joined the Labour party in 1971 and served on the Westminster City Council 1982–6. Elected to parliament as MP for Hackney North and Stoke Newington in 1987, she became the first black woman member of the House of Commons.

Changing places

3 Planning for writing a report

In this unit you will be writing a report on facilities for people who are disabled in the area where you live and the area where you go to school. For the purposes of this report, think about any ways people could be helped that are not available at present, as well as making a note of good ideas that already exist and which could be copied in other places.

Investigation stage

You will need to find out more information before you start your report. This could involve:

- discussing the issue with other people
- interviewing a person who is disabled about how they view the situation in the local area
- noticing any problems that people who are disabled might face in your local area and making a note of **where** it is and **what** the problem is.

ADVICE

▲ If you have not had experience of being in a wheelchair, talk to someone who has that experience, or imagine what it would be like on a typical day when you go to school/go shopping/go to the cinema/use public transport.

▶ Do you ever use the words 'blind', 'deaf' or 'dumb' as insults?
▶ What is your opinion of using these words in this way?

WORDS

▲ **curb** *noun* a raised edge or border; *North America* a kerb.
▲ **dropped curb** *noun* a sloping gradient usually replacing a sharp vertical curb.
▲ **ramp** *noun* a sloping surface between two different levels, especially one that can be used instead of steps.
▲ **tail lift** *noun* platform, usually at the back of a vehicle, which can be lowered to ground level; this enables wheelchair users to stay in their wheelchair while being transported.

ADVICE

▲ You could start taking a selection of photographs of problems or solutions, which you could then use to illustrate your report.
▲ Alternatively you could draw diagrams or cartoons to illustrate problems or solutions.

WORDS

▲ **blind** *adjective* **1** not able to see. **2** unable or unwilling to understand or appreciate something unwelcome or undesirable.
▲ **deaf** *adjective* **1** unable to hear at all or unable to hear well. **2** not willing to listen to advice, appeals, criticism, etc.
▲ **disabled** *adjective* said of a person having a physical or mental handicap.
▲ **dumb** *adjective* **1** not having the power of speech. **2** *colloquial, especially US* foolish, unintelligent.
Some of the above uses of the words are derogatory.
▲ **derogatory** *adjective* showing, or intended to show, disapproval, dislike, scorn or lack of respect.

8 REPORT WRITING

Content of a report

4 Using close observations to generate ideas

For this activity it will help if you 'get into the skin' of the people whose point of view you are considering.

- Look at the photographs opposite. Identify any problems that people who are disabled might have in each case, or any help they are being given. For each photograph, think about different groups and what problems might arise/what solutions are provided.
- Now draw up a list of groups of people you could consider, starting with those in the table below. Think of particular groups who might have particular problems, e.g. young and disabled people attending the local school.
- Draw up a second list of possible problems in public areas (outside the home), starting with those in the table below.

Group of people	Possible areas causing problems
People who are partially hearing/deaf	Crossing roads
	Doorways/Emergency exits
People who are partially sighted/blind	Emergency exits
	Gradients – how steep a ramp is
	Pavement curbs/steps/stairs
People who use wheelchairs for mobility	Public transport
	Ramps/gradients – how steep a ramp is
Young and disabled people	Shops, pubs, cinemas, libraries, banks, eating places
	Using local schools

> **WORDS**
> ▲ **get into someone's skin** to try to imagine what it would be like to experience life from that person's point of view.

> **ADVICE**
> ▲ Start with the ideas listed in the table on the left, but:
> • Be more precise – what exactly could cause the problems, and for whom?
> • Add any extra ideas you think are worth considering.

5 Using lateral thinking to generate solutions

- For each problem you have identified so far, and any others you now think of, imagine what solutions might be possible. This may be a solution you have seen being used, or a solution you come up with in your group.
- Use a table like the one below, using as many rows as you need.

Problem	Possible solutions
1 Pavement curbs too high for	At pedestrian crossing points, have a smooth slope rather than a sharp, high edge wheelchair users – a dropped curb
2	

> **ADVICE**
> ▲ Don't be too critical of each other at this stage – think laterally.
> ▲ Include existing solutions as well as new solutions.

> **WORDS**
> ▲ **lateral thinking** *noun* a form of thinking which seeks new and unusual ways of approaching and solving problems, and does not merely proceed by logical steps from the starting point of what is known or believed.

> **ADVICE**
> ▲ In the table you will probably be writing in note form. Keep the best ideas for your actual report, but remember that in this you will need to write in full sentences, not in note form.

152

Changing places

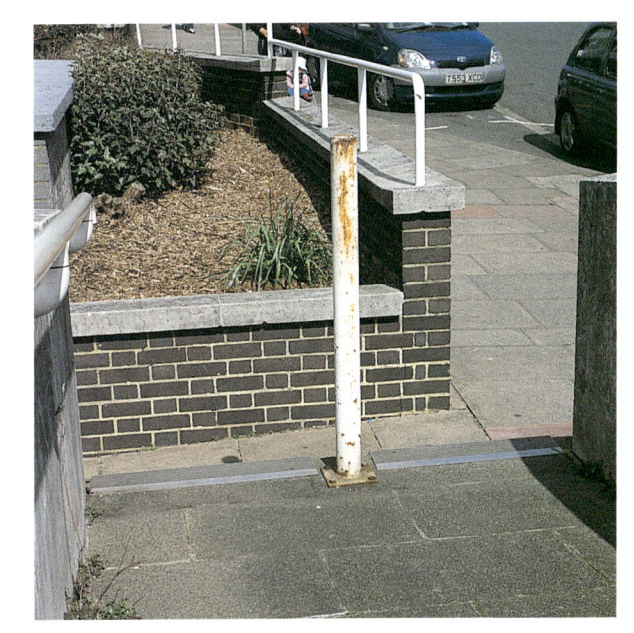

153

8 REPORT WRITING

6 Planning the structure of your report

The activities so far should have helped you to explore the kinds of areas your report could cover. You are now at the stage when you can begin to organise these ideas more logically and systematically.

▶ List each problem you have identified according to the group of people most affected by that problem. For example, the roadside curb is probably of most concern to wheelchair users.

▶ Start with the groups listed in the table below, but add others as you find you need to.

People who are partially hearing/deaf	People who are partially sighted/blind	People who use wheelchairs to get around	People who have problems with arthritis etc.	Young and disabled people

Now see how your report could have a different structure if you used a different way of organising your ideas.

▶ List the problems according to the places where they arise.

Roads/streets and pavements	Public transport	Shops, pubs, cinemas, etc.	Access to and inside local schools

▶ Which organisation of ideas did you find easier to work on?
▶ Which organisation of ideas would work better in your report?
▶ What other ways of organising the ideas can you think of?

7 Planning the content of a report

▶ Place the following parts of a report into the order you think is most logical.
   A Date, and name of author of report (i.e. your name)
   B Introduction, including who the report is being prepared for and why
   C Possible solutions to problems
   D Recommendation
   E The present situation
   F Title
▶ Where would the items in Activity 6 occur in this contents list?

ADVICE

▲ In writing your report you may find it helpful to use subheadings. These could match the organisation of ideas you have decided would work best for you from Activity 6.

154

Changing places

Compilation of a report

8 Preparing to write a report

You should already have a fairly clear idea of what you want to include in your report. The details below summarise the essential points you need to have in mind.

▶ You have been asked to write a report for the local council on facilities for people who are disabled in your local area. This should include an investigation of:
- access to buildings such as schools, libraries, hospitals, cinemas, shops
- issues surrounding the inside of buildings open to the public, e.g. ease of access through doorways, access if there are steps, availability of lifts
- ease of use of public transport – buses/trams/trains, etc.

You should include:
- descriptions/photos/diagrams/cartoons of actual problems for people who are disabled in your area
- descriptions/photos/diagrams/cartoons of good examples of provision for people who are disabled inside or outside your area
- recommendations for how the situation can be improved.

▶ Choose a layout that suits the kind of report you want to make. Whatever you choose, the basic sequence for your report should be:
- Clear title for your report
- Statement of the aim of the report – to report to the local council on existing facilities for people who are disabled and what needs to be done to improve matters
- Areas causing problems
- Possible solutions
- Recommendations
- Date and author's (your) name.

> **ADVICE**
>
> ▲ What is the difference between 'Possible solutions' and 'Recommendations'?
> - In the 'Possible solutions' section of the report, you should be coming up with plenty of ideas for the types of changes that would help people who are disabled. These should match the problems you have identified in the 'Areas causing problems' section.
> - In the 'Recommendations' section of your report, you need to be more **selective**: which changes do you think are the **most** important or urgent or cost-effective? Rank these top recommendations in order of priority, making clear why you have come to your decisions.

9 Style guide

One of the most difficult things to get right in a report is the style. For example, in a report you should not use 'I'. This activity is designed to show you how you can write in the kind of style that is appropriate for a report.

Passive and active

It is a good idea to say who should do what, and not suggest 'they' should do something, when the reader is not clear who 'they' refers to. (You may not be sure who is responsible yourself.) However, in some cases it is helpful not to state who is responsible. In this case, you can use the **passive voice**.

Active voice	Passive voice
They should construct a ramp to allow access without using steps.	A ramp should be constructed to allow access without using steps.
We definitely need a lift at this location.	If a lift was provided at this location, access would be much more straightforward.
Blind people have no special traffic lights at this crossing.	No special traffic lights have been provided for blind people at this crossing.

8 REPORT WRITING

Appropriate style

Match one sentence in the left-hand column with its equivalent in the right-hand column.

Active voice	Passive voice
1 I don't think anyone should have to put up with this.	A The need to make the public more aware of possible problems is proved by examples of people who are blind tripping over objects such as bicycles left on pavements.
2 I saw a blind lady tripping over a bicycle that had been left lying on the pavement by someone with no consideration for others.	B It is strongly recommended that the highest priority should be given to these proposals.
3 I think the present situation is an absolute disgrace.	C Evidence gathered during the investigation stage of this report revealed that lack of lifts at some schools prevents some people who use wheelchairs from attending their local school.
4 My friend who uses a wheelchair to get around can't come to our school as there aren't any lifts.	D Many aspects of the present situation give cause for serious concern.
5 These are brilliant ideas and should be acted on NOW!!	E Some people who are disabled are clearly having to cope with an intolerable situation.

Here are some sentences from reports written by pupils who have tackled this unit. These sentences have been chosen because they do not match the requirements of report writing.

▶ Match up each sentence in the left-hand column with advice for change in the right-hand column:

Sentences not in report style	Advice on report writing
1 On road crossings there are lights but no sounds to let you know when to cross.	A Write in full sentences, not in note form.
2 But would you feel safe being carried up and down the stairs?	B Use the passive voice rather than the active voice at times.
3 Evidence gathered shows us some of the problems faced by people who are partially sighted.	C Use a formal rather than a conversational style.
4 We definitely need a lift at this location.	D Explain who 'they' refers to.
5 No special traffic lights for blind people.	E Avoid using second person pronoun.
6 If an alarm went off, they couldn't hear it.	F Avoid using questions and exclamations.
7 At a pedestrian crossing, have a slight slope instead of a sharp, high-edged curb.	G Avoid using first person singular or plural pronouns.
8 People who're blind also have a few problems.	H Avoid using first person singular or plural pronouns.

10 The not-causing-offence guide

People who are disabled are, very naturally, sensitive about the way they refer to themselves and the way others refer to them. The terms that are found acceptable do change, but you could use the following guidelines unless you have good reasons for choosing a different form of words.

Don't write …	Do write …
deaf and dumb	*(deaf:)* people who are partially hearing/people who are hard of hearing/people who have a hearing problem/people who are deaf/people who are hearing impaired
	or *(dumb:)* people (not deaf) with a speech problem
spastic	people with cerebral palsy
suffering from …	having …
the disabled	people who are disabled

People who are 'hearing impaired' range from the partially hearing, who hear varying degrees of speech sounds, to people who are profoundly deaf, who may only hear one or two speech sounds. People who have *no* hearing are *not* 'partially hearing' or 'hard of hearing', and they may wish to be referred to as 'deaf'. This is obviously an area where you must be very aware of what other readers may think, and take extra care over the way you express yourself.

Note: The reason some people with hearing difficulties were labelled 'deaf and dumb' was that because they couldn't *hear* clearly they couldn't learn how to *pronounce* words clearly. People whose hearing is good learn how to speak by imitating others, and you can't imitate what you can't hear clearly.

ADVICE

▲ **Guideline:** Put *people* first! *People* who use wheelchairs, *people* who are blind, *people* who are disabled …

11 Writing a report

▶ Write a report on facilities in public places in your area for people who are disabled.

ADVICE

▲ Think clearly about:
- your audience – the local council
- your purpose – to inform of the present situation and recommend changes
- your style – formal English, not in the first person, using standard English
- the tense – use the present tense to describe the existing situation
- the layout – your text should be presented with subheadings etc. so that it looks like a report, ending with clear priorities for change.

▲ 'Your area' could include where you go to school and/or where you live.

8 REPORT WRITING

Self-assessment

12 Judging your own performance

▶ From the list below:
  a select three points on which you feel you have made the most progress
  b select one point on which you most need to improve.
  I can use research skills to find out about a person, note important facts, and name my sources.
  I can research background information for a report effectively.
  I can describe the present situation for people who are disabled in my area clearly.
  I can 'read' photographs and work out problems and solutions from them.
  I can recommend good ways for improving the situation for people who are disabled.
  I can write in a way that is not likely to cause offence.
  I can write in a style that is appropriate for a report.
  I can organise the structure of a report in an appropriate way.
  I can write in a way that is likely to inform and persuade the reader.

13 Improving your skills in English

▶ Select one or two skills you need to concentrate on to improve your skills in writing. (The descriptions of levels are a guide only.)

	Writing skill	From	To
1	Ideas are organised appropriately for a report	Level 3	Level 4
2	Writing is thoughtful, and ideas are sustained and developed in interesting ways	Level 3	Level 4
3	Writing conveys meaning clearly, using the more formal style required by a report	Level 4	Level 5
4	Vocabulary choices are imaginative and words are used precisely	Level 4	Level 5
5	Uses an impersonal style appropriate for a report	Level 5	Level 6
6	Uses a range of sentence structures and varied vocabulary to create effects	Level 5	Level 6
7	Writing is confident and shows an appropriate choice of style for a report	Level 6	Level 7
8	Ideas are organised and coherent, with grammatical features and vocabulary accurately and effectively used	Level 6	Level 7
9	Writing is coherent and gives a clear point of view	Level 7	Level 8
10	The use of vocabulary and grammar enables fine distinctions to be made or emphasis achieved	Level 7	Level 8
11	Writing has shape and impact, and control of the style appropriate for a report	Level 8	E.P.
12	The report is coherent, reasoned and persuasive	Level 8	E.P.

9 Creating and shaping stories
The Monkey's Paw

Your focus
The content of this unit is designed to:
- help you understand the choices authors make to create effects
- give you the skills to use the same techniques yourself.

Your target
By the end of this unit you should be more able to:
- recognise techniques that writers use in narrative
- appreciate the wider context in which a story is written
- write an effective story of your own.

Your move

- Reading
- Writing
- 11 Improving your skills in English
- 10 Judging your own performance
- Self-assessment
- Independent writing
- 9 Writing and commenting on your own story
- Introduction
- 1 Exploring techniques writers use in fiction
- 2 Reading between the lines
- The Monkey's Paw 1
- 3 Exploring the structure of the story
- 4 Mapping the tension in the story
- **Creating and shaping stories**
- The Monkey's Paw 2
- 8 Exploring endings
- 7 Exploring the wider context
- 5 Exploring adverbs
- 6 Exploring point of view

9 CREATING AND SHAPING STORIES

Introduction

1 Exploring techniques writers use in fiction

The following is the opening of a novel by Jan Mark, *Heathrow Nights*.
▶ Read it for enjoyment, then explore any techniques you think Jan Mark is using here to make your reading more enjoyable.
▶ Make a note of the line reference, the relevant quotation, the technique if relevant, and be ready to comment to the other groups on the effect of the quotations you have selected.

> **WORDS**
>
> ▲ **intercept** *verb* to stop, deflect or seize on the way from one place to another. *Sport* to seize or cut off (a pass) on its way from one opponent to another.
> ▲ **honcho** *noun, chiefly North American, informal* an important man; a boss.

One

We intercepted the letters. I don't know if the others read theirs, I opened mine standing there in the hall, with the rest of the envelopes on the carpet, fanned out, face down, just as they had been when they landed. With a criminal instinct I didn't know I possessed I'd marked all their positions before I scooped them up, picked out mine and put them back again.

Only it wasn't mine.

I started to take it out of the envelope addressed to Mrs S. Jagger, with the school's name printed along the top, the school not having yet caught up with the fact that she is no longer Mrs S. Jagger but Mrs S. Hague. The school, in the person of the head honcho McPherson, has a lot of catching up to do. If he wanted to avoid people like me doing what I was at that very moment doing, he should have used a plain envelope. If he had *really* thought about it he'd have used e-mail, but for all the stuff about IT in the prospectus, and the hardware cluttering up the place, bad news still goes out on paper and falls into the hands of promising crims: me, Curtis and Adam. Very bad news, all three of us.

Mr Hague and the new Mrs Hague were still in bed, it being Saturday, but Mum was sure to have heard the postman crashing about, so I didn't stop to read McPherson's letter, I just glanced at the first lines: *Dear Mrs Jagger, I regret to inform you that your son Russell ...*

I knew the rest. McPherson had given it to us in very plain prose the previous morning. Overhead the floorboards creaked. Mum was getting up, fairy-footed. Hague hits the mat like boots dropping from a great height. I slid the letter back into the envelope and tore it across, from top to bottom, the two halves into four, the four into eight. After that it wouldn't tear, but by then Mum was closing the bathroom door and I was in the kitchen, filling the kettle.

When she came downstairs I was ladling coffee into the cafetière, laying out biscuits. I heard her go along the hall to pick up the post; seven envelopes, a Jiffy bag and a magazine, shrink-wrapped to keep the germs out. *The* letter was not there, it never had been, it did not exist. There were some scraps of paper in my back pocket, to be disposed of later. Can't imagine where they came from, it's amazing the junk that collects in back pockets.

Mum came into the kitchen, already sorting the mail into his'n'hers. 'Nothing for you, sorry.' There never is anything for me. Then she saw what I was doing. 'Coffee in bed? Oh, Russ, that's nice of you.'

5

10

15

20

25

▶ What are the most important pieces of information the author includes in this opening, do you think? Select five, and be prepared to defend your choice.
▶ Make predictions for what you think might happen later in the story. You must start with evidence from the opening of the novel printed above.

The Monkey's Paw   W. W. Jacobs

1

Without the night was cold and wet, but in the small parlour of Laburnum Villa the blinds were drawn and the fire burned brightly. Father and son were at chess, the former, who possessed ideas about the game involving radical changes, putting his king into such sharp and unnecessary perils that it even provoked comment from the white-haired old lady knitting placidly by the fire.

'Hark at the wind,' said Mr White, who, having seen a fatal mistake after it was too late, was amiably desirous of preventing his son from seeing it.

'I'm listening,' said the son, grimly surveying the board as he stretched out his hand. 'Check.'

'I should hardly think he'd come tonight,' said his father, with his hand poised over the board.

'Mate,' replied the son.

'That's the worst of living so far out,' bawled Mr White, with sudden and unlooked-for violence; 'of all the beastly, slushy, out-of-the-way places to live in, this is the worst. Pathway's a bog, and the road's a torrent. I don't know what people are thinking about. I suppose because only two houses in the road are let, they think it doesn't matter.'

'Never mind, dear,' said his wife, soothingly; 'perhaps you'll win the next one.'

Mr White looked up sharply, just in time to intercept a knowing glance between mother and son. The words died away on his lips, and he hid a guilty grin in his thin grey beard.

'There he is,' said Herbert White, as the gate banged to loudly and heavy footsteps came towards the door.

The old man rose with hospitable haste, and opening the door, was heard condoling with the new arrival. The new arrival also condoled with himself, so that Mrs White said, 'Tut, Tut!' and coughed gently as her husband entered the room, followed by a tall, burly man, beady of eye and rubicund of visage.

'Sergeant-Major Morris,' he said, introducing him.

The sergeant-major shook hands, and taking the proffered seat by the fire, watched contentedly while his host got out whisky and tumblers and stood a small copper kettle on the fire.

At the third glass his eyes got brighter, and he began to talk, the little family circle regarding with eager interest this visitor from distant parts, as he squared his broad shoulders in the chair and spoke of wild scenes and doughty deeds; of wars and plagues and strange peoples.

'Twenty-one years of it,' said Mr White, nodding at his wife and son. 'When he went away he was a slip of a youth in the warehouse. Now look at him.'

'He don't look to have taken much harm,' said Mrs White, politely.

'I'd like to go to India myself,' said the old man, 'just to look round a bit, you know.'

'Better where you are,' said the sergeant-major, shaking his head. He put down the empty glass, and sighing softly, shook his head again.

'I should like to see those old temples and fakirs and jugglers,' said the old man. 'What was that you started telling me the other day about a monkey's paw or something, Morris?'

'Nothing,' said the soldier, hastily. 'Leastways nothing worth hearing.'

WORDS

▲ **without** *preposition archaic* on the outside (of). 1
▲ **hark** *verb* to listen to it or them attentively. 5
▲ **intercept** *verb* to stop, deflect or seize on the way from one place to another. 15
▲ **bang to** *verb* shut with a loud noise. 17
▲ **condole** *verb* (followed by *with*) to express sympathy with someone in grief, pain, etc. 19
▲ **rubicund** *adjective* reddish colour. 22
▲ **visage** *noun* the face. 22
▲ **doughty** *adjective* hardy, resolute. 28
▲ **fakir** *noun* holy man. 35
▲ **leastways** *adverb informal* at least, anyway, at any rate. 37

9 CREATING AND SHAPING STORIES

'Monkey's paw?' said Mrs White, curiously.

'Well, it's just a bit of what you might call magic, perhaps,' said the sergeant-major, offhandedly.

His three listeners leaned forward eagerly. The visitor absent-mindedly put his empty glass to his lips and then set it down again. His host filled it for him.

'To look at,' said the sergeant-major, fumbling in his pocket, 'it's just an ordinary little paw, dried to a mummy.'

He took something out of his pocket and proffered it. Mrs White drew back with a grimace, but her son, taking it, examined it curiously.

'And what is there special about it?' inquired Mr White as he took it from his son, and having examined it, placed it upon the table.

'It had a spell put on it by an old fakir,' said the sergeant-major, ' a very holy man. He wanted to show that fate ruled people's lives, and that those who interfered with it did so to their sorrow. He put a spell on it so that three separate men could each have three wishes from it.'

His manner was so impressive that his hearers were conscious that their light laughter jarred somewhat.

'Well, why don't you have three, sir?' said Herbert White, cleverly.

The soldier regarded him in the way that middle age is wont to regard presumptuous youth. 'I have,' he said quietly, and his blotchy face whitened.

'And did you really have the three wishes granted?' asked Mrs White.

'I did,' said the sergeant-major, and his glass tapped against his strong teeth.

'And has anybody else wished?' persisted the old lady.

'The first man had his three wishes. Yes,' was the reply; 'I don't know what the first two were, but the third was for death. That's how I got the paw.'

His tones were so grave that a hush fell upon the group.

'If you've had your three wishes, it's no good to you now, then, Morris,' said the old man at last. 'What do you keep it for?'

The soldier shook his head. 'Fancy, I suppose,' he said, slowly. 'I did have some idea of selling it, but I don't think I will. It has caused enough mischief already. Besides, people won't buy. They think it's a fairy tale, some of them; and those who do think anything of it want to try it first and pay me afterwards.'

'If you could have another three wishes,' said the old man, eyeing him keenly, 'would you have them?'

'I don't know,' said the other. 'I don't know.'

He took the paw, and dangling it between his forefinger and thumb, suddenly threw it upon the fire. White, with a slight cry, stooped down and snatched it off.

'Better let it burn,' said the soldier solemnly.

'If you don't want it, Morris,' said the other, 'give it to me.'

'I won't,' said his friend, doggedly. 'I threw it on the fire. If you keep it, don't blame me for what happens. Pitch it on the fire again like a sensible man.'

The other shook his head and examined his new possession closely. 'How do you do it?' he inquired.

WORDS

▲ **proffer** *verb* to offer for acceptance. 44
▲ **grimace** *noun* distorted facial expression, as from disgust. 44
▲ **wish** *noun* something desired or hoped for. 50
▲ **wont** *adjective* accustomed (to do something). 54
▲ **presumptuous** *adjective* bold, forward. 54
▲ **doggedly** *adverb* in an obstinately determined way. 75

The Monkey's Paw

'Hold it up in your right hand and wish aloud,' said the sergeant-major, 'but I warn you of the consequences.'

'Sounds like the *Arabian Nights*,' said Mrs White, as she rose and began to set the supper. 'Don't you think you might wish for four pairs of hands for me?'

Her husband drew the talisman from his pocket, and then all three burst into laughter as the sergeant-major, with a look of alarm on his face, caught him by the arm.

'If you must wish,' he said, gruffly, 'wish for something sensible.'

Mr White dropped it back in his pocket, and placing chairs, motioned his friend to the table. In the business of supper the talisman was partly forgotten, and afterward the three sat listening in an enthralled fashion to a second instalment of the soldier's adventures in India.

'If the tale about the monkey's paw is not more truthful than those he has been telling us,' said Herbert, as the door closed behind their guest, just in time for him to catch the last train, 'we sha'n't make much out of it.'

'Did you give him anything for it, father?' inquired Mrs White, regarding her husband closely.

'A trifle,' said he, colouring slightly. 'He didn't want it, but I made him take it. And he pressed me again to throw it away.'

'Likely,' said Herbert, with pretended horror. 'Why, we're going to be rich, and famous and happy. Wish to be an emperor, father, to begin with: then you can't be henpecked.'

He darted round the table, pursued by the maligned Mrs White, armed with an antimacassar.

Mr White took the paw from his pocket and eyed it dubiously. 'I don't know what to wish for, and that's a fact,' he said, slowly. 'It seems to me I've got all I want.'

'If you only cleared the house, you'd be quite happy, wouldn't you?' said Herbert, with his hand on his shoulder. 'Well, wish for two hundred pounds, then; that'll just do it.'

His father, smiling shamefacedly at his own credulity, held up the talisman, as his son, with a solemn face, somewhat marred by a wink at his mother, sat down at the piano and struck a few impressive chords.

'I wish for two hundred pounds,' said the old man distinctly.

A fine crash from the piano greeted the words, interrupted by a shuddering cry from the old man. His wife and son ran towards him.

'It moved,' he cried, with a glance of disgust at the object as it lay on the floor. 'As I wished, it twisted in my hand like a snake.'

'Well, I don't see the money,' said his son, as he picked it up and placed it on the table, 'and I bet I never shall.'

'It must have been your fancy, father,' said his wife, regarding him anxiously.

He shook his head. 'Never mind, though; there's no harm done, but it gave me a shock all the same.'

They sat down by the fire again while the two men finished their pipes. Outside, the wind was higher than ever, and the old man started nervously at the sound of a door banging upstairs. A silence unusual and depressing settled upon all three, which lasted until the old couple rose to retire for the night.

WORDS

▲ **talisman** *noun* stone or other small object, supposed to have magic powers to protect its owner from evil, bring good luck or work magic. 83

▲ **henpecked** *adjective* harassed and tormented by persistent nagging, especially a man by his wife. 96

▲ **malign** *verb* slander or defame. 97

▲ **antimacassar** *noun* a covering for the back of a chair to stop it getting dirty; *anti* = preventing + *macassar* an oil once used on hair. cf. *antifreeze, antilock system*. 97

▲ **shamefacedly** *adverb* acting in a way that shows a sense of shame. 102

▲ **credulity** *noun* tendency to believe something on little evidence, gullibility. 102

9 CREATING AND SHAPING STORIES

'I expect you'll find the cash tied up in a big bag in the middle of your bed,' said Herbert, as he bade them goodnight, 'and something horrible squatting up on top of your wardrobe watching you as you pocket your ill-gotten gains.'

He sat alone in the darkness, gazing at the dying fire, and seeing faces in it. The last face was so horrible and so simian that he gazed at it in amazement. It got so vivid that, with a little uneasy laugh, he felt on the table for a glass containing a little water to throw over it. His hand grasped the monkey's paw, and with a little shiver he wiped his hand on his coat and went up to bed.

2

In the brightness of the wintry sun next morning as it streamed over the breakfast table he laughed at his fears. There was an air of prosaic wholesomeness about the room which it had lacked on the previous night, and the dirty, shrivelled little paw was pitched on the sideboard with a carelessness which betokened no great belief in its virtues.

'I suppose all old soldiers are the same,' said Mrs White. 'The idea of our listening to such nonsense! How could wishes be granted in these days. And if they could, how could two hundred pounds hurt you, father?'

'Might drop on his head from the sky,' said the frivolous Herbert.

'Morris said the things happened so naturally,' said his father, 'that you might if you so wished attribute it to coincidence.'

'Well, don't break into the money before I come back,' said Herbert as he rose from the table. 'I'm afraid it'll turn you into a mean, avaricious man, and we shall have to disown you.'

His mother laughed, and following him to the door, watched him down the road; and returning to the breakfast table, was very happy at the expense of her husband's credulity. All of which did not prevent her from scurrying to the door at the postman's knock, nor prevent her from referring somewhat shortly to retired sergeant-majors of bibulous habits when she found that the post brought a tailor's bill.

'Herbert will have some more of his funny remarks, I expect, when he comes home,' she said, as they sat at dinner.

'I dare say,' said Mr White, pouring himself out some beer; 'but for all that, the thing moved in my hand; that I'll swear to.'

'You thought it did,' said the old lady soothingly.

'I say it did,' replied the other. 'There was no thought about it; I had just – What's the matter?'

His wife made no reply. She was watching the mysterious movements of a man outside, who, peering in an undecided fashion at the house, appeared to be trying to make up his mind to enter. In mental connection with the two hundred pounds, she noticed that the stranger was well dressed, and wore a silk hat of glossy newness. Three times he paused at the gate, and then walked on again. The fourth time he stood with his hand upon it, and then with sudden resolution flung it open and walked up the path. Mrs White at the same moment placed her hands behind her, and hurriedly unfastening the strings of her apron, put that useful article of apparel beneath the cushion of her chair.

She brought the stranger, who seemed ill at ease, into the room. He gazed at her furtively, and listened in a preoccupied fashion as the old lady apologized for the appearance of the room, and

WORDS

▲ **simian** *adjective* resembling a monkey or ape. 123
▲ **prosaic** *adjective* lacking imagination, matter-of-fact. 127
▲ **wholesomeness** *noun* having the properties of healthiness. 127
▲ **betoken** *verb* indicate, signify. 129
▲ **avaricious** *adjective* extreme greed for money. 137
▲ **bibulous** *adjective, humorous* liking alcohol too much, or drinking too much of it. 141
▲ **apparel** *noun* clothing. 155

her husband's coat, a garment which he usually reserved for the garden. She then waited as patiently as her sex would permit, for him to broach his business, but he was at first strangely silent.

'I – was asked to call,' he said at last, and stooped and picked a piece of cotton from his trousers. 'I come from Maw and Meggins.'

The old lady started. 'Is anything the matter?' she asked breathlessly. 'Has anything happened to Herbert? What is it? What is it?'

Her husband interposed. 'There, there, mother,' he said, hastily. 'Sit down, and don't jump to conclusions. You've not brought bad news, I'm sure, sir,' and he eyed the other wistfully.

'I'm sorry – ' began the visitor.

'Is he hurt?' demanded the mother, wildly.

The visitor bowed in assent. 'Badly hurt,' he said, quietly, 'but he is not in any pain.'

'Oh, thank God!' said the old woman, clasping her hands. 'Thank God for that! Thank –'

She broke off suddenly as the sinister meaning of the assurance dawned upon her and she saw the awful confirmation of her fears in the other's perverted face. She caught her breath, and turning to her slower-witted husband, laid her trembling old hand upon his. There was a long silence.

'He was caught in the machinery,' said the visitor at length in a low voice.

'Caught in the machinery,' repeated Mr White, in a dazed fashion, 'yes.'

He sat staring blankly out at the window, and taking his wife's hand between his own, pressed it as he had been wont to do in their old courting days nearly forty years before.

'He was the only one left to us,' he said, turning gently to the visitor. 'It is hard.'

The other coughed, and rising, walked slowly to the window. 'The firm wished me to convey their sincere sympathy with you in your great loss,' he said, without looking around. 'I beg that you will understand I am only their servant and merely obeying orders.'

There was no reply; the old woman's face was white, her eyes staring, and her breath inaudible; and on the husband's face was a look such as his friend the sergeant-major might have carried into his first action.

'I was to say that Maw and Meggins disclaim all responsibility,' continued the other. 'They admit no liability at all, but in consideration of your son's services, they wish to present you with a certain sum as compensation.'

Mr White dropped his wife's hand, and rising to his feet, gazed with a look of horror at his visitor. His dry lips shaped the words, 'How much?'

'Two hundred pounds,' was the answer.

Unconscious of his wife's shriek, the old man smiled faintly, put out his hands like a sightless man, and dropped, a senseless heap, to the floor.

3

In the huge new cemetery, some two miles distant, the old people buried their dead, and came back to a house steeped in shadow and silence. It was all over so quickly that at first they could hardly realise it, and remained in a state of expectation as though of something else to happen – something else which was to lighten this load, too heavy for old hearts to bear.

But the days passed, and expectation gave place to resignation – the hopeless resignation of the old, sometimes miscalled apathy. Sometimes they hardly exchanged a word, for now they had

---

WORDS

▲ **garment** *noun* an article of clothing. 159
▲ **wistfully** *adverb* in a sadly thoughtful way. 167
▲ **assent** *noun* agreement. 170
▲ **assurance** *noun* statement, assertion. 172
▲ **pervert(ed)** *verb* distort(ed). 173
▲ **inaudible** *adjective* not loud enough to be heard. 183
▲ **steep(ed)** *verb* soak(ed), saturate(d). 195
▲ **apathy** *noun* absence of enthusiasm for things generally considered interesting or moving. 199

9 CREATING AND SHAPING STORIES

166

nothing to talk about, and their days were long to weariness.

It was about a week after that the old man, waking suddenly in the night, stretched out his hand and found himself alone. The room was in darkness, and the sound of subdued weeping came from the window. He raised himself in bed and listened.

'Come back,' he said, tenderly. 'You will be cold.'

'It is colder for my son,' said the old woman, and wept afresh.

The sound of her sobs died away on his ears. The bed was warm, and his eyes heavy with sleep. He dozed fitfully, and then slept until a sudden wild cry from his wife awoke him with a start.

'*The paw!*' she cried wildly. 'The monkey's paw!'

He started up in alarm. 'Where? Where is it? What's the matter?'

She came stumbling across the room towards him. 'I want it,' she said quietly. 'You've not destroyed it?'

'It's in the parlour, on the bracket,' he replied, marvelling. 'Why?'

She cried and laughed together, and bending over, kissed his cheek.

'I only just thought of it,' she said, hysterically. 'Why didn't I think of it before? Why didn't *you* think of it?'

'Think of what?' he questioned.

'The other two wishes,' she replied, rapidly. 'We've only had one.'

'Was not that enough?' he demanded, fiercely.

'No,' she cried, triumphantly; 'we'll have one more. Go down and get it quickly, and wish our boy alive again.'

The man sat up in bed and flung the bedclothes from his quaking limbs. 'Good God, you are mad!' he cried, aghast.

'Get it,' she panted; 'get it quickly, and wish – Oh, my boy, my boy!'

Her husband struck a match and lit the candle. 'Get back to bed,' he said unsteadily. 'You don't know what you are saying.'

'We had the first wish granted,' said the old woman, feverishly; 'why not the second?'

'A coincidence,' stammered the old man.

'Go and get it and wish,' cried his wife, quivering with excitement.

The old man turned and regarded her, and his voice shook. 'He has been dead ten days, and besides he – I would not tell you else, but – I could only recognise him by his clothing. If he was too terrible for you to see then, how now?'

'Bring him back,' cried the old woman, and dragged him towards the door. 'Do you think I fear the child I have nursed?'

He went down in the darkness, and felt his way to the parlour, and then to the mantelpiece. The talisman was in its place, and a horrible fear that the unspoken wish might bring his mutilated son before him ere he could escape from the room seized upon him, and he caught his breath as he found that he had lost the direction of the door. His brow cold with sweat, he felt his way round the table, and groped along the wall until he found himself in the small passage with the unwholesome thing in his hand.

Even his wife's face seemed changed as he entered the room. It was white and expectant, and to his fears seemed to have an unnatural look upon it. He was afraid of her.

'*Wish*,' she cried, in a strong voice.

WORDS

▲ **hysterically** *adverb* in an extremely emotional way. 214
▲ **quake** *verb* shake or tremble from fear. 221
▲ **aghast** *adjective* overcome with amazement or horror. 222
▲ **ere** *conjunction, old use* before. 236
▲ **unwholesome** *adjective*, harmful to physical or moral health. 239

9 CREATING AND SHAPING STORIES

'It is foolish and wicked,' he faltered.

'*Wish*!' repeated his wife.

He raised his hand. 'I wish my son alive again.'

The talisman fell to the floor, and he regarded it fearfully. Then he sank trembling into a chair as the old woman, with burning eyes, walked to the window and raised the blind.

He sat until he was chilled with the cold, glancing occasionally at the figure of the old woman peering through the window. The candle-end, which had burned below the rim of the china candlestick, was throwing pulsating shadows on the ceiling and walls, until, with a flicker larger than the rest, it expired. The old man, with an unspeakable sense of relief at the failure of the talisman, crept back to his bed, and a minute or two afterwards the old woman came silently and apathetically beside him.

Neither spoke, but lay silently listening to the ticking of the clock. A stair creaked, and a squeaky mouse scurried noisily through the wall. The darkness was oppressive, and after lying for some time screwing up his courage, he took the box of matches, and striking one, went downstairs for a candle.

At the foot of the stairs the match went out, and he paused to strike another; and at the same moment a knock, so quiet and stealthy as to be scarcely audible, sounded on the front door.

The matches fell from his hand and spilled in the passage. He stood motionless, his breath suspended until the knock was repeated. Then he turned and fled swiftly back to his room, and closed the door behind him. A third knock sounded through the house.

'What's that?' cried the old woman, starting up.

'A rat,' said the old man in shaking tones, ' – a rat. It passed me on the stairs.'

His wife sat up in bed listening. A loud knock resounded through the house.

'It's Herbert!' she screamed. 'It's Herbert!'

She ran to the door, but her husband was before her, and catching her by the arm, held her tightly.

'What are you going to do?' he whispered hoarsely.

'It's my boy; it's Herbert!' she cried, struggling mechanically. 'I forgot it was two miles away. What are you holding me for? Let go. I must open the door.'

'For God's sake don't let it in,' cried the old man, trembling.

'You're afraid of your own son,' she cried, struggling. 'Let me go. I'm coming, Herbert; I'm coming.'

There was another knock, and another. The old woman with a sudden wrench broke free and ran from the room. Her husband followed to the landing, and called after her appealingly as she hurried downstairs. He heard the chain rattle back and the bottom bolt drawn slowly and stiffly from the socket. Then the old woman's voice, strained and panting.

'The bolt,' she cried loudly. 'Come down. I can't reach it.'

But her husband was on his hands and knees groping wildly on the floor in search of the paw. If he could only find it before the thing outside got in. A perfect fusillade of knocks reverberated through the house, and he heard the scraping of a chair as his wife put it down in the passage against the door. He heard the creaking of the bolt as it came slowly back, and at the same moment he found the monkey's paw, and frantically breathed his third and last wish.

The knocking ceased suddenly, although the echoes of it were still in the house. He heard the chair drawn back, and the door opened. A cold wind rushed up the staircase, and a long loud wail of disappointment and misery from his wife gave him the courage to run down to her side, and then to the gate beyond. The street lamp flickering opposite shone on a quiet and deserted road.

WORDS

▲ **pulsate** *verb* to expand and contract rhythmically. 250

▲ **apathetically** *adverb* done in a manner expressing lack of interest or enthusiasm. 253

▲ **fusillade** *noun* simultaneous or rapid fire of guns, etc. 280

▲ **reverberate** *verb* re-echo, resound. 280

▲ **cease** *verb* end. 284

The Monkey's Paw 1

2 Reading between the lines

The first essential in developing reading skills is being able to **locate** relevant detail in the text – often referred to as 'search and find'. The next stage, which you can develop through practice, is **inference** or 'reading between the lines'.

The first activity is designed to help you practise your skills in inference. In some cases you will be asked to come up with ideas about why the author has written the text in a certain way. Of course you cannot prove why an author has written in a certain way, but it will help you develop your own skills in writing if you explore the possible reasons for shaping texts in particular ways.

An author will often use the start of a story to introduce **characters**:
- a In line 10, Mr White *bawled ... with sudden and unlooked-for violence*. What explanation does the author hint at for why he acts in this way?
- b The husband talks about the 'beastly' place they live in (line 11). The wife talks about the game of chess (line 14). Why?
- c What does the author suggest about the relationship between the mother and the son from line 15?
- d What are Mrs White's first impressions of the sergeant-major (lines 19–22)?
- e What can you tell about Mrs White from what she says and how she says it in line 31?
'He don't look to have taken much harm,' said Mrs White, politely.
- f What is the effect of the author's choice of the adverb 'hastily' in line 37?
- g The son calls the sergeant-major 'sir' (line 53), the father calls him 'Morris' (74), and the mother does not refer to him by name (lines 56, 58 etc.).
How do these three different forms of addressing the sergeant-major reflect the different relationships?
- h How does the way Herbert behaves, before the father makes the wish, show his attitude (lines 89–104)?

The opening is also an opportunity for the author to give the reader an idea of the **setting**.
- i Use lines 1–13. What kind of place do they live in? What time of day is it? Why do you think this setting has been chosen for this story?
- j Now look back at line 5. How has the author made the introduction of the setting seem natural?

The opening lines set the **mood** of the writing. In a story such as this, the writer will be aiming to create and build **suspense** and **tension**.
- k Why do you think the author doesn't tell us who the visitor is at first (line 8)?
- l What is suggested about the visitor before he appears (lines 17 and 18)?
- m When the spell is first mentioned, the hearers laugh (line 51). Why do you think the author includes this detail?
- n In what other ways does the writer build up a sense of mood and atmosphere? Track the most impressive examples throughout the story.

WORDS

▲ **inference** *noun* judgement based on facts, observation and deduction.
▲ **deduction** *noun* thinking out or judging on the basis of what one knows or assumes to be fact.
▲ **setting** *noun* the time and place in which the action of a text is described as happening.
▲ **mood** *noun* the atmosphere or feeling created by the choice of words in a text.
▲ **suspense** *noun* tension or excitement created by an eager desire to know the outcome of a plot.
▲ **tension** *noun* a feeling or state of nervous and excited anticipation or suspense.
▲ **Gothic** *adjective* belonging or relating to a type of literature dealing with mysterious or supernatural events in an eerie setting, popular in the 18th century.
▲ **eerie** *adjective* strange and disturbing or frightening.

9 CREATING AND SHAPING STORIES

3 Exploring the structure of the story

- Why do you think the story is divided into three sections? Why are the divisions at these particular places, do you think? (lines 125–126, 193–194)
- Use a table like the one below. Rate the level of tension at different points in the story:
  *0 = minimal tension, 10 = maximum tension.

> **ADVICE**
>
> ▲ The highest point of tension in the story, for you or your group, should be rated as 10

Lines	Quotation	Rating: 0–10?*
37	'Nothing,' said the soldier hastily. 'Leastways nothing worth hearing.'	
59–60	'The first man had his three wishes. Yes,' was the reply. 'I don't know what the first two were, but the third was for death. That's how I got the paw.'	
71–72	He took the paw, and dangling it between his forefinger and thumb, suddenly threw it upon the fire. White, with a slight cry, stooped down and snatched it off.	
106–107	A fine crash from the piano greeted the words, interrupted by a shuddering cry from the old man. His wife and son ran towards him.	
122–125	The last face was so horrible and so simian that he gazed at it in amazement... he felt on the table for a glass containing a little water... His hand grasped the monkey's paw...	
171	'Oh, thank God!' said the old woman, clasping her hands. 'Thank God for that! Thank –'	
191	'Two hundred pounds,' was the answer.	
219–220	'No,' she cried triumphantly; 'we'll have one more. Go down and get it quickly, and wish our boy alive again.'	
229–230	'He has been dead ten days, and besides he – I would not tell you else, but – I could only recongise him by his clothing.'	
245	He raised his hand. 'I wish my son alive again.'	
258–259	At the foot of the stairs the match went out, and he paused to strike another; and at the same moment a knock, so quiet and stealthy as to be scarcely audible, sounded on the front door.	
271	'For God's sake don't let it in,' cried the old man, trembling.	
282–283	He heard the creaking of the bolt as it came slowly back, and at the same moment he found the monkey's paw, and frantically breathed his third and last wish.	

- Are there any other key moments in the story that you think should be included in this chart? Make a note of them, as they will be helpful when you come to draw a graph of the tension at various points in the story.

The Monkey's Paw

4 Mapping tension in the story

You may have seen reviews of films which include a graph to suggest how involved the audience will be at different points in the film. A graph from the magazine *Total Film* is printed on the right. It shows the 'predicted interest curve' for the film *The Others*, starring Nicole Kidman.

▶ Draw a graph for *The Monkey's Paw*, giving an indication of the reader's pulse rate as it changes through the story.
Use a layout like the one below.

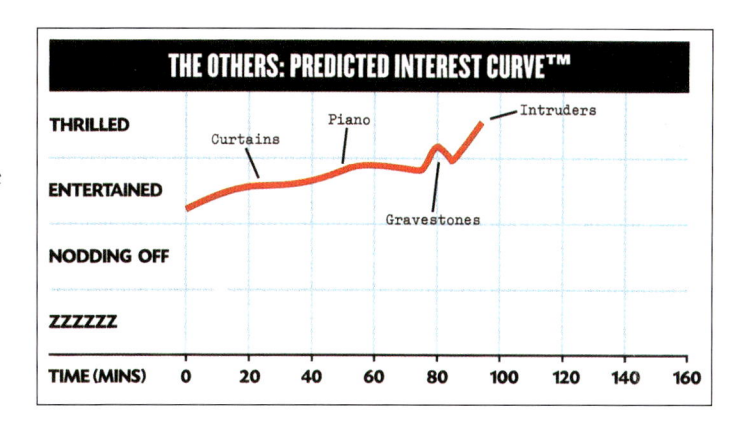

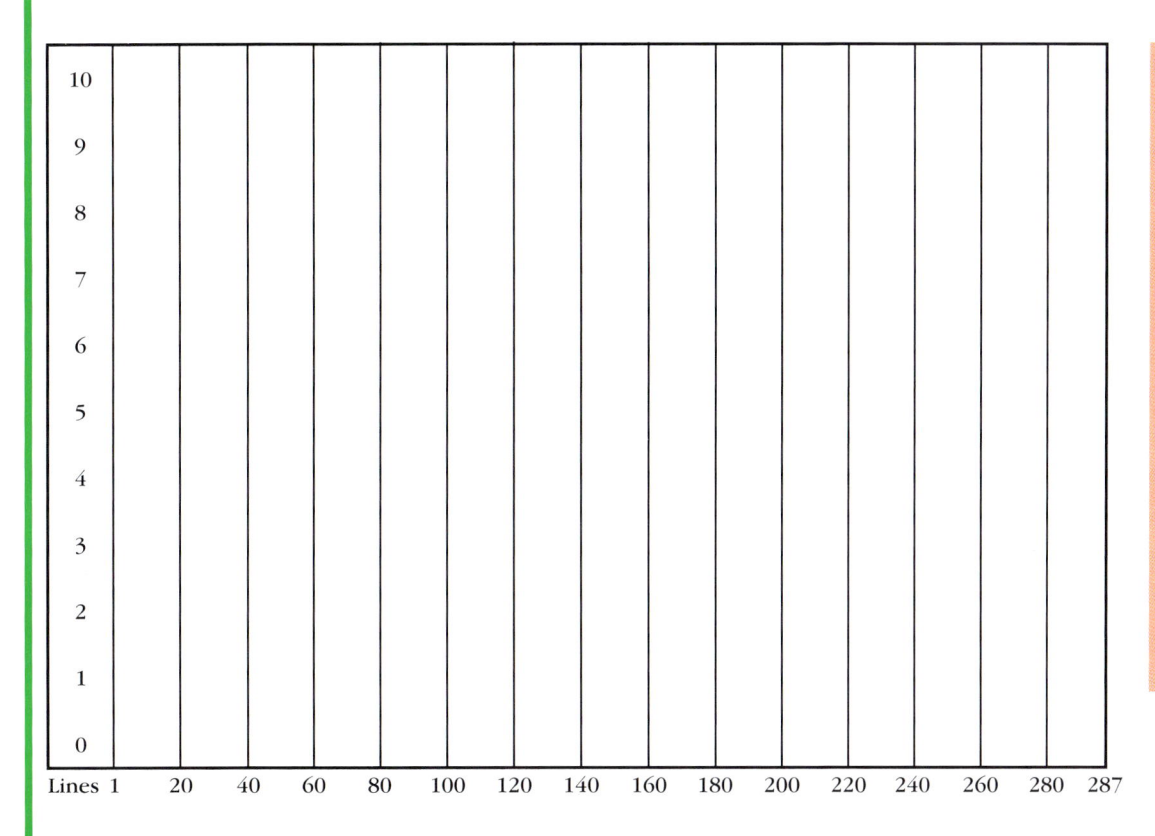

THE OTHERS: PREDICTED INTEREST CURVE™

THRILLED — Curtains, Piano, Intruders
ENTERTAINED — Gravestones
NODDING OFF
ZZZZZZ
TIME (MINS) 0 20 40 60 80 100 120 140 160

Lines 1 20 40 60 80 100 120 140 160 180 200 220 240 260 280 287
(y-axis: 0 to 10)

ADVICE
▲ The highest point of tension in the story should be shown near the top line of the graph.
▲ The graph should start in the bottom left-hand corner, imagining the situation before even the title has been read.
▲ You may like to start by plotting the ratings you have given in Activity 3 onto your own graph.

Using the ratings chart from Activity 3:
▶ Mark your ratings with a * for the given line numbers.
▶ Add any ratings for line numbers you chose in addition to those given in Activity 3.
▶ Join up the stars in pencil.
▶ Does this line represent all your reactions to the whole story?
▶ Were there any points where your pulse rate dropped that are not marked? (Think of the next morning after the visit of the soldier; the period after the son's death.)
▶ Now amend your graph to show the ups and downs – where tension is not so high as well as the high points.

▶ Could a story be kept on a high level of tension all the time?
▶ What is the effect of an author creating different levels of tension during the story?

9 CREATING AND SHAPING STORIES

The Monkey's Paw 2

5 Exploring adverbs

▶ In groups of four, prepare to act out the following scene, paying particular attention to the **adverbs**. You may wish to *exaggerate* the point, or you may wish to try to act it *realistically*, but make sure the other groups know which you have chosen without you telling them.

'I should like to see those old temples and fakirs and jugglers,' said the old man. 'What was that you started telling me the other day about a monkey's paw or something, Morris?'

'Nothing,' said the soldier **hastily**. 'Leastways nothing worth hearing.'

'Monkey's paw?' said Mrs White **curiously**.

'Well, it's just a bit of what you might call magic, perhaps,' said the sergeant-major, **offhandedly**.

His three listeners leaned forward **eagerly**. The visitor **absent-mindedly** put his empty glass to his lips and then set it down again.

ADVICE

▲ You need to look up any words you are not sure of before speaking the lines.
▲ Morris = soldier = sergeant-major = visitor.
▲ Old man = Mr White.
▲ The son does not speak in these lines, but does show body-language.

6 Exploring point of view

An author is like a director of a film, selecting which angle to use at a particular moment in the story. Will the reader/viewer imagine/see a stranger walking up a rough path to an isolated house? Or will the reader/viewer imagine/see a family waiting inside a house, with the family hearing but not seeing the stranger approach? As a reader or viewer we tend to take sides with the person/people whose point of view we are sharing.

▶ From whose point of view is *The Monkey's Paw* told?
▶ Are any characters' viewpoints privileged (favoured) in any way?
▶ Look again at the following lines and decide whose viewpoint is privileged in any way.
▶ Use a table like the following and be prepared to justify your conclusions.

ADVICE

▲ Imagine the story as a film. When someone is not in a particular room etc., do we go with the people leaving, or stay with the people staying?
▲ Start by deciding if the viewpoint of the family or of Sergeant-Major Morris is privileged at the beginning of the story.

Lines	Incident	Whose viewpoint is privileged in the text?	If you were making a film, how would you want to show this scene?
17–23	The visitor arrives.		
86–94	The visitor leaves.		
115–125	The couple retire for the night.		
201–207	The wife cannot sleep.		
234–241	The wife asks for the monkey's paw.		
254–262	Knocks at the front door.		
272–287	Wife *vs* husband.		

The Monkey's Paw

7 Exploring the wider context

- What word choices might suggest that this text was written before the First World War (1914–1918)?
- Having read the whole story, what do you notice about this sentence?
  'Well, I don't see the money,' said his son, as he picked it [the monkey's paw] *up and placed it on the table, 'and I bet I never shall.'* (lines 110–111)
- Why do you think the author has Mr White saying: *'It seems to me I've got all I want.'* ? (line 99)
- What does this quotation show about Mrs White?
  'And if they could, how could two hundred pounds hurt you, father?' (lines 131–132)
- What is ironic about this comment from the son, imagining the father receiving the two hundred pounds?
  'I'm afraid it'll turn you into a mean, avaricious man, and we shall have to disown you.' (line 137)
- Why do you think the author has Mrs White *unfastening the strings of her apron* at line 155?
- Do you think the author implies any criticism of any of the characters for the way they behave? Be prepared to back up your point of view with a quotation or evidence of some kind.
- Is there any suggestion of female stereotyping in the way Mrs White is presented? If so, is the author showing a woman behaving stereotypically, or is the author being stereotypical in the way he presents women?

ADVICE

▲ In many cases here, there are no single correct answers. In your group, discuss each question and then decide which answer you feel matches the text most fully.

WORDS

▲ **irony** *noun* term used to describe a situation that seems satisfactory or desirable on the surface, but which 'fate' seems to have twisted into something that is quite the reverse; term used to describe an outcome of events which seems to mock or twist an earlier statement or expectation.

8 Exploring endings

- Authors end their stories in a whole variety of ways. Some of the possible decisions for authors to make about endings are listed below. Some stories may include more than one of these possibilities.
- In a comment column in a table like the one below, write down the titles of any novels or short stories you know that end in each way listed. Make notes on how well you like this kind of ending.

ADVICE

▲ Start with a short story or novel you have recently read on your own or in class, such as *The Monkey's Paw*.
▲ If you need to, add an extra row to your table.

Choice of ending	Comment
Coming to a cliff-hanger ending, leaving room for a sequel.	
Ending the main events of the story, but letting the reader know what happens to the characters later in their 'lives'.	
Ending the main plot, but leaving some of the sub-plots unresolved.	
Giving alternative routes through a story, with alternative endings.	
Leaving the ending open, so that the reader decides the most likely development/uses knowledge based on how characters have behaved so far to predict how they will behave in the future.	
The good end happily, the bad unhappily.	
Tying up all the loose ends.	

CREATING AND SHAPING STORIES

▶ Using a table like the one below, make notes on some of the stories you have read over the past three years. Choose about ten, and work out what sort of ending each one of them had.

Date read	Title	Author	Type of ending
	Next Term We'll Mash You	Penelope Lively	
	Aliens Don't Eat Bacon Sandwiches	Helen Dunmore	
	The Monkey's Paw	W. W. Jacobs	

▶ Do different types of story (animal, detective, horror, school, sports...) have different types of ending?
▶ Select two or three types of story that typically end in a particular way. Decide in your group the match between *type of story* and *type of ending* you think you can convince other groups about most effectively.

ADVICE

▲ You could include *Next Term We'll Mash You* (*Level Best 1*, Unit 9) and *Aliens Don't Eat Bacon Sandwiches* (*Level Best 2*, Unit 9), if you have read them. Include novels and short stories you have read in class and those you have read on your own.

Independent writing

9 Writing and commenting on your own story

▶ Write your own story, which could be autobiographical, fictional, or a combination of the two.

Deciding on your ending

▶ What type of ending from the list in Activity 8 (or one not mentioned) would suit your story best?
▶ In your commentary, explain why you think your ending matches your story.

ADVICE

▲ If you decide to tell a story involving the supernatural in any way, you would be well advised to make nearly everything fairly normal. Notice that in *The Monkey's Paw*, most details of the house, the family and the visitor are totally realistic and believable. You are more likely to convince a reader that something is true if you have gained their trust in the reality of the events you describe first.

ADVICE

▲ You might like to think about including one or two of the following ideas, but if you have a story of your own in mind you may wish to ignore these suggestions:
- a letter home from school
- arriving first at the post
- e-mail
- step-parents
- a story designed to create a particular type of mood and atmosphere, which you negotiate with your teacher.

▲ You might like to experiment with third person narrative. If so, at each significant point in the story, decide:
- which character the 'camera' will follow
- whose thoughts will be expressed, if anyone's.

In your commentary, explain the reasoning behind your decisions.

▲ Your story is likely to sound very strange unless there is some consistency in viewpoint, but you could experiment and comment on your findings.

174

Self-assessment

10 Judging your own performance

▶ From the list below:
  a select three points on which you feel you have made the most progress
  b select one point on which you most need to improve.
  I can make predictions based on details in the text.
  I can identify and comment on the ways in which authors introduce characters.
  I can identify and comment on the ways in which authors set the scene in the opening of a story.
  I can identify and comment on the ways in which authors create mood and atmosphere.
  I can effectively track the level of tension created by an author at various points in a story.
  I understand how adverbs can be used to build up an idea of character.
  I can identify and comment on the way a story privileges a particular point of view.
  I can identify and comment on word choice which helps to date a text.
  I can identify and comment on the use of irony.
  I can make judgements, backed up by reference to the text, on how far a character is presented stereotypically.
  I can recognise and comment on different types of endings and their effect on the reader.
  I can write a story of my own, selectively using techniques I have identified in the work of other authors.

11 Improving your skills in English

▶ Select one or two skills you need to concentrate on to improve your skills in reading. Then do the same for your writing skills. (The descriptions of levels are a guide only.)

	Reading skill	From	To
1	Show understanding of significant ideas, themes, events and characters, beginning to use inference and deduction	Level 3	Level 4
2	Refer to the text when explaining views; locate and use ideas and information	Level 3	Level 4
3	Select essential points and use inference and deduction where appropriate	Level 4	Level 5
4	Identify key features, themes and characters and select sentences, phrases and relevant information to support views	Level 4	Level 5
5	Identify different layers of meaning and comment on their significance and effect	Level 5	Level 6
6	Give a personal response to literary texts, referring to aspects of language, structure and themes in justifying views	Level 5	Level 6
7	Show understanding of the ways in which meaning and information are conveyed in a range of texts	Level 6	Level 7
8	Articulate personal and critical responses to texts, showing awareness of their thematic, structural and linguistic features	Level 6	Level 7
9	Show appreciation of, and comment on, a range of texts	Level 7	Level 8

9 CREATING AND SHAPING STORIES

10	Evaluate how authors achieve their effects through the use of linguistic, structural and presentational devices	Level 7	Level 8
11	Confidently sustain responses to a demanding range of texts, developing ideas and referring in detail to aspects of language, structure and presentation	Level 8	E.P.
12	Make apt and careful comparison between texts, including consideration of audience, purpose and form	Level 8	E.P.

	Writing skill	From	To
1	Writing is lively and thoughtful, with ideas often sustained in interesting ways	Level 3	Level 4
2	Vocabulary choices are adventurous and words are used for effect	Level 3	Level 4
3	Writing is varied and interesting, conveying meaning clearly	Level 4	Level 5
4	Vocabulary choices are imaginative and words are used precisely; simple and complex sentences are organised into paragraphs	Level 4	Level 5
5	Writing often engages and sustains the reader's interest	Level 5	Level 6
6	Pupils use a range of sentence structures and varied vocabulary to create effects	Level 5	Level 6
7	Writing is confident and shows an appropriate choice of style	Level 6	Level 7
8	Characters and settings are developed. Grammatical features and vocabulary are accurately and effectively used	Level 6	Level 7
9	Writing shows selection of specific features or expressions to convey particular effects and to interest the reader	Level 7	Level 8
10	Narrative writing shows control of characters, events and settings, and structural and presentational devices	Level 7	Level 8
11	Writing has shape and impact, and shows control of style, maintaining the interest of the reader throughout	Level 8	E.P.
12	Narratives use structure as well as vocabulary for a range of imaginative effects; a variety of grammatical constructions and punctuation are used accurately and appropriately and with sensitivity	Level 8	E.P.

10 Exploring Shakespeare
Macbeth

Your focus

The content of this unit is designed to:
- help you understand Shakespeare for yourself
- help you understand the context Shakespeare was writing in
- help you speak a part effectively.

Your target

By the end of this unit you should be more able to:
- understand some of the changes to the English language over time
- understand some of the techniques Shakespeare uses in writing for the theatre
- appreciate how the language of a Shakespeare play comes to life when performed.

Your move

- Speaking and listening
- Reading
- Self-assessment

Exploring Shakespeare

- Act 1 Scene 1
  - 1 Creating atmosphere in performance
  - 2 Finding out how an audience becomes involved
- Act 1 Scenes 2–3
  - 3 Exploring an early scene
  - 4 Exploring the reactions of Banquo and Macbeth
- Act 1 Scene 4
  - 5 Who will be king after Duncan?
- Act 1 Scenes 5–7
  - 6 Exploring Lady Macbeth's reaction
  - 7 Exploring Macbeth's conscience
  - 8 Exploring Lady Macbeth on Macbeth
- Images of Act 1
  - 9 Illustrating an image
  - 10 Comparing a graphic novel version with a performance
  - 11 Exploring one frame in more detail
  - 12 Making predictions
  - 13 Judging your own performance
  - 14 Improving your skills in English

177

10 EXPLORING SHAKESPEARE

Act 1 Scene 1

1. Creating atmosphere in performance

▶ Prepare a reading of the following lines in your group. They make up the whole of Act 1 Scene 1 of *Macbeth*.

▶ Your aim should be:
- to create a sense of danger and mystery – without making your audience laugh
- to say the words clearly enough for an audience to hear them well
- to rehearse a few times so that you can present your version to the other groups.

Act 1
Scene 1 *An open place.*
Thunder and lightning. Enter three WITCHES.

1ST WITCH	When shall we three meet again?	
	In thunder, lightning, or in rain?	
2ND WITCH	When the hurlyburly's done,	
	When the battle's lost and won.	
3RD WITCH	That will be ere the set of sun.	5
1ST WITCH	Where the place?	
2ND WITCH	Upon the heath.	
3RD WITCH	There to meet with Macbeth.	
1ST WITCH	I come, Graymalkin!	
2ND WITCH	Paddock calls.	
3RD WITCH	Anon!	10
ALL	Fair is foul, and foul is fair:	
	Hover through the fog and filthy air.	

Witches vanish

WORDS

▲ **hurlyburly** *noun* the noisy activity of crowds of people; confusion or uproar. 16th century, from *hurling* and *burling*, a rhyming compound based on hurling in its obsolete meaning of 'uproar'.

▲ **ere** *preposition, conjunction, old use* before.

▲ **heath** *noun* an area of open land, usually with dry sandy acidic soil, dominated by low-growing evergreen shrubs, especially heathers.

▲ **Graymalkin** a grey cat, a common witches' familiar.

▲ **familiar** *noun* a demon or spirit, especially one in the shape of an animal, that serves a witch.

▲ **Paddock** a toad.

▲ **anon** *adverb, old use* some time soon.

▲ **fair** *adjective* **1** just, not using dishonest methods or discrimination. **2** *old use* beautiful.

▲ **foul** *adjective* **1** disgusting; filthy; **2** unfair or treacherous *by fair means or foul*.

▲ **obsolete** *adjective* no longer in use.

2. Finding out how an audience becomes involved

▶ The lines you have performed may not seem to make much sense, but find out how much information is contained in them by trying to answer these questions:

1. When will the witches meet next? (Search for two answers here.)
2. Where will the witches meet next?
3. Who will the witches meet with?
4. How might an audience know these three performers are intended to be witches?
5. What reasons might there be for Shakespeare giving the witches the line:
   Fair is foul, and foul is fair?
6. What reasons might there be for Shakespeare not revealing why the witches want to meet Macbeth?
7. How is the atmosphere created, apart from by the use of words?

Act 1 Scenes 2–3

3. Exploring an early scene – Scene 2

After reading Scene 2 below, discuss the following questions in your group.
- How could a director help an audience understand who is who by seeing them enter? Think about their order of appearance and their costume.
- What make-up must the Sergeant have? (Look at the stage directions and also lines 42–44.)
- Suggest possible reasons why it is useful for Shakespeare to use a messenger (the Sergeant) at this point in the play.
- Duncan is King of Scotland. How does an audience find this out?
- King Duncan's army is fighting against two enemies:
  - use lines 9–13 to briefly describe one enemy
  - use lines 31–33 to briefly describe a second enemy.
- Macbeth is described in lines 16–24. Write down three details that reveal something about the kind of man who is being presented to the audience at this point in the play.
- Look closely at lines 33–35. King Duncan asks the Sergeant if Macbeth and Banquo were not 'dismay'd' by the attack from the Norwegians. The Sergeant says 'Yes' (implying they were dismayed). Suggest possible reasons for Shakespeare having the Sergeant say this.
- Lines 33–44 are not all strictly 10 syllables to the line. In your group, brainstorm some possible reasons for this. Select the best reason to present to the other groups. (Look at lines 34, 38 and 41.)
- What does 'Norway' in line 52 refer to?
- What does the audience find out about the Thane of Cawdor?

Scene 2 *A camp near Forres.*
Alarum within. Enter KING DUNCAN, MALCOLM, DONALBAIN, LENNOX, *with* Attendants, *meeting a bleeding* Sergeant.

DUNCAN	What bloody man is that? He can report,	
	As seemeth by his plight, of the revolt	
	The newest state.	
MALCOLM	This is the sergeant	
	Who like a good and hardy soldier fought	5
	'Gainst my captivity. Hail, brave friend!	
	Say to the King the knowledge of the broil	
	As thou didst leave it.	
SERGEANT	Doubtful it stood,	
	As two spent swimmers, that do cling together	
	And choke their art. The merciless Macdonwald –	10
	Worthy to be a rebel, for to that	
	The multiplying villainies of nature	
	Do swarm upon him – from the Western Isles	
	Of kerns and gallowglasses is supplied;	

ADVICE

▲ Think about:
- how 'Yes' fits in with the next line
- what is happening at lines 40–44.

▲ If a series of lines runs smoothly, it may suggest a sense of calm and order, with nothing disturbing that calm and order.

▲ If a series of lines runs unevenly, it may suggest the unsettled state of mind of the speaker.

▲ It may help you to try reading the speeches of Duncan and the Sergeant in lines 33–35 aloud in your group.

ADVICE

▲ Lines in Shakespeare are usually 10 syllables long. Lines such as 3 and 7 are **shared** between two speakers.

	And Fortune, on his damned quarrel smiling,	
	Show'd like a rebel's whore. But all's too weak;	15
	For brave Macbeth – well he deserves that name –	
	Disdaining Fortune, with his brandish'd steel,	
	Which smok'd with bloody execution,	
	Like valour's minion, carv'd out his passage	
	Till he fac'd the slave;	20
	Which ne'er shook hands, nor bade farewell to him,	
	Till he unseam'd him from the nave to th' chops,	
	And fix'd his head upon our battlements.	
DUNCAN	O valiant cousin! worthy gentleman!	
SERGEANT	As whence the sun 'gins his reflection	25
	Shipwrecking storms and direful thunders break,	
	So from that spring whence comfort seem'd to come,	
	Discomfort swells. Mark, King of Scotland, mark:	
	No sooner justice had, with valour arm'd,	
	Compell'd these skipping kerns to trust their heels,	30
	But the Norweyan Lord, surveying vantage,	
	With furbish'd arms, and new supplies of men,	
	Began a fresh assault.	
DUNCAN	Dismay'd not this	
	Our captains, Macbeth and Banquo?	
SERGEANT	Yes;	
	As sparrows eagles, or the hare the lion.	35
	If I say sooth, I must report they were	
	As cannons overcharg'd with double cracks;	
	So they doubly redoubled strokes upon the foe.	
	Except they meant to bathe in reeking wounds,	
	Or memorize another Golgotha,	40
	I cannot tell –	
	But I am faint; my gashes cry for help.	
DUNCAN	So well thy words become thee, as thy wounds:	
	They smack of honour both. – Go, get him surgeons.	
	Exit Sergeant, attended.	
	Enter ROSS.	
	Who comes here?	
MALCOLM	The worthy Thane of Ross.	45
LENNOX	What a haste looks through his eyes!	
	So should he look that seems to speak things strange.	
ROSS	God save the King!	
DUNCAN	Whence cam'st thou, worthy thane?	
ROSS	From Fife, great King,	
	Where the Norweyan banners flout the sky	50
	And fan our people cold.	
	Norway himself, with terrible numbers,	
	Assisted by that most disloyal traitor	
	The Thane of Cawdor, began a dismal conflict;	
	Till that Bellona's bridegroom, lapp'd in proof,	55
	Confronted him with self-comparisons,	
	Point against point rebellious, arm 'gainst arm,	

	Curbing his lavish spirit; and, to conclude,	
	The victory fell on us.	
DUNCAN	Great happiness!	
ROSS	That now	60
	Sweno, the Norways' king, craves composition;	
	Nor would we deign him burial of his men	
	Till he disbursed, at Saint Colme's Inch,	
	Ten thousand dollars to our general use.	
DUNCAN	No more that Thane of Cawdor shall deceive	65
	Our bosom interest. Go pronounce his present death,	
	And with his former title greet Macbeth.	
ROSS	I'll see it done.	
DUNCAN	What he hath lost, noble Macbeth hath won.	
	Exeunt.	

WORDS

▲ **rebel** *noun* someone who openly resists or fights against authority.
▲ **kern** *noun, old use* lightly-armed Irish soldier.
▲ **gallowglass** *noun, old use* heavily-armed footman in army of Irish or from Scottish isles.
▲ **disdain** *verb* reject because of a feeling of scorn or contempt.
▲ **nave** *noun, Shakespearean usage* navel.
▲ **chops** *plural noun* the jaws or mouth.
▲ **valiant** *adjective* outstandingly brave and heroic.
▲ **worthy** *adjective* admirable, excellent or deserving.
▲ **captain** *noun* a leader or chief.

4 Exploring the reactions of Banquo and Macbeth

▶ To help you understand the next part of the play, coloured fonts have been used:
- The first two predictions of the witches: that Macbeth will be Thane of Glamis and Thane of Cawdor.
- The third prediction of the witches: that Macbeth will become King 'hereafter' – some time in the future.
- The thoughts Macbeth has of murdering the King so that he may become King.

Macbeth was Thane of Glamis when the play started.
The witches name Macbeth Thane of Glamis, Thane of Cawdor and as future King.
After the witches vanish, Ross arrives with news that King Duncan has honoured Macbeth with the title Thane of Cawdor.
Macbeth now thinks to himself: 'if what the witches say is true, I could be King. But will it happen by Fortune/Chance?' The alternative, which he can barely dare to think about, would involve murdering the present king, Duncan.

MACBETH:	*[Aside]* Glamis, and Thane of Cawdor!
	The greatest is behind. *[To Ross and Angus]* Thanks for your pains.
	[Aside to Banquo] Do you not hope your children shall be kings,
	When those that gave the Thane of Cawdor to me
	Promis'd no less to them?

10 EXPLORING SHAKESPEARE

BANQUO:	[Aside to Macbeth] That, trusted home,	120
	Might yet enkindle you unto the crown,	
	Besides the Thane of Cawdor. But 'tis strange;	
	And oftentimes, to win us to our harm,	
	The instruments of darkness tell us truths;	
	Win us with honest trifles, to betray's	125
	In deepest consequence. –	
	[To Ross and Angus] Cousins, a word, I pray you.	
MACBETH:	[Aside] Two truths are told,	
	As happy prologues to the swelling act	
	Of the imperial theme – I thank you, gentlemen.	
	[Aside] This supernatural soliciting	130
	Cannot be ill; cannot be good. If ill	
	Why hast it given me earnest of success,	
	Commencing in a truth? I am Thane of Cawdor.	
	If good, why do I yield to that suggestion	
	Whose horrid image doth unfix my hair	135
	And make my seated heart knock at my ribs	
	Against the use of nature? Present fears	
	Are less than horrible imaginings.	
	My thought, whose murder yet is but fantastical,	
	Shakes so my single state of man	140
	That function is smother'd in surmise,	
	And nothing is but what is not.	
BANQUO:	Look how our partner's rapt.	
MACBETH:	[Aside] If chance will have me King, why, chance may crown me,	
	Without my stir.	
BANQUO:	New honours come upon him,	145
	Like our strange garments, cleave not to their mould	
	But with the aid of use.	

- Banquo is giving Macbeth a warning in lines 122–126. What do you think he is warning Macbeth about?
- What does Macbeth say is the physical effect on him when he just thinks about killing the king?
- Draw a diagram of the stage at the point Macbeth delivers his soliloquy (130–142). As director, indicate where Angus, Banquo, Macbeth and Ross are standing and which way each man is facing. Make clear in your diagram where the audience is.
- In your group, rewrite what Macbeth says in lines 144–145 in a way that will express his ideas as clearly as possible for the other groups. (*If chance … my stir*).
- In your group, rewrite what Banquo says in lines 145–147 in a way that will express his ideas as clearly as possible for the other groups.
- Try to find a tone of voice for Macbeth for each of the following:
  - text printed in green
  - text printed in blue
  - text printed in red.
- In pairs, try reading/performing these lines so that they would be as clear as possible to someone who has not studied the play at all.

WORDS

▲ **aside** *noun* words said by a character in a play which the audience can hear, but which some other characters 'cannot' hear.

Act 1 Scene 4

5 Who will be king after Duncan?

▶ Read Act 1 Scene 4 (up to line 47).
Look again at lines 11–14. Duncan is saying that it is impossible to work out what a person is thinking just by observing their face. He trusted the previous Thane of Cawdor absolutely, and he turned out to be a traitor.
▶ Who do you think Duncan now trusts?
▶ Why do you think Shakespeare chose to have Macbeth enter at this point?

Look again at lines 22–27.
▶ What do you think could be going through Macbeth's mind as he says this? Draw a 'thought bubble' and write in it what you believe Macbeth might be thinking here. How might an actor playing Macbeth hint at these thoughts by tone of voice and/or body language?

Look again at lines 35–39.
▶ Duncan is naming his oldest son, Malcolm, as his successor as king when he dies. What do you think could be going through Macbeth's mind as he hears Duncan say this? Draw a 'thought bubble' and write in it what you believe Macbeth might be thinking here. How might an actor playing Macbeth hint at these thoughts through body language?

Scene 4 *Forres. The palace.*
Flourish. Enter DUNCAN, MALCOLM, DONALBAIN, LENNOX, *and* Attendants.

DUNCAN	Is execution done on Cawdor? Are not Those in commission yet return'd?	
MALCOLM	My liege, They are not yet come back. But I have spoke With one that saw him die; who did report That very frankly he confess'd his treasons, Implor'd your Highness' pardon, and set forth A deep repentance. Nothing in his life Became him like the leaving it: he died As one that had been studied in his death To throw away the dearest thing he ow'd, As 'twere a careless trifle.	5 10
DUNCAN	There's no art To find the mind's construction in the face. He was a gentleman on whom I built An absolute trust. *Enter* MACBETH, BANQUO, ROSS, *and* ANGUS. O worthiest cousin! The sin of my ingratitude even now Was heavy on me. Thou art so far before That swiftest wing of recompense is slow To overtake thee. Would thou hadst less deserv'd, That the proportion both of thanks and payment Might have been mine! Only I have left to say,	 15 20

183

	More is thy due than more than all can pay.	
MACBETH	The service and the loyalty I owe,	
	In doing it, pays itself. Your Highness' part	
	Is to receive our duties: and our duties	
	Are to your throne and state, children and servants,	25
	Which do but what they should by doing everything	
	Safe toward your love and honour.	
DUNCAN	Welcome hither:	
	I have begun to plant thee, and will labour	
	To make thee full of growing. Noble Banquo,	
	That hast no less deserv'd, nor must be known	30
	No less to have done so, let me infold thee	
	And hold thee to my heart.	
BANQUO	There if I grow,	
	The harvest is your own.	
DUNCAN	My plenteous joys,	
	Wanton in fulness, seek to hide themselves	
	In drops of sorrow. Sons, kinsmen, thanes,	35
	And you whose places are the nearest, know	
	We will establish our estate upon	
	Our eldest, Malcolm, whom we name hereafter	
	The Prince of Cumberland: which honour must	
	Not unaccompanied invest him only,	40
	But signs of nobleness, like stars, shall shine	
	On all deservers. From hence to Inverness,	
	And bind us further to you.	
MACBETH	The rest is labour, which is not us'd for you.	
	I'll be myself the harbinger, and make joyful	45
	The hearing of my wife with your approach;	
	So, humbly take my leave.	

Act 1 Scenes 5–7

6 Exploring Lady Macbeth's reaction

In the following extract, font colour has again been used to help you understand the text:
- Information based on the witches' predictions.
- The possibility of Macbeth and Lady Macbeth becoming King and Queen.
- Murdering to become King.
- The human side of Macbeth's character.

WORDS

▲ **illness** *noun*, *old use* evil, wickedness.

Scene 5 *Inverness. MACBETH's castle.*
Enter LADY MACBETH, *reading a letter.*

LADY MACBETH:	'They met me in the day of success; and I have learn'd by the perfect'st report they have more in them than mortal knowledge. When I burn'd in desire to question them further, they made themselves air, into which they vanish'd. Whiles I stood rapt in the wonder of it, came missives from the King, who all-hail'd me, "Thane of Cawdor"; by which title, before, these weird sisters saluted me, and referr'd me to the coming on of time, with "Hail, King that shalt be!" This have I thought good to deliver thee, my dearest partner of greatness, that thou mightst not lose the dues of rejoicing by being ignorant of what greatness is promis'd thee. Lay it to thy heart, and farewell.'	5
	Glamis thou art, and Cawdor; and shalt be	10
	What thou are promis'd. Yet do I fear thy nature;	
	It is too full o' th' milk of human kindness	
	To catch the nearest way. Thou wouldst be great;	
	Art not without ambition, but without	
	The illness should attend it. What thou wouldst highly,	15
	That wouldst thou holily; wouldst not play false,	
	And yet wouldst wrongly win.	
	Thou'dst have, great Glamis, that which cries,	
	'Thus thou must do' if thou have it;	
	And that which rather thou dost fear to do	20
	Than wishest should be undone. Hie thee hither,	
	That I may pour my spirits in thine ear,	
	And chastise with the valour of my tongue	
	All that impedes thee from the golden round	
	Which fate and metaphysical aid doth seem	25
	To have thee crown'd withal.	
	Enter a Messenger	
	What is your tidings?	
MESSENGER:	The King comes here tonight.	
LADY MACBETH:	Thou'rt mad to say it.	
	Is not thy master with him? who, were't so,	
	Would have inform'd for preparation.	

▶ Lines 1–9 are written in prose. Suggest a reason why, and explain the main differences in the way a performer should act in lines 1–9 compared with the later lines.

▶ Why do you think Shakespeare shows Macbeth concentrating on the supernatural in the letter to his wife?

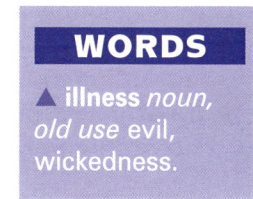

10 EXPLORING SHAKESPEARE

▶ What reasons can you think of for Macbeth saying 'what greatness is promis'd **thee**' rather than '**me**' or '**us**'? (line 9)

Lady Macbeth is presented as believing Macbeth is at fault in two ways.
▶ Use the text printed in green to say in your own words what he has too much of, according to Lady Macbeth.
▶ Use the text printed in red to say in your own words what he has too little of, according to Lady Macbeth.

Lady Macbeth can be seen as over-reacting to the Messenger's news. (lines 26–29)
▶ What suggests she is over-reacting?
▶ How does Lady Macbeth try to cover up for her 'mistake'?
▶ Give tone of voice directions for:
  - line 27: *Thou'rt mad to say it.*
  - lines 28–29: *Is not thy master with him? who, were't so, Would have inform'd for preparation.*
▶ Having looked at the scene in some detail, now suggest what tone of voice you think would be most appropriate for the parts of lines 11–26 printed in:
  - green
  - red
  - blue.

ADVICE

▲ You may need to try out different tones of voice before you catch the appropriate tone. Notice particularly how the tone of voice might change when the colour changes.

7 Exploring Macbeth's conscience

▶ Match up Shakespeare's text with the modern English versions.
▶ Write down the modern version opposite the Shakespeare text in a table like the one below.
▶ Highlight the words you found most useful in making the match.

1
But in these cases,
We still have judgement here; that we but teach
Bloody instructions, which being taught return,
To plague th'inventor. This even-handed justice
Commends th'ingredience of our poison'd chalice
To our own lips.

2
He's here in double trust:
First, as I am his kinsman and his subject –
Strong both against the deed;

3
then, as his host,
Who should against his murderer shut the door,
Not bear the knife myself.

4
Besides, this Duncan
Hath borne his faculties so meek, hath been
So clear in his great office, that his virtues
Will plead like angels, trumpet-tongu'd, against
The deep damnation of his taking-off;

5
And pity, like a naked new-born babe,
Striding the blast, or heaven's cherubin hors'd
Upon the sightless couriers of the air,
Shall blow the horrid deed in every eye,
That tears shall drown the wind.

Macbeth

6	I have no spur To prick the sides of my intent, but only Vaulting ambition, which o'erleaps itself, And falls on th'other.	
7	He hath honour'd me of late (*to his wife*)	
8	and I have bought Golden opinions from all sorts of people, Which would be worn now in their newest gloss, Not cast aside so soon. (*to his wife*)	

A	Duncan has been such a good king that there would be an outcry against the sin of his murder.	**E**	If Duncan was murdered, everyone would cry with pity at such cruelty.
B	Duncan has recently rewarded me with the title of Thane of Cawdor.	**F**	If we use violence to start with, others may use violence against us.
C	I am his host, and should be there to *prevent* anyone killing the king, not using the knife on the king *myself*.	**G**	I have built up a good reputation among many people recently and want to enjoy it, not risk it.
D	I am related to him and owe duty to him as my king – both strong reasons against killing him.	**H**	The only thing making me want to act in this way is the kind of ambition that often leads to failure rather than success.

8 Exploring Lady Macbeth on Macbeth

In the 'adage', or story with a moral, that Shakespeare refers to, the cat wants to eat a fish but is not prepared to get its feet wet in the process.
In the following passage:
▶ Identify where Lady Macbeth is comparing Macbeth to the cat that wants to eat a fish.
▶ Identify where Lady Macbeth is comparing Macbeth to the cat that doesn't want to get its feet wet.

> LADY MACBETH   Was the hope drunk
>   Wherein you dress'd yourself? Hath it slept since,
>   And wakes it now to look so green and pale
>   At what it did so freely? From this time
>   Such I account thy love. Art thou afeard
>   To be the same in thine own act and valour
>   As thou art in desire? Would'st thou have that
>   Which thou esteem'st the ornament of life,
>   And live a coward in thine own esteem,
>   Letting 'I dare not' wait upon 'I would',
>   Like the poor cat i' th' adage?

▶ Having separated the two parts of the argument, try to identify a tone of voice that would be appropriate for each.
▶ Try reading the lines, changing tone of voice as appropriate, and perhaps using facial expression to help convey her feelings.

10 EXPLORING SHAKESPEARE

Images of Act 1

9 Illustrating an image

▶ Find a way of drawing a picture/cartoon to help someone understand one of the following images:
Page 182: *Scene 3 lines 145–147* BANQUO: New honours come upon him,/Like our strange garments, cleave not to their mould,/But with the aid of use.
Page 184: *Scene 4 lines 28–29* DUNCAN: I have begun to plant thee, and will labour/To make thee full of growing.
Page 185: *Scene 5 lines 21–23* LADY MACBETH: Hie thee hither,/That I may pour my spirits in thine ear,/And chastise with the valour of my tongue

▶ Now try out ways of speaking the text. The way you say the lines must help an audience understand the power of the image on first hearing. You may wish to use body language.

ADVICE
▲ Look at the context of the speech before making any decisions.

10 Comparing a graphic novel version with a performance

The following is a graphic novel version of Act 1 of the play.
▶ As you study it, think about the different impression of the play you would have if you saw it performed.

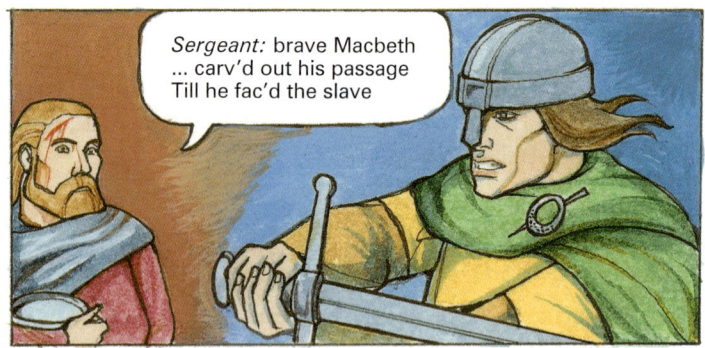

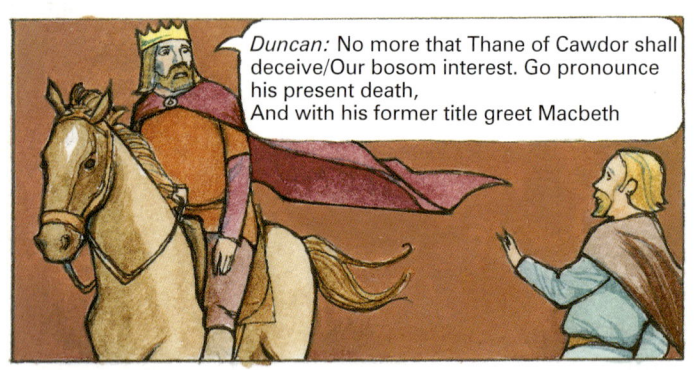

Witch 1: Where the place?
Witch 2: Upon the heath.
Witch 3: There to meet with Macbeth.

Sergeant: brave Macbeth ... carv'd out his passage Till he fac'd the slave

Duncan: No more that Thane of Cawdor shall deceive/Our bosom interest. Go pronounce his present death, And with his former title greet Macbeth

Witch 1: All hail, Macbeth! Hail to thee, Thane of Glamis!
Witch 2: All hail, Macbeth! Hail to thee, Thane of Cawdor!
Witch 3: All hail, Macbeth! That shalt be King hereafter!

Witch 1: Lesser than Macbeth, and greater.
Witch 2: Not so happy, yet much happier.
Witch 3: Thou shalt get kings, though thou be none.

Ross: He bade me, from him, call thee Thane of Cawdor.
Banquo: What! Can the devil speak true?

Macbeth: This supernatural soliciting/Cannot be ill; cannot be good
We will establish our estate upon Our eldest, Malcolm, whom we name hereafter The Prince of Cumberland
The Prince of Cumberland! That is a step On which I must fall down, or else o'er-leap, For in my way it lies.
Lady Macbeth: Yet do I fear thy nature; It is too full o' th' milk of human kindness, To catch the nearest way.
The King comes here tonight.
Thou'rt mad to say it.
Come, you spirits That tend on mortal thoughts, unsex me here; And fill me, from the crown to the toe, top-full Of direst cruelty.
See, see, our honour'd hostess!
I have no spur To prick the sides of my intent, but only Vaulting ambition, which o'erleaps itself, And falls on th'other.
We will proceed no further in this business.
When you durst do it, then you were a man; And to be more than what you were, you would Be so much more the man.

10 EXPLORING SHAKESPEARE

▶ What are the advantages and disadvantages of a graphic text novel compared with a performance of *Macbeth*?

ADVICE

▲ Think about:
- being able to go back if you don't understand
- being clear about who is who
- having a sense of atmosphere
- hearing the tone of voice of the speaker
- seeing how facial expressions and body language change.

11 Exploring one frame in more detail

Compare frame 9 with the following text, which provides the context.
▶ How do the two versions affect your understanding?
Macbeth is telling the King he will tell his wife the good news that the King will be staying at their castle:

MACBETH   I'll be myself the harbinger, and make joyful
                  The hearing of my wife with your approach;
                  So, humbly take my leave.

DUNCAN   My worthy Cawdor!

MACBETH   [*Aside*] The Prince of Cumberland! That is a step,
                  On which I must fall down, or else o'er-leap,
                  For in my way it lies. Stars, hide your fires;
                  Let not light see my black and deep desires.
                  The eye wink at the hand; yet let that be
                  Which the eye fears, when it is done, to see. [*Exit*]

ADVICE

▲ Think of the Shakespeare version performed on stage.

▶ Experiment with different ways of speaking this text.
▶ Should the actor playing Macbeth hint that Macbeth is hiding something in the first three lines?
▶ How loudly should Macbeth's *aside* be spoken?
▶ Should Macbeth's tone of voice in his *aside* be sinister or frightened or confident? Why?

12 Making predictions

An audience in a theatre will inevitably predict what will happen next, if the story of the play is not known.
▶ Work out what an audience that does not know the story might predict will happen next, based on what has been seen and heard so far.
▶ Will Macbeth become king? Do you have any evidence?
▶ If Macbeth becomes king, what will happen then? Do you have any evidence?

Macbeth

Self-assessment

13 Judging your own performance

▶ From the list below:
  a select three points on which you feel you have made the most progress
  b select one point on which you most need to improve.
  I can perform an extract from a play, helping to create atmosphere.
  I recognise some of the techniques a playwright uses to create atmosphere.
  I understand the contribution that make-up, costume, lighting and scenery can make to a play.
  I appreciate how a playwright communicates necessary information to an audience.
  I understand some of the ways an audience learns about a character.
  I understand how line length in Shakespeare can be used to create particular effects.
  I can make logical decisions about the sequence of a text, backing up these decisions with clear evidence.
  I understand that what a character says in a play may be different from what they are thinking.
  I can make sensible predictions based on evidence in the text so far.
  I can evaluate the strengths and weaknesses of different versions of the same story.
  I can understand and comment on the way a written text is transformed when produced on stage.
  I can identify key features of a Shakespeare play when performed on stage.

14 Improving your skills in English

▶ Select one or two skills you need to concentrate on to improve your skills in speaking and listening. Then do the same for your reading skills. (The descriptions of levels are a guide only.)

	Speaking and listening skill	From	To
1	Talk and listen with confidence in an increasing range of contexts, developing ideas thoughtfully	Level 3	Level 4
2	In discussion, listen carefully, making contributions and asking questions that are responsive to others' ideas and views	Level 3	Level 4
3	Talk and listen confidently in a wide range of contexts, varying expression and vocabulary	Level 4	Level 5
4	In discussion, pay close attention to what others say, ask questions and develop ideas and make contributions that take account of others' views	Level 4	Level 5
5	Adapt talk to demands of different contexts with increasing confidence	Level 5	Level 6
6	Take an active part in discussion, showing understanding of ideas and sensitivity to others	Level 5	Level 6
7	Confident in matching talk to the demands of different contexts	Level 6	Level 7
8	In discussion, make significant contributions, evaluate others' ideas and vary how and when to participate	Level 6	Level 7
9	Maintain and develop talk purposefully in a range of contexts; use appropriate intonation and emphasis	Level 7	Level 8
10	Make a range of contributions which show perceptive listening and sensitivity to the development of the discussion	Level 7	Level 8

10 EXPLORING SHAKESPEARE

11	Select and use structures, styles and registers appropriately in a range of contexts, varying vocabulary and expression confidently for a range of purposes	Level 8	E.P.
12	Initiate and sustain discussion through the sensitive use of a variety of contributions; take a leading role in discussion, listening with concentration and understanding to varied and complex speech	Level 8	E.P.

	Reading skill	From	To
1	Show understanding of significant ideas, themes, events and characters, beginning to use inference and deduction	Level 3	Level 4
2	Refer to the text when explaining views, locating and using ideas and information	Level 3	Level 4
3	Select essential points and use inference and deduction where appropriate	Level 4	Level 5
4	Identify key features, themes and characters; select sentences, phrases and relevant information to support views	Level 4	Level 5
5	Identify different layers of meaning and comment on their significance and effect	Level 5	Level 6
6	Give a personal response, referring to aspects of language, structure and themes in justifying views	Level 5	Level 6
7	Show understanding of the ways in which meaning and information are conveyed in a range of texts	Level 6	Level 7
8	Articulate personal and critical response to texts, showing awareness of their thematic, structural and linguistic features	Level 6	Level 7
9	Appreciate and comment on a range of texts	Level 7	Level 8
10	Evaluate how authors achieve their effects through the use of linguistic, structural and presentational devices	Level 7	Level 8
11	Confidently sustain responses, developing ideas and referring in detail to aspects of language, structure and presentation	Level 8	E.P.
12	Make apt and careful comparison between texts, including consideration of audience, purpose and form	Level 8	E.P.